Swimming in the
Steno Pool

Also by Lynn Peril

*Pink Think: Becoming a Woman
in Many Uneasy Lessons*

*College Girls: Bluestockings, Sex Kittens,
and Coeds, Then and Now*

TO SAM !!

Swimming

in the

Steno Pool

A Retro Guide to Making It in the Office

LYNN PERIL   SQUARE
8/29/18

Lynn Peril

W. W. Norton & Company
New York London

For information about permission to reproduce
selections from this book,
write to Permissions, W. W. Norton & Company, Inc.,
500 Fifth Avenue, New York, NY 10110

For information about special discounts for bulk purchases,
please contact W. W. Norton Special Sales at specialsales@
wwnorton.com or 800-233-4830

Manufacturing by Courier Westford
Book design by Judith Stagnitto Abbate / Abbate Design
Production manager: Devon Zahn

Library of Congress Cataloging-in-Publication Data

Peril, Lynn.
Swimming in the steno pool : a retro guide to
making it in the office / Lynn Peril. — 1st ed.
p. cm.
Includes bibliographical references and index.
ISBN 978-0-393-33854-6 (pbk.)
1. Secretaries. 2. Vocational qualifications. I. Title.
HD8039.S58P47 2011
651—dc22
                                                    2010044289

W. W. Norton & Company, Inc.
500 Fifth Avenue, New York, N.Y. 10110
www.wwnorton.com

W. W. Norton & Company Ltd.
Castle House, 75/76 Wells Street, London W1T 3QT

1 2 3 4 5 6 7 8 9 0

To my darling aunt,

Norma Voorhorst (1927–2008)

Contents

Acknowledgments

I've been graced with mostly good bosses and wonderful colleagues throughout my working life, Eileen Lenihan and Anne MacDonald chief among them.

June Morrall put me in touch with Lynn Kalajian McCloskey and Rosie Murray, who in turn graciously shared their memories of the Grace Ball Secretarial School in San Francisco, California.

Karen Finlay, Jessica MacGregor, Jane Townley, and Tomiko Wood all provided love, enthusiasm, and snacks at exactly the right moments in time. Barbara Nielsen also let me interview her about working as an executive assistant. Mary Ann Irwin taught me the difference between secretaries and word processors. Mary Ricci and Carrie Swing bravely read drafts—and Carrie inspired my author photo.

Meredith Jones, John Marr, Mickey McGowan, Brian Nevill, and Enid Westberg all donated secretarial femoribilia to my archives. My brother, Doug, turned me on to the television program *3's a Crowd*. With Kim Cooper's help, I was able to do research at the Los Angeles Public Library. Sunny Buick, Laurent Bigot, et Jon Von Zelowitz helped with translation.

I love Johnny Bartlett for much more than his photography and design skills.

Faye Bender is still the best agent a woman could have.

Editors Annalee Newitz at io9.com, Josh Glenn at hilobrow.com, Deb Stoller, Laurie Henzel, and Emily Rems (all at *Bust* magazine) waited calmly as their deadlines passed while I finished just one more draft of *Steno Pool*.

Alane Salierno Mason (who in the 1980s didn't get an internship at *The New Yorker* because she failed the typing test) and Denise Scarfi were the editorial tag team at W. W. Norton who pushed this project past the finish line. I can't thank them enough for their skills and their patience.

Regarding the latter, it's difficult enough to write a book under the best of circumstances, let alone when your heart is aching: both my aunt Norma Voorhorst and my brother-in-law, Jude Bartlett, died while I was writing this book. Norma was the first corporate secretary I ever met; Jude was more than willing to tell you everything he knew about photocopiers—and that was a lot. I miss them both more than I can say.

Finally, three cheers for secretaries and administrative assistants everywhere! Without you, the work would never get done.

Swimming in the
Steno Pool

Introduction

Out of the Kitchen and into the Office:
The Birth of the Secretary

Secretaries are marvelous people. They are ornamental and they are useful. They take down what you say and improve upon it. They know where to put in the double l's, the commas and the paragraphs. They hold the mad letters until tomorrow. They answer the telephone, sidetrack the bores and put through those on the important list. They remember the birthdays and anniversaries. They remind you that it's time to get going for the lunch date. They see when you need a haircut.

W. H. Kiplinger, "Salute to Secretaries" (1967)

The cover of *How to Be a Super-Secretary,* an informational pamphlet published by Remington Rand's Typewriter Division in 1949, features a cartoon drawing of a bright-eyed woman holding a pad and pencil, her softly smiling lips forming a perfect, rosy cupid's bow. Inside the little pink booklet, the same perky spokeswoman demonstrates the dos and don'ts of super-secretarydom, many of which suspiciously resembled the relationship advice handed out in mid-twentieth-century women's magazines. A super-secretary cheerily acted as "a one-woman publicity campaign" for the boss, gave "him encouragement when he is feeling low," and made "him feel he's a pretty wonderful person." She, on the other hand, remained silent about her "own personal troubles" and had "just one mood" in the office: "fair and sunny . . . no matter how you feel." There was a reward for such constant enthusiasm: according to the booklet, the super-secretary would "experience a new typing thrill" the moment she laid her carefully manicured fingertips on the Remington Electric DeLuxe typewriter.[1]

Let me tell you from personal experience, typing has never once given me a thrill. In fact, at the beginning of my career it was more likely to give me nightmares, as, having been perhaps a tiny bit untruthful about my skills at my job interview, I habitually typed "Sub Francusi" instead of "San Francisco," a decided liability for a secretary based in that fair city. That's right: I'm a secretary. Surprised? Ask around the cubicles at any office and you'll find all kinds of creative types taking refuge from a bad economy—or simply using their day job to finance their films, blogs, or novels-in-progress. This certainly isn't my first tour of duty; office work in one form or another has supported or supplemented my writing career for over twenty years. I've been an administrative assistant in a small, not-for-profit art gallery, a word processor in a law firm (yes, my typing got a lot better), and a humble civil servant—and I've temped at too many places to mention.

I'm just one of approximately four million secretaries in the United States, a figure that doesn't include word processors, typists, data entry clerks, receptionists, and others who perform secretarial tasks in addition to those of their regular job. We are overwhelmingly female—a statistic that has changed little if at all during the last century. Among our ranks are—in addition to the artists and writers—women who will one day establish their own businesses or get their professional degrees. Others work solely to support their families. Many are college educated. I've even met one or two Herculean single moms who work forty hours a week (or close to it), go to school, and raise children.[2]

For over a century now, secretarial work has been extolled as a wonderful career opportunity for women—and excoriated as dead-end busy work. Both characterizations are true. Long before the Ivy League business schools opened their doors to women in the 1970s, an enterprising secretary could use her

Remington Rand promoted its tips for super-secretaries with a full-page advertisement in a 1954 issue of The Secretary *magazine.*

experience in the steno pool ("a stuffy inside room where . . . wretched girls may spend their whole working lives, with disfiguring earphones clamped to their heads, transcribing stupid letters and still more ghastly statistical reports," according to *Good Jobs for Good Girls* (1949), a tongue-in-cheek guide to marrying the boss) as the first rung on the ladder of corporate success. But for every woman who climbed out of the steno pool and into an executive position were many others who were stymied by what came to be known in the mid-1980s as the glass ceiling: an unacknowledged but unsurpassable barrier based solely on gender. Still more were shunted into a secretarial career because there were few other choices.[3]

Secretary, Stenographer, Typist—and the Pool

Secretarial manuals were careful to define the differences between secretaries, stenographers, and typists. Each position had its own job description, and there was a definite hierarchy among them. In a small office, all three positions might be filled by one woman; in a large office, not every steno or typist ever made it out of the pool.

TYPISTS were the low women on the totem pole. They did exactly what their job title said: they typed up documents from stenographic notes or recordings on Dictaphone cylinders or tapes, or made sense out of marked-up hard copy.

STENOGRAPHERS took dictation, usually by hand in a face-to-face meeting with the dictator. They might type up their own notes, or hand them off to a typist. As far back as 1920, it was recognized as "the profession over which the legend should be written, 'Abandon hope, all ye who enter here.'" In some offices, however, working as a stenographer was preliminary to a secretarial position. [*]

SECRETARIES provided support to executives. Among other duties, they answered phones, set meetings, greeted callers, wrote letters (signed with their boss's signatures or their own), and did the 101 other things necessary to keep the office running. Executive, personal, or confidential secretaries were at the top of the heap—sometimes to the point of having their own secretaries or assistants. According to a National Secretaries Association conference attendee in 1949, "A stenographer . . . is paid to do; a secretary is paid to think." [†]

In some very large offices, typists, stenographers, and secretaries worked in POOLS. "Here you will be assigned a desk in one of many rows, all facing a supervisor—you know, similar to a classroom!" explained the *Gregg*

---

[*] Maud Robinson Toombs, "When a Woman Reaches Forty," *San Francisco Chronicle*, September 26, 1920, SM3.
[†] "Secretaries Quash Idea They Like to Romance with Their Bosses," *Los Angeles Times*, October 2, 1949, 21.

Writer in 1946. "When a stenographer is needed, Miss Supervisor will introduce you to the man for whom you will work. . . . He may give you two letters, or he may dictate for two hours."‡ In offices where executives used Dictaphones, completed wax cylinders or tapes were sent directly to the pool and a stenographer might not ever see the dictator's face. Often, newly hired secretaries were started in the pool, where their skills and personalities could be assessed before they were assigned to an individual executive.

‡ "Try the Stenography Department," *Gregg Writer*, March 1946, 354.

Office work has allowed me to publish a zine, get a graduate degree, and write three books, but I still have a hard time not adding the words—aloud or mentally—"just a" or "only a" in front of the word "secretary" when people ask me what I do. I doubt I'm the only one. I mean, can you blame us? Freed from a lot of grunt work thanks to copiers and computers, today's secretary is responsible for a greater array of complex tasks than her predecessors, but the word "secretary" is considered so demeaning that most offices shelved it long ago in favor of "administrative assistant." Indeed, "diminished image" and low pay were given as two reasons for a secretarial shortage that began in the late 1970s.

The Secretarial Mystique

Anyone who hasn't resided under a rock for the past century is well aware of that image: the husband-hunting, pencil-pushing, coffee-getting, dumb-bunny, sex-bomb secretary depicted in advertisements, novels, movies, television shows, comic books, and just about every other form of pop culture for a lot longer than you probably realize. Consider the stereotype of the gorgeous but dumb secretary. I discovered the following joke in a magazine from 1914, but it could easily have found its way into a 1960s or '70s sketch comedy show like *Laugh-In*. Imagine a dapper man in a tuxedo and Goldie Hawn in a bikini and body paint. Goldie speaks first:

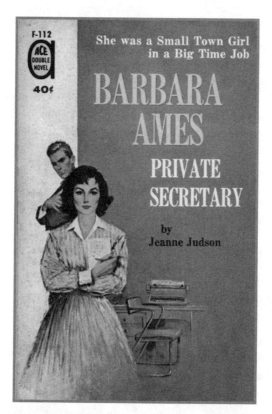

The road wasn't far from Barbara Ames, Private Secretary *(1960), a "respectable" romance for women . . .*

"Have you done anything for spelling reform?"
"Yes. I fired my blond stenographer."

A drummer snaps off a rim shot—it's on to the next gag. (You may be somewhat relieved to know that the magazine article containing this joke complained about "the frivolous treatment of the stenographer in popular literature" and the "alleged comic" effect of this joke in particular.)[4]

Then there's the sloe-eyed incubus who tempts or actually seduces her

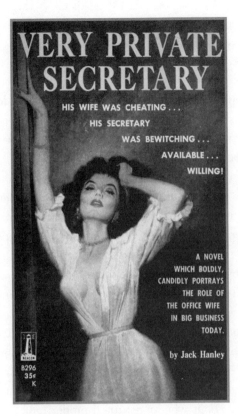

... *to* Very Private Secretary *(1960), a*
"dirty" book for men.

boss, an "innocent" married man. Regarding the latter scenario, no female
occupation, with the possible exceptions of librarian and stewardess, has
had more soft- and hard-core pornography devoted to it. Time for a little
dictation—winking emphasis on the first syllable, please—courtesy of *Office
Wife* (1961), a spicy novel for adults:

> Stella arrived that afternoon, dark-eyed, her lips curved into that same
> little taunting smile Rick had seen the previous Friday in the secretarial
> pool. . . . In her long, slender fingers she held a freshly-sharpened pencil

and a flat stenographer's pad, flipped open to a fresh and unused page. Her nails, Rick noted, were unusually long for a girl who had to type all day. His mind asked the question: I wonder how they'd feel digging into my back?[5]

Trust me, you don't have to dig far to find much filthier depictions of boss-secretary relationships. The power differential inherent in the relationship between boss (dominant) and secretary (submissive) made it a natural for all sorts of sadomasochistic scenarios.

But if the librarians and stewardesses gave her a run for the money at the adult-book store, without question no working woman had as many advice guides written for her as did the secretary. In addition to practical information (how to change typewriter ribbons, lists of frequently misspelled words, hints on grammar, and so on), the secretarial manuals devoted page after page to the secretary's proper dress and appropriate behavior. It was as if the secretary, by stepping into the "man's world" of business, had to have her femininity constantly reinforced lest she forget "her place" in the world—and make no mistake, the sort of advice dished out in *How to Be a Super-Secretary* and a plethora of textbooks and guidebooks, newspaper columns, trade publications, and general-interest magazines aimed at the secretary did just that. As a longtime collector of examples of what I like to call "pink think" (a set of ideas and attitudes about what constituted proper female behavior that was adhered to, consciously or not, by advice writers, manufacturers of toys and other consumer products, experts in many walks of life, and the public at large, particularly during the mid-twentieth century), I love these materials. Simultaneously earnest, kitschy, and offensive, they paint a disturbing picture of subservient, man-pleasing femininity that suggested what a wife was to a husband, and what a secretary was to her boss (minus the sex, but more about that later). This was the fabled "office wife," a term that stuck like glue, even though it was loathed by guidebook writers and working secretaries alike, and provided plenty of ammunition for pop-culture merchants of all stripes.

I'm not sure whether I'm more appalled by the fact that *The Secretary and Her Job* (1939) dove right into "Serving Refreshments" on page 5—long before it addressed such basics as answering the phone (page 34) or taking shorthand (all the way back on page 127)—or tickled by the sheer ludicrousness of the advice given therein:

> If your employer has a bar in his office he will doubtless mix the drinks himself, but he may ask you to play hostess. . . . You can't be expected to know all the details of the fine art of bartending, so you might do as one secretary does: inside the roll top of the bar she keeps a small booklet containing the most common recipes.[6]

This is *Mad Men*–style secretarying at its finest—though if you're a fan of that television show (set in a fictional 1960s advertising agency), you know that the executives tend to pour their own booze, often before lunch. Would that my boss had cause to mix up a Manhattan for a guest—and of course one for me too (I am, after all, a liberated secretary).

Naturally, I'm kidding—sort of. Cocktail mixing was a bit of an anomaly, but otherwise the advice to the "perfect," "super," or "ideal" secretary contained in the manuals that form the basis of this book remained amazingly consistent over the years. "Invariably courteous, gentle, cheerful, tactful, sunny, courageous, optimistic, [the secretary] creates the atmosphere of the office," explained *Vocations for the Trained Woman* (1910). In the words of a *Ladies' Home Journal* writer in 1916, it was the secretary's job to radiate the office "with sunshine and sympathetic interest." In 1931, the *New York Times* even proclaimed the secretary "doubtless the nearest thing to the old-fashioned wife . . . modern civilization affords. . . . She may be counted upon to smile appreciatively at his jokes, even to hold his pencils admiringly." *So You Want to Be an Executive Secretary* (1963), a classic of the secretarial advice genre, went further still when it suggested that a good secretary combined "the best features of an executive's wife, his mother and his best friend—without any of their faults":

> Like his wife, she is proud of his successes, but never mentions his defeats.
>
> Like his mother, she is proud of his virtues, but conveniently forgets his vices.

Like his best friend, she listens to his problems sympathetically and confidentially, and never argues with him.[7]

While it may induce gagging in today's administrative assistants, and probably did in more than a few secretaries back then as well, this type of twaddle would have been all too familiar to young women who grew up in the mid-twentieth century. It was in fact just a literary hop, skip, and jump from teen girls guide to secretarial school textbook. "Boys are like anybody else," explained *On Becoming a Woman* (1959). "If you make them feel clever, talented, important, they like you for it, because it makes them like themselves." *Charm: The Career Girl's Guide to Business and Personal Success* (1964) simply extrapolated similar advice to the office: "Look for his [the boss's] good points; overlook his bad ones. . . . Be an appreciative audience and a bond of good feeling will develop between you."[8]

Taken all together, the guidebooks and pop-culture portrayals formed a mystique as pervasive and perverse as the one Betty Friedan wrote about—which makes it all the more surprising that prior to the late nineteenth century, all secretaries (or clerks, as they were called) were men.

The Nineteenth-Century Office: No Women Allowed!

Today, when a laptop and a wireless card make it possible to conduct international business on the city bus, it's all but impossible to imagine an office of 150 years ago. Back then, the economy was still based in agriculture, though heavy industry was knocking on the door, especially in places like the Northeast. A few insurance companies and banks had offices in more than one city, but "big business" as we know it didn't yet exist—most businesses served people in and around the towns where they were based. The boss wrote his own letters in longhand—or he might dictate to a personal secretary who used one of many forms of shorthand (phonetic systems of rapid writing that used either letters or symbols to indicate sounds instead of words) to record his thoughts.

If multiple copies of a document were needed, they had to be duplicated by hand. An unlikely visitor from the twenty-first century would no doubt find the lack of phones, faxes, and computers jarring—imagine how quiet the office must have been!—and she or he would certainly miss the coffee machine. But perhaps most shocking to modern sensibilities would be the absence of women—who, given their "separate spheres" of influence, kept the home fires burning while their menfolk inhabited the public world of commerce. "Man is and should be head of his own department, in the management of his business for the support of his family," explained the *Workingman's Advocate* newspaper in 1870. "Woman should be head in her own department, in the management of household affairs, and in the care and government of the children."[9]

The person who did the brunt of the work in the antebellum office was the clerk. His workload varied with the size of the office he worked in and the type of business it conducted, but a good clerk was a jack-of-all-office-trades: he drafted letters, copied documents, kept the books, filed, and took care of the thousand and one things that came up in the course of the business day. This sounds like a day in the life of a female secretary in the twentieth century, but there's a major exception. A nineteenth-century clerkship was a sort of business apprenticeship that allowed the clerk to see how a firm ran from top to bottom; if he got along with his boss and performed his duties well, a clerk could reasonably expect to move up the ladder into a solid management position, perhaps even into the boss's chair after he retired. The same expectation held true for bookkeepers and even for office boys, who, if they were dependable, might find themselves taken on as clerks. Thus a lowly office boy could legitimately dream of taking over the company—there was no glass ceiling to hold him back.[10]

T-Girls: The First Female Office Workers

Women first entered the office in 1862, thanks to a staffing shortage caused by the Civil War. With most of the men he would otherwise hire facing each other on the battlefields surrounding Washington, D.C., Treasury Department head Elias Spinner took the novel step of hiring women to trim paper money. They had such dainty little fingers, after all. "A woman can use scissors better than a man," he told his boss, Treasury Secretary Salmon P. Chase, "and she will do it cheaper." Prophetic words, indeed.[11]

Women could count too. When Spinner's new note trimmers proved "physically and mentally . . . more than a match for any man in the room," he hired female clerks to tally the finished bills. "I knew that women, with their more nimble fingers could count faster than men," he recalled, mentioning in passing the vaunted manual dexterity that in decades to come made women such geniuses at typing, piecework, putting together widgets on the factory line, and other low-paying tasks—but, as Gloria Steinem later pointed out, dexterity was never considered a positive job attribute when it came to a highly paid position like brain surgeon. Spinner deemed the hiring of women "a complete success," not least because many of them did "as much work, if not more," and did it "as well, if not better" than some of the male clerks, who were paid twice as much. Other government departments took note and started to hire women too.[12]

Job-Stealing Sluts?

By coming into the office, Spinner's clerks had quietly stormed a barricade; some women worked as law copyists in nineteenth-century Washington, for example, but they maintained decorum by having the work brought to their houses. The women who worked at the Treasury directly challenged the long-standing belief that a middle-class woman's place was in the home. Not everyone agreed that this was a good idea.

To some, the entrance of women into office work was no less than the thin edge of a blade held to the throats of honest working men while wily women stole their jobs straight out from under them. The *Workingman's Advocate* complained in 1866 that the government "stooped to the hiring of female clerks to do the work of its Departments because they could be got for a smaller sum than males." The government was guilty as charged, but

A Case History of Poaching Jobs from Men

(U) nlike typing, stenography had a long history of male practitioners. In 1906, the author of *Starting in Life: What Each Calling Offers Ambitious Boys and Young Men* warned his readers that, save for the as yet mostly male bastion of the newspaper office, the woman stenographer had "become an office fixture and necessity." Women had even infiltrated the ranks of court reporters, where they had been long considered too delicate to hear the litany of greed, murder, lust, and corruption, not to mention the occasional indecency of language, they might be subjected to when taking trial testimony. The reason for women's success as stenographers was "obvious," the author concluded. "So long as the woman continues to work at a lower price than is paid to the man for a similar service, the man cannot compete with the woman on what may be assumed to be the woman's ground." He thus warned boys "to pause and reflect, and then to pause again, and to continue to reflect, for several days or weeks, before entering a profession which has comparatively few prizes to offer, and has very little substantial reward even for those who draw a prize." The women, it seemed, had devalued what once had been a man's noble calling.[*]

[*] Nathan C. Fowler Jr., *Starting in Life: What Each Calling Offers Ambitious Boys and Young Men* (Boston: Little, Brown, 1906), 119, 126.

even in its hallowed halls, dissenting voices were heard. Treasury Secretary Chase okayed Spinner's request to hire women, but his successor was less than thrilled with developments since then. "There are too many tea pots in the Treasury of the nation," grumbled Secretary Hugh McCulloch. McCulloch focused his ire on the nineteenth-century equivalent of the travel mug that sits on many desks today, and made it a symbol of women's unfitness for government service—how dare they turn the Treasury into a ladies' tea room?[13] An underlying (and long-lived) assumption, often despite compel-

What Really Happened at the Treasury Department?

In the spring of 1864, Representative James H. Brooks made a spectacular accusation from the floor of the House of Representatives. The Treasury Department, he said, had become a "house for orgies and bacchanals." An investigative committee was quickly convened under the leadership of Representative (later President) James A. Garfield. Under the spotlight was a division headed by one Spencer M. Clark, who, it was said, hired women based on their looks rather than their ability. Witnesses further alleged that Clark, who was married, "plied some of these women with oysters and ale and made 'improper' overtures" to them. A former Treasury employee claimed Clark had offered her first $100, then ten times that amount, for a tryst with her (she refused both offers). Three others said they had spent the night with him on more than one occasion, testimony corroborated by a "disinterested" third party who lived in the same house as two of the women. But when one of the three women who testified that she had slept with Clark passed away unexpectedly during the trial, a postmortem found "incontestable evidence" that she died a virgin.

Spencer Clark denied all the charges, and on June 30, 1864, Garfield's committee cleared the Treasury Department of "gross immorality." It concluded that Clark had been the victim of "a conspiracy" on the part of one Colonel Lafayette C. Baker "and the three prostitutes associated with him, by the aid of coerced testimony" to destroy Clark's reputation. Baker had botched the investigation of the theft of $30,000 from the Treasury the previous December, leading to the imprisonment of an innocent "midlevel official," who sued Baker the moment he was let out of jail. When the Treasury Department refused to back him up, Baker produced the women's affidavits. After the charges were dismissed, in the words of historian Kerry Segrave, "Baker continued to claim 'whitewash.'"

As Segrave points out, it's impossible to know exactly what happened, other than that the women were "branded as liars" and labeled sexually promiscuous. The latter charge was powerful enough to smear female Treasury workers in general, albeit via whispered rumors, for the next half-century.*

* Kerry Segrave, *The Sexual Harassment of Women in the Workplace, 1600–1993* (Jefferson, NC: McFarland, 1994), 103–4.

ling evidence to the contrary, was that women worked for "pin money" to buy furbelows like tea pots, while men were serious workers who needed salary and wages to support their families. When women entered the workforce, they usurped jobs that "rightfully" belonged to husbands and fathers—and often drove down wages in the process.

Poaching men's jobs was bad enough, but there were also whispers about the Treasury women's morality. After all, they worked side by side with men, men who might lead them to ruin—or, even more deliciously naughty, vice versa! Rumors flew so thick and fast that less than a decade after Spinner hired his first female employees, the author of a salacious guide to Washington listed "treasury courtesans" among *The Sights and Secrets of the National Capital* (1869). Such "black sheep" were "greatly in the minority," he noted, though they were "still believed to be numerous." (The notion that the Treasury Department was a den of iniquity died hard. During the Wilson administration's attempt to clean up Washington's red light district in the second decade of the twentieth century, a madam told a judge, "Your honor, everybody knows I run the second best house in the city . . . the Treasury runs the best.")[14]

Early generations of female office clerks ignored slander to their reputations for the same reason workers have always put up with less-than-stellar working conditions: they needed the money. A female clerk was paid half of what a male clerk was—but that was still double the salary of a public school teacher, enough for a woman to "live respectably, but not luxuriously" if she was thrifty.[15] As a result, women flocked to government jobs. The 1880 census showed there were 1,412 female clerks in government offices; a decade later, the number of women working in Washington as clerks, copyists, stenographers, and typists had more than doubled.

The private sector lagged by comparison when it came to hiring women—at least at first. In 1870, for example, there were only five female shorthand writers in New York City. A mere twenty years later, however, 60 percent of American stenographers and typists were women; by 1900, the number was 77 percent; by 1920—in the wake of World War I, when women filled places formerly held by men at the front—it was 90 percent. Two things helped this rapid acceleration: the blizzard of paperwork generated by the birth of big business, and the introduction of a commercially available, practical typewriter.[16]

A Woman's Best Friend Is Her Typewriter

If the scissors helped woman breach the office door, the typewriter cemented her place behind the desk. The frontispiece of *The Story of the Typewriter* (1923) is a sepia-toned composite photo showing white-haired Christopher Latham Sholes seated at a table with the "writing machine" he invented, while a line of smiling women dressed in Grecian tunics and with fashionably if anachronistically bobbed hair march across what looks like an arctic icescape behind and above him. "EMANCIPATION" reads the opposite page, over a statement from the inventor himself: "I feel that I have done something for the women who have always had to work so hard. This will enable them more easily to earn a living." That women's hard-fought and recently won right to vote might be a better example of "emancipation" and that Sholes was by various reckonings either the 52nd, 76th, or 112th inventor of a typing machine are mere quibbles of history: the picture shows how the union of woman and typewriter, just fifty years after its invention, already had been cast into mythology.[17]

Spectral women typists line up to pay their respects to typewriter inventor Christopher Latham Sholes, circa 1920s.

Sholes patented his version of the typewriter in 1873, and gun maker E. Remington & Sons brought it to market the following year. Created to free humankind from what one writer called "the bondage of the pen," the typewriter was nevertheless slow to be adopted in offices. Priced at $125, it was expensive, and until the development of a shift-key model in 1878, users could only type in capital letters. There was also a question of etiquette, which deemed handwriting more polite than mechanical type. "I do not think it necessary . . . to have your letters to me taken to the printers' and set up like a handbill. I will be able to read your writing, and I am deeply chagrined

"Miss Remington" displays a come-hither look, 1908.

to think you thought such a course necessary," read the handwritten reply to a typed missive sent by an early adopter in the insurance industry. But once the mechanical bugs were fixed, typewriter sales took off—etiquette be damned. Remington sold a mere four hundred machines during the first year of production; thirteen years later, in 1887, it manufactured fifteen hundred a month, and the public still clamored for more.[18]

Sex appeal helped bolster sales when Remington hired cute young women to demonstrate its first machines to potential customers. This strategy hooked no less a fish than Mark Twain, who bought a Remington No. 1 in 1874 after watching a "type girl" blaze through fifty-seven words a minute at a Boston showroom (a feat he was unable to repeat at home). Sales were also helped by the fact that, despite the alluring presence of the saucy

No Christmas
This Year

will be complete without a present, and no practical present can be made that will give more real good for the coin paid than a practical low-priced typewriter like the "WORLD," sold for $15.00. Available at once for the boy or his father, the girl or her mother. You want a catalogue? We send it. Type-writer Dept., POPE MFG. CO., Boston, New York, Chicago.

Another example of the typewriter's early nongendered appeal. Mom, Sis, Dad, and Little Brother all wanted a World Typewriter for Christmas, 1890.

type girls, there was no early consensus about who should operate this new form of technology. The typewriter was, in the words of academics, "gender neutral," unlike, say, the "female" iron and the "male" razor. A Remington ad from December 1875 therefore touted the machine as a "CHRISTMAS PRESENT for a boy or girl," then expounded on its utility to women. "No invention has opened for women so broad and easy an avenue to profitable and suitable employment as the 'Type-Writer,' and it merits the careful consideration of all thoughtful and charitable persons interested in the subject of work for women."[19] Typing was "suitable employment" because it had never been a male-only occupation, and women who sought work as typists were not perceived as stealing jobs from men.

By the turn of the twentieth century, the association between woman and machine was so complete that the term "typewriter" could mean either the physical object or the woman who operated it, and the "pretty typewriter"

"My Pretty Typewriter"

The following gem appeared in *Judge's Library*, "A Monthly Magazine of Fun," in 1903. It touched three lodestones of secretarial humor (beauty, incompetence, insubordination) and finished up with a boffo twist at the end. Perhaps not surprisingly, the author chose to remain anonymous.

MY PRETTY TYPEWRITER

I have a pretty typewriter,
As pretty as can be,
I'm very much in love with her,
And she as much with me.

I tell what I'd have her say,
But not what she must do;
For this I find the only way
She'll be dictated to.

Sometimes she makes a lover "stare,"
When I would have him *start*,
But never strikes a wrong note on
The key-board of my heart.

had become a stock character in jokes and humorous stories. A few commentators even complained—prematurely as it turned out—that she had replaced the mother-in-law as a figure of fun. Young female typewriters were also subject to the same sort of suggestive sniggering the women at the Treasury Department faced, no doubt thanks in part to Remington's sexy type girls. The author of an 1894 guide to the sights of New York City did his best to defend typewriters' reputations: "On few subjects have more jokes

She dotes on her old "No. 2,"
This girl who's one with me;
She chose the number so because
We hadn't room for three.

And must I tell you now her name?
I'd quite as lief as not.
This pretty typewriter of mine
Is—just—my—daughter—Dot.*

* Anonymous, *Judge's Library*, vol. 166–177, 1903.

been made, and ill-natured slurs cast, than on the 'pretty typewriter.' It is doubtless true that some unprincipled adventuresses, and some weak and silly girls, have entered this occupation. But the overwhelming majority of the women who operate typewriting machines are modest, industrious, and worthy of all encouragement," he concluded.[20]

Once again, there was a consensus that women's nimble fingers—so good with the scissors—made them better typists than men. "The type-writer is especially adaptable to feminine fingers," confided the English author of *A Manual of the Type-Writer* (1888). "They seem to be made for type-writing." In response to a 1913 *Scientific American* article that asked "Are Men Better Typists Than Women?" C. E. Smith, the author of *Practical Course in Touch Typing* (1904), argued that men's "extremely large and strong fingers" were a liability when it came to the typewriter keyboard, especially "when all the fingers of the hands are employed in striking the keys, which is the only scientific method of operating a typewriter." Were men better typists than women? After testing six women and five men, *Scientific American* conceded that the result was pretty much a draw.[21]

As in the modern office, familiarity with the latest technology paid off: a skilled typewriter in the late nineteenth century made as much as seven dollars a week, a dollar more than an ordinary office clerk.[22]

Women swarm a giant typewriter, fondling its keys and other suggestively shaped parts (look at the woman perched at the upper left), in this postcard from San Francisco's Panama-Pacific Exposition of 1915. The typewriter was genderless no more.

Around the same time that the typewriter was becoming standard office equipment, the American business model expanded from regional to national (and eventually to international), leaving a flood of paperwork in its wake. "Speed and efficiency" became managerial bywords as employers, aided by new technologies, streamlined office tasks into numerous subspecialties, a process known as "rationalization." Where once a single clerk performed a number of different chores, now there was a stenographer, a file clerk, and a typist, each dedicated to her particular practice. "Her" because most men didn't want these new jobs: they were tedious, didn't pay well enough, and, worst of all, offered little room for advancement.

Women filled these occupations. *The Private Secretary: His Duties and Opportunities* (1916) was written on the cusp of the male secretary's transformation into the ivory-billed woodpecker of office life (i.e., seldom seen but rumored to exist). In its pages, author and business educator Edward Jones Kilduff boldly suggested that the "knowledge of stenography and typewriting" was not an "essential requirement for the private secretary in the *higher type of position*" because the lucky man who found himself occupying such a position could expect "typists to do the typing for the chief and also for the secretary." These lowly typists were women. Kilduff used a fictional man Friday, Frank Campbell, as an exemplar of proper secretarial behavior. Instead of asking him to get his steno pad, Campbell's boss asks him to "send in Miss Andrews for dictation." Later, when summoned by "the chief," Campbell tells "Miss Ray"—the stenographer to whom he is giving dictation—that he'll be back in a moment. The implication was the *"higher type"* of office hired "wide-awake" men to act as secretaries/junior executives, while female typists and stenos, possessed of little more ambition than to marry and leave the workforce as quickly as possible, pounded out the drudge work. [23]

The work may have been dull, but the office provided a clean, safe work space, as opposed to the grim and potentially dangerous factory. (Not that middle-class women were looking for factory jobs; by the 1860s, these were already considered the bastion of working-class, immigrant women, as was domestic service. And not that the office was always safe. In 1899, the *New York Times* reported that an eighteen-year-old typist at a toy company died from blood poisoning after she popped a fever blister with fingers stained with typewriter ribbon ink.) Unlike nursing and teaching, secretarial work didn't require higher education. Many girls learned office skills while in high school business courses. For others, a year at a commercial business school provided enough training to become a stenographer or typist. Working in an office also carried a higher status than sales clerking, another popular area of female employment at the turn of the twentieth century. From the employer's standpoint, women made good workers because men wanted promotions and higher wages; as an office manager explained in 1917, "girls do not have these demands"—or so management perceived.[24]

• • •

Today, advances in office technology mean more bosses do their own typing or use voice-recognition software that replaces the Dictaphone, secretary, and word processor. Thanks to the internet, some small offices turn to "virtual assistants" who answer phones and type letters sometimes hundreds of miles from their employers, and at a fraction of the price of a full-time employee (not least because they don't require a benefits package). Will there be a place for the secretary—I mean, administrative assistant—in the "paperless" office of the future?

If there is, let's hope she can move past at least one enduring image. None of the women I've worked with over the years faintly resembled the "old-fashioned wife" who cheerfully dusted the boss's desk and ran to get him coffee—I knew one who dislodged her persnickety boss's pencils from their perfect formation when he was out to lunch—but they did slyly ask, "Is your husband in?" if they needed to talk to each other's bosses. When I worked as a word processor, my friend the legal secretary explained the difference between our positions this way. "Oh, honey," she said when I told her I had good working relationships with all the attorneys at the firm, "that's because word processing is the mistress; secretaries are the wives."

It doesn't seem to matter how powerful a woman is; if she works for a man, she's susceptible to this matrimonial image. In April 2004, then national security advisor Condoleezza Rice made a telling slip of the lip at a New York party: "As I was telling my husb—," she began before catching herself. "As I was telling President Bush," she continued.[25]

So You Want to Be a Secretary: Preparing for and Getting a Job

The royal road to the future for a young woman starts at the secretary's desk. From it, as a base of operations, she can campaign for an eligible male in her vicinity or for advancement in her position. First, however, she has to be a successful secretary to stay at the desk long enough to accomplish either or both of these goals.

"A Secretary Is Set to Wed or Get Ahead,"
New York Times, April 23, 1956

I fell into the secretarial pool by chance. At the tender age of twenty-four I moved from Milwaukee, Wisconsin, to San Francisco, California, armed with a degree in art history but no idea where I would live or how I would support myself. (You could go far on mere enthusiasm back in the 1980s; it also helped that housing prices were much, much lower.) After a brief but horrible job in a filthy health-food store in Berkeley, I dusted off my extremely rusty typing skills and started working as an office temp in the city.

Though it would be years before I admitted it to myself, by doing so I had proved my parents right. "Take typing," they said, as I planned my high school schedule. "You'll always have something to fall back on." Boys took typing too, but there was an unstated assumption—at least when I was stuck behind a manual typewriter in Mrs. Schmidt's class in the mid-1970s—that for them, at least, typing was an expedient to get them through college term papers. Once they graduated, they would hire other people, mostly female, to do their typing for them. (I myself did little typing in college because I talked a boyfriend's legal-secretary mother into doing it for me. No money exchanged hands—a fact that bothered me not a whit back then. Alas, even the free personal typing service couldn't stop me from dumping her son, and I was finally forced to hunt and peck through my final semesters.)

"Employment 'Insurance'"

As a legion of young and not-so-young women discovered long before I did, for better or worse, typing and its squiggly partner, shorthand, were what guidebook author and secretarial school administrator Lucy Graves Mayo called "Employment 'Insurance'"—and my parents called "something to fall back on." Secretarial skills were proven moneymakers for women—not that a secretary, stenographer, or typist was going to retire rich, unless she married well or was extremely wise when it came to investments. But if a woman needed a paid position, she could almost always get one if she could type and take shorthand. *Good Housekeeping* magazine, usually a stalwart of the stay-at-home mom, explained the importance of secretarial skills with steely eyed practicality in 1952. "Knowledge of a solidly grounded trade" was "one of the greatest assets" a woman could possess. She could practice "such a trade before marriage, fall back on it during family economic crises if necessary, and use it gratefully when home responsibilities become almost nonexistent and a life of dependence on married children faces her. . . . Stenography and typing always are useful."[1]

Useful they undoubtedly were, but until attitudes about women in the professions began to change in the mid-1970s, secretarial skills presented a catch-22 for many college-educated women: typing and stenography got them jobs, but the jobs they got were far from the positions for which they

Who needed a liberal arts education when one could experience the same sort of collegiate bonding at a secretarial school? Students at the Hartford Secretarial School smile for the photographer, circa 1940s.

trained. Today's young, college-educated female job seeker knows (as does her male counterpart) that computer skills and a basic knowledge of popular software applications are prerequisites for most entry-level positions—but she doesn't expect to be shunted into the secretarial pool if she applies as, say, a beginning engineer or copywriter. This, however, is exactly what happened to earlier generations of diploma-holding women, who watched from behind their typewriters as male applicants—the vast majority of whom didn't type—took the plum positions. In 1922, a young woman explained how she and the other members of her college women's club made the difficult discovery that "nine jobs out of ten offered to girls just starting out in the business world today require[d] stenography."

> If they find they can't get a job unless they know stenography, they buckle down and learn it. . . . And of course some professions are still practically closed to women. I wanted to study engineering but I found that none of the college courses in that subject were open to women.[2]

Had she graduated with her wished-for degree in engineering, she may well have discovered that the only positions open to her were those that involved a typewriter and a steno pad. In the late 1930s, a group of "educators and employers, scientists and personnel directors" convened to discuss the problem faced by "college girls disconsolate over three degrees in chemistry but lack of a job." They concurred that the "average, undistinguished girl chemist" was better off learning "auxiliary skills" like typing and shorthand, the better to use secretarial work "as an entering wedge" to the profession. (A woman chemist who was asked for her opinion of the plan responded with "something closely approximating wrath." For a "really able woman chemist bent on maintaining her professional dignity," she asserted, it was "definitely derogatory to permit herself to have anything to do with a typing job.")[3]

Many women simply resigned themselves to what the *New York Times* in the 1930s characterized as "the octopus-like tendency of the typewriter to wrap its arms around her and refuse to let her rise above it." A 1950s-era secretarial manual hopefully suggested that "after year or two" working "for the purpose of saving up for training in one of the professions," a girl might find "office work a fascinating career in itself," but that was guidebook speak at its best. More likely, she found a weekly paycheck a balm against the seemingly insurmountable combination of personnel offices that wouldn't promote—or hire—women, and experts who extolled secretarial work as a naturally feminine career path. "Despite all the progress women have made in the business world, it is still the exception to find a woman holding a big executive job; rare to find a high-pressure, high-salaried woman salesman or a top-flight

The School of Shorthand advertised to newly graduated men and women in the 1911 edition of the University of Michigan's Michiganesan *yearbook.*

woman lawyer," explained Rae Chatfield Ayer, a secretary arguing against the proposition "Are Men Better Secretaries?" in the *Rotarian*, the membership publication of the businessmen's service organization, Rotary, in 1940:

> Most girls realize this, and take the next best thing, a secretarial job.
> A sensible girl realizes that such a position is a "natural" for her and that she might as well accept it and not bang her head against the stone walls of manmade business.[4]

Today's sensible girl is no doubt banging her head on her desk after reading Ayer's ambition-bursting advice, but Ayer was far from alone in her assertions. "Sometimes career choice is a compromise between idealism and realism," wrote Lucy Mayo in *You Can Be an Executive Secretary* (1965). "You might, for instance, choose to be a lawyer's or a doctor's or a scientist's secretary because you once hoped to be a lawyer or a doctor or a scientist." The suggestion that secretarial work was a coordinate "woman's career" by which she could take part in the profession of her choice was a common one for most of the twentieth century. It didn't matter if a girl had a report card filled with As and Bs—chances were good that her high school guidance counselor would urge her to look into a secretarial career. (I apparently just missed this era at my own private, college-prep high school. A highly intelligent friend who graduated four years ahead of me reports that it happened to her. By contrast, my own mandatory senior year meeting with the guidance counselor in 1979 was remarkable only for the fact that no useful information whatsoever was imparted to me.) "I was more or less socialized to be a secretary. . . . If I wasn't going to be a teacher, I'd have to be a secretary or a nurse," said a newly liberated secretary in 1975. Others were funneled into secretarial programs in high school, got decent-enough jobs after graduation, and never quit.[5]

The Feminine Secretary

In a nutshell, biology was destiny in the office as surely as it was in the bedroom. Journalist Dorothy Thompson expressed a prevailing viewpoint in *Ladies' Home Journal* in 1952: "*all* women are, or aspire to be, wives and mothers also, and our society is still organized on the assumption that the conduct of the home is every woman's *natural* function." For a woman to ignore the "natural" roles of wife and stay-at-home mother by stepping outside the house and into men's work was to invite psychological discord, not to mention social opprobrium. Working women ran the risk of being "masculinized" by their experience, and thus turned into men's rivals instead of their helpmeets. As a result, women "insensibly" developed "the characteristics of aggression, dominance, independence and power," a role reversal that drove them "steadily deeper into personal conflict soluble only by psychotherapy," according to the authors of *Modern Woman: The Lost Sex* (1947), an influential work of pop psychology later excoriated by Betty Friedan as an agent of the feminine mystique. Women who worked outside the home could remain "psychologically balanced" only if they found ego satisfaction in "nurturing activities" such as "teaching, nursing, doctoring, social service work, guidance, catering, decorating, play direction, [or] furnishing."[6]

A wife's foray into the working world could wreak mental and emotional havoc on her spouse too. The husband's morale suffered when he was "faced with evidence that his efforts at supporting the family" were so unsatisfactory

The secretarial mystique goes international. Here, a French guidebook blurs the line between boss and husband. "I'm a Secretary . . . at the Office, and at Home Too!"

that his wife took "the reins in her hands in order to provide" for them. With his role of primary breadwinner usurped, a husband tended to drift like a rudderless ship, and as a consequence, his once-proud ego deflated like a dinghy with a slow leak. By contrast, the "natural and normal strategy" by which a woman retained her husband's "respect and regard" involved what one marriage manual, *Happiness for Husbands and Wives* (1968), called "a complementary relationship" in which she recognized him "as 'head of the house'" and he served as "an intermediary between the family and outside world."[7]

Luckily for both single and married women, secretarial work was innately feminine, requiring skills practically hardwired into the female brain. Women made better secretaries than men, Rae Chatfield Ayer declared, because the boss, a man, needed "steady respect, even admiration from those about him—and these things a woman, because she is a woman, can give him. . . . woman's success as a secretary is not due to masculine qualities in her, but the converse." Office work came "naturally to a woman," the founder of Brazil's first secretarial school told the *Chicago Tribune* in 1943. "It is typical of our feminine nature to like to take care of things—a natural expression of a woman." A secretary used "all the skills that most women naturally possess—language facility, organizational ability, willingness to pay attention to fine detail, intuitiveness, tact, warmth in handling people." Because the job required she use these feminine qualities, a woman could "derive great comfort and satisfaction from her role as secretary. Personally, I enjoy doing in the office many of the same things that I enjoy doing in my own home, and I feel that the better secretary I am, the better all-round person I am," wrote Lucy Graves Mayo in *Wendy Scott, Secretary* (1961), a career romance novel for teen girls that read like a police procedural for the desk set. Writing to a young audience she hoped to entice into the profession (and perhaps lure a few of them to the secretarial school she worked for), Mayo stressed that secretarial work was "'primarily a woman's field. In it you are not competing with men; you are *complementing* them.' . . . Complementing men is a function that has been woman's natural one ever since the incident of Adam's rib!" a sentiment with which the evangelical Christian author of *Happiness for Husbands and Wives* would no doubt have thoroughly agreed.[8]

The Career Girl's Consort

Most mid-century guidebooks and women's magazines assured their female readers that a wife who worked outside the home emasculated her husband as effectively as a veterinarian wielding a scalpel over a stray tom cat. Yet there was a distinct lack of male-penned articles equivalent to those like "Have I Stolen My Husband's Birthright?" (*Woman's Home Companion*, 1927) and "My Job versus My Husband's Pride" (*McCalls*, 1977). Of course, given the rigid gender roles espoused by mid-century prescriptive literature and pop culture, a man who wrote about his wife's work outside the house essentially admitted to his own emasculation.

Humor helped one author defuse this sticky situation. In the late 1950s, Bart McDowell's former journalist wife went back to work as a freelance copywriter and he chronicled the experience in a memoir, *I Was a Career Girl's Consort* (1960). Even though the book jacket got maximum mileage from humorous role-turnabout imagery (both the front cover illustration and the author photo featured an apron-wearing husband and a briefcase-toting wife), McDowell made it clear from the first chapter that his wife worked outside the home because she needed the stimulation, not because he couldn't support her and their children. Their struggles to balance childcare and household chores (in particular his pathetic attempts to cook dinner) may sound modern to today's two-career couples, as does his obvious pride in his talented spouse, but ultimately the bulk of the book focused on storylines that had little to do with the consequences of his wife working outside the home (planning a wedding for one of their ongoing line of nannies, for example). In this way, McDowell had his cake and ate it too: he wrote about his working wife, yet never turned in his business suit for a frilly apron—except for comic effect.

Keeper of Secrets?

One of the earliest definitions for the word "secretary" (the *Oxford English Dictionary* traces it to the late fourteenth century) is "one who is entrusted with private or secret matters; a confidant; one privy to a secret."[*] Indeed, keeping mum about upcoming projects and sensitive information—some of it personal—was and remains an important part of the administrative assistant's duties. Yet despite the fact that women have been firmly identified with the position of secretary since they filled the vast majority of secretarial job slots during the early decades of the twentieth century, the tenets of stereotypical "femininity" dictate that they are unable to keep their gums from flapping once some tasty gossip comes along. "Perhaps the worst feminine fault," wrote Elizabeth Mac-Gibbon in *Manners in Business* (1936), "is talking too much. A great deal of the office gossip, which can be so devastating, and which leads to so many misunderstandings and hurt feelings, is due to the fact that women's tongues are loose at both ends."[†]

[*] *Oxford English Dictionary*, 2d ed, 1989, at http://dictionary.oed.com.ezproxy.sfpl.org/cgi/entry/50218064?query_type=word&queryword=secretary&first=1&max_to_show=10&sort_type=alpha &result_place=1&search_id=MXO7-KsuCvM-8185&hilite=50218064 (accessed December 12, 2007).
[†] Elizabeth Gregg MacGibbon, *Manners in Business* (New York: Macmillan, 1936), 78–79.

Secretarial Schools

Office work had an advantage over teaching and nursing, two other traditionally "feminine" occupations, in that entry-level positions didn't require a great deal of training—or a college degree. "Although a secretary need not be a genius, she should have above-average intelligence. Endowed with that, and a stable personality, a woman can acquire all the qualifications necessary for success provided she has a sincere desire to serve," opined Sybil Lee

Gilmore in *The Successful Secretary* (1951). "Secretary" was second on *The Seventeen Book of Young Living*'s list of "Careers without College" in 1961, wedged between "air-lines hostess or reservationist" and "interior decorating." A high school business course, a couple of semesters in night school, or even six weeks in one of the lightning-fast classes some business colleges offered for women who had to find a job pronto—any of these gave enough training in shorthand and typing for the average person to start applying for jobs in the steno pool, or as a typist or clerk. But if a young woman had both time and money to go to a school that specialized in secretarial training, she might forge her "way to a better job," in the words of *The Seventeen Book of Young Living*. There was probably a plethora of secretarial schools from which to

A coed group of high school students practice typing sometime during the second decade of the twentieth century.

In an era when professions such as law, medicine, and architecture were still largely closed to women, no shortage of secretarial schools promised an entrée into the business world. Glamour, *March 1963.*

choose right in her hometown. All she needed to do was pick up the phone book, newspaper, or a women's magazine like *Good Housekeeping* or *Glamour*, whose back pages were filled with ads for secretarial schools and business colleges that offered courses in shorthand, typing, the use of business machines, bookkeeping, and other office skills. Some, like the Nancy Taylor Secretarial Schools, went beyond the basic good grooming tips that were part of most course curricula and provided additional training in charm and personality development for "that finishing school look." The Grace Downs Air Career School even offered an "Airline Secretarial" course that, among other accomplishments, prepared its graduates to "take dictation in the terminology of the Air Age." Finding the right program from the many available was "like choosing anything from a hat to a husband—chiefly a matter of determining clearly in advance what you need and want, and then hunting until you find it," according to a mid-twentieth-century secretarial expert.[9]

By the time that advice was given, commercial schools had been around for close to a century. Unlike the university business schools of today, which train the executives of tomorrow in management techniques, these offered young men raised on Horatio Alger stories instruction in the basic clerical skills they needed to open their own businesses: commercial math, book-keeping, and penmanship (legible handwriting being a highly important skill before the invention of the typewriter). Some also offered courses in stenography, and after the 1880s, most included typewriting in the curriculum.[10]

Given the fact that coeducation still struck fear into the hearts of many educators and parents (perhaps the main "objection . . . to be considered," wrote an observer in 1905, was "summed up in the word 'love-making'"), it's amazing that many nineteenth-century business colleges not only accepted women but went so far as to actively recruit them. Some advertised that their programs would unlock women's heretofore untapped intellectual capabilities; others, that commercial education offered a level of independence and awareness of "the workaday world" that no woman should be without— especially at a time when the "problem" of unmarried spinsters or old maids, who otherwise remained unemployed at the family home until the end of their days, was much discussed. With the introduction of typewriting courses in the 1880s, the schools simply pointed to the new clerical opportunities for women in the changing business world—and began to offer "amanuensis courses" that taught both typing and shorthand to future secretaries ("amanuensis" being a fancy word for "one who copies or writes from the dictation of another").[11]

Perhaps feeling the pinch of competition, the 1880s was also the decade when universities began offering "comprehensive, professional" business degree programs for future corporate presidents. These programs were largely closed to women, who, in turn, began to dominate the student body at the more technically oriented private business colleges. Historian Lisa M. Fine discovered that during the 1892–1893 school year, 90 percent of the students enrolled in the amanuensis course at Chicago's Metropolitan Business College were women—who comprised only 25 percent of the entire student body. It was also around this time that the first specialized typing and shorthand schools appeared—the forerunners of the secretarial colleges.[12]

But not all secretarial or business colleges were alike, and it's clear from contemporary evidence that many of them promised more than they could deliver. The "amount of fraud and the variety of crookedness in the teaching of shorthand . . . in Boston is amazingly large," noted the author of an 1890 letter to the editor of the *Phonographic Journal*. "Young girls, with little or no education to fit them for any employment demanding discretion, knowledge of English grammar or simple mathematics, have been crowding by thousands into cheap so-called typewriting and stenographic 'colleges'; and after a few months' crude endeavor are let loose upon the business world believing that they can take the place of experience, education, and responsibility. Painful disappointment has been the lot of many," reported the *Chicago Herald* the following year.[13] *The Ambitious Woman in Business* (1916) huffed about "fly-by-night 'business schools'" that claimed to train students in both stenography and typewriting in a mere thirty days, while *The Girl and the Job* (1919) offered "a word of warning" to young women about the shady practices of some less-than-reliable business schools. These included "sending representatives to the homes of graduates to solicit pupils" and the "curious system of rotation" by which recent graduates were placed into jobs, then "after a month or two, for no very definite reason," were replaced "by a girl just graduated, who, too, had been promised a position by the school." Thirty-two years later, an article describing what a prospective student should look for in a secretarial school told of two young woman graduates from such programs: one landed a job as a stenographer and was quickly promoted, the other had a hard time finding a placement, and when she did, it was as "one of those general office slaveys" who were never promoted. The difference? "One girl had received her secretarial training in a good secretarial school; the other in a poor one." Nor was this an isolated case. "Far too many able and ambitious girls" were not getting ahead "as well as they should because of inadequate secretarial preparation."[14]

The Right Kind of Education

Secretarial school also provided what some experts considered the "right kind" of education for women—who, after all, had little need for a bachelor of arts when their role in life (according to the same experts) was to trap a bachelor boy into marriage. A liberal arts degree would only frustrate them. Writing in the *Rotarian* in 1938, Henry C. Link, Ph.D., a pioneer in the field of employment psychology, warned parents who sent their daughters to liberal arts colleges of the dire consequences that could follow such a rash decision. An unhappy freshman in "a leading women's college" begged her parents for a vocational examination, which Link administered. "While bright enough for a liberal arts education, there were factors in her makeup that pointed toward the need for a more practical, more disciplined education." He recommended she train to become a nurse—and not a moment too soon, as a few weeks later, the girl, who chose to finish out her freshman year at her current school, suffered a nervous breakdown and had to leave college. She was just one of "many student casualties due to the wrong kind of education." Along with nursing, secretarial studies provided the right kind of education. "Quite often we find it desirable, on the basis of a complete psychological examination, to suggest the substitution of a college major in secretarial work or dietetics, for a major in sociology or political science." Young women who graduated with the latter types of degrees "found themselves prepared for nothing in particular." As a result, they had to "do some straight thinking. Often it ends in their going back to school, this time, perhaps to a secretarial school."[15]

Link's psychological tests sound like pseudo-science at its scary-funny best, but one didn't have to go far in the mid-twentieth century to find women willing to testify against their college education in favor of secretarial studies. Seven years after her graduation in 1957, an analytical chemist bitterly reported that women analysts were the "second class citizens" of chemistry and that if she ever worked again, she "might tech but would more likely do stenographic work. This is women's work, traditional and respectable." Around the same time, a twenty-six-year-old "secretary-research assistant" at a Los Angeles television station, who had attended both UCLA and the Sorbonne, explained that "college may give you a wonderful foundation for life but it's not much help in getting a job. I wouldn't have gotten this job without having secretarial skills." She didn't use her shorthand "more than once a week, but if a girl doesn't have it she won't get the job." (But even she was annoyed with previous employers who "were always impressed with my education but didn't necessarily want me to use it.")[16]

For a young woman, secretarial studies were the gender-appropriate equivalent of medical school—at least according to a 1966 article in *Junior Secretary*, "A Magazine for First-Year Secretarial Students" published by the Gregg Shorthand empire: "Just as a young man goes to medical school to be a doctor, so you study now to be a secretary. And, as he can use his medical basics to launch him into a specialty—so, too, can you use a thorough knowledge of shorthand."[17]

Katharine Gibbs School:
The Harvard of Secretarial Education

If medical school represented a pinnacle of educational success for young men, its equivalent for the shorthand set was the Katharine Gibbs School. According to a 1941 ad, Gibbs was "the choice of thoughtful fathers anxious to see their daughters fortunately placed in the business world" and offered "happy away-at-school experiences with thorough preparation for secretarial careers." This was a far cry from a liberal arts college, where a daughter majoring in "sociology, political economy, or economics" might "come home inspired with radical plans for a *world* economy, but quite unable to make a practical contribution to the economy of the *home*," as employment psychologist Henry Link explained in 1938.[18]

A young woman emphatically was not going to be radicalized by the cur-

Loads of responsibility in glamorous surroundings: the Gibbs Girl had it all, 1957.

riculum at Gibbs—at least not if the administration could help it. Left a widow with two sons and no means of support after her husband was killed in a yachting accident in 1909 (technically a yacht-painting accident—the mast he was working on collapsed beneath him), forty-six-year-old Katharine Gibbs first tried her hand at a dressmaking career. When that proved unsuccessful, she and her sister enrolled in a stenography course at Boston's Simmons College. Businessman John Simmons founded the college that bore his name in 1899, with the belief that "women should be able to earn independent livelihoods and lead meaningful lives," and offered a curriculum that combined a liberal arts and technical education. For example, in 1902, along with what the *New York Times* referred as the "mere shorthand and typewriting lessons of the secretarial course," there was "instruction in English, German, French, and Spanish, making the training acquired by the

Simmons graduate . . . something quite different from that received at any purely 'business college.'"[19]

The course at Simmons galvanized Gibbs. Returning home, she took one thousand dollars raised from the sale of her jewelry and in 1911 opened the Providence Secretarial School for Educated Women. A newspaper article published on the occasion of the Katharine Gibbs School's fiftieth anniversary noted that the school was "the first *secretarial*—as opposed to stenographic— school" for women only (the school didn't accept men until the late 1960s). Only high school graduates were accepted (the "Educated Women" of the school's name), a requirement that winnowed out ill-prepared students (not to mention immigrants), who flocked to other commercial business schools. Apparently drawing on her experience at Simmons, the curriculum at Gibbs included—in addition to the old standbys of shorthand and typing—business law, business math, and English. The school was wildly successful; by 1918 there were branches in New York and Boston. By providing women the skills to be secretaries instead of mere stenographers, Gibbs hoped to expand the opportunities for women in the business world at large. "A woman's career is blocked by lack of openings, by unjust male competition, by prejudice and, not least, by inadequate salary and recognition," she wrote in 1924.[20]

This makes its founder sound like a proto-feminist—and she certainly blazed a trail for herself as a businesswoman—but the Katharine Gibbs School quickly gained a reputation as a secretarial finishing school, turning out perfect secretaries in white gloves and hats whose thorough knowledge of shorthand and typing was surpassed only by their loyalty to the boss. According to a *BusinessWeek* profile in the early 1960s, Gibbs operated "like a New England prep school" untouched "by progressive education." The average student load amounted to fifty hours a week: twenty-five in class, twenty-five as homework. "It was hideous," recalled a student who arrived at Gibbs in 1960. "They had it worked so you had to spend four hours a day practicing to get through the next day's classes." A student from the 1950s remembered a typing test where the young woman next to her made a mistake at the beginning, put in another piece of paper to start over—and was expelled. The goal of such stringent testing, along with constant drilling (in shorthand as well as typing), was to make these basic skills automatic, thus leaving the student secretaries' minds "free to cope with the broader aspects of their jobs."[21]

"Broader aspects" included the "dignity and good taste" that, according to a mid-twentieth-century Katharine Gibbs School catalog, were "essential attributes" of what was popularly called the Gibbs Girl. Combined, these qualities made for a "prestige appearance" that reflected not only beauty but also "good judgment and intelligence." In other words, there was a dress code. In the early 1960s, it called for "street dresses rather than skirts and blouses; light use of cosmetics and jewelry; high heels and stockings; and for outdoors, hat and gloves." Twenty years later, long after other schools had given up in the battle against jeans, Gibbs students were forbidden to wear them. Even denim skirts were frowned upon—if a young woman showed up wearing one, she was sent home to change, as was a young woman who showed up on the first day of school one year in the 1980s wearing a leather miniskirt (a Gibbs official alleged that three months later this rebel was "at the head of her class and wearing a business suit").[22]

The dress code was simply the most visible aspect of Gibbs's finishing-school atmosphere. For most of its existence, Gibbs trained its girls to be no less than office geishas: skilled in typing and shorthand but with such crucial knowledge as "how to sound pleasant over the telephone . . . [and] how to chitchat about current events at the boss' cocktail parties." Classes in "personality development" promised to impart "tact, resourcefulness, a well-modulated voice, and good taste in dress and grooming," in addition to supplementary lectures on etiquette as well as the secretary's "special responsibilities in personal business contacts." After all, as Gibbs vice president Marion Beck rhetorically asked the *BusinessWeek* reporter in 1961, "What earthly good can a girl be to an executive if he has to hide her in a closet?" Another staff member (the "lecturer on office manners") noted that the Gibbs girl was trained to be "at all times an understatement—nobody likes a pushy female."[23]

Gibbs and other secretarial school graduates were a step ahead of those who couldn't get jobs with their useless liberal arts degrees. In *You Can Be an*

Wendy Scott, Secretary,
by Lucy Graves Mayo (1961)

he vast majority of novels that featured secretaries as protagonists merely used the office as a backdrop. The heroine took some shorthand, typed a letter or two, then married the boss—after many trials and tribulations, of course. There was little information about the nuts and bolts of office protocol or even what secretaries did if they weren't mooning after the boss. One young-adult novel, *Wendy Scott, Secretary,* was an exception to the rule. Penned by Lucy Graves Mayo, Katharine Gibbs School staff member and later author of *You Can Be an Executive Secretary* (1965), the book followed the travails of Wendy Scott, a high school senior torn between becoming a secretary after graduation or going to college. When her father loses his job, Wendy decides to attend the Kathleen Briggs secretarial school (a thinly disguised stand-in for Mayo's employer).

Wendy Scott, Secretary offered plenty of examples of mid-twentieth-century office wifery: during Career Day at Wendy's high school, a visiting secretary explains how she and her coworkers "officiate as office hostess to their executive's callers"; a publishing executive tells Wendy that the attributes of the "perfect" secretary he wants to hire include the ability to "look after (unobtrusively) the publisher's private affairs . . . keep his checkbook balanced, shop for him (particularly gifts for his family and friends)." But teens who read *Wendy Scott* also learned about secretarial school classes, resumes, dictation, and typing tests, and that some entry-level jobs were better than others.[*]

Then there's Wendy's classmate, Judy. Though her boyfriend has presented her with an engagement ring, Judy wants to use what she's learned at Briggs in the real world. When her fiancé tells her he doesn't want her to work after the wedding, Judy realizes he's not "the kind of

---

[*] Lucy Graves Mayo, *Wendy Scott, Secretary* (New York: Dodd, Mead, 1961), 54, 171–72.

man I want. Maybe I just don't want to be married to *any* man yet. I guess I'm not ready to stop bein' Judy Marlowe. Come to think of it, I haven't really *started* to be me."[†]

A character who wanted a bit of independence, and refused to settle for the first diamond ring that came along, was a departure from most teenage career romances, which generally ended with the protagonists quitting their careers as soon as they received a proposal of marriage. Which isn't to say *Wendy Scott* broke all precedent when it came to romance—at the end of the book Judy is engaged to a doctor (who believes in working wives) and Wendy's boyfriend is dropping hints about marriage.

It is, however, guaranteed that *Wendy Scott, Secretary* is the only teen career-romance novel to ask the following question: "Tell me again, Wendy, when is an introductory gerund phrase *not* the subject of a sentence?"[‡]

[†] Ibid., 167.
[‡] Ibid., 143.

Executive Secretary, Gibbs School administrator Lucy Mayo told the story of a recent college graduate who made the rounds but remained unemployed. Then she added "good, basic secretarial skill" to her resume, *et voila*:

> Now I can DO [Mayo quoted the newly hired grad], not just talk about doing. And I can hardly wait to go back to all those places that wanted no part of me when a college diploma was my major "qualification." "Can you type, write shorthand, file and find?" they asked me. And when my answer was "No, but . . ." the doors closed. Well, they are opening now, and it's because of what I can DO.[24]

When Mayo penned the example of the college graduate and her newly minted office skills, she meant it to give hope as well as provide a strategy to women who were either unemployed or felt stuck in their current positions. Whether her reader's degree was from college or high school, an uppercased affirmation on the title page of Mayo's book explained the benefits of holding secretarial skills in an era when the "career woman" was still considered a dubious character: "IF YOU CAN TYPE, IF YOU CAN LEARN SHORTHAND, THIS BOOK WILL HELP YOU ENJOY YOUR JOB AND EARN MORE MONEY."

The Lost Art of Shorthand

Typing on a manual or electric typewriter was vastly more labor intensive than tapping out a letter on a computer keyboard (one little mistake, youngsters, and you often had to go back and do it all over), but it's not as mystifying as the all-but-dead practice of shorthand. For generations of office workers, the steno pad was as symbolic of the secretary's job as the stethoscope was of the physician's. To be caught without one would have been an unthinkable dereliction of duty. Shorthand was the very "foundation of successful secretarial practice," in the words of an early 1960s Katharine Gibbs School catalog.[25]

A stenographer might write the word "people" as "pepl"—only in most forms of shorthand it's written in some combination of curving lines or circles and dots. Don't worry if this sounds confusing: shorthand is completely unintelligible to the uninitiated. Even speedwriting, an "easier" form of shorthand created in the mid-twentieth century that used letters instead of symbols, resulted in gibberish: "Your rebate check will reach you in a few days" turned into "u rba ck l rec u n a fu ds\" (the slash represented a period). All shorthand systems could be tricky to learn and required constant practice to stay sharp, but a skilled practitioner could easily take down 120 words per minute during dictation (the average speaking rate is about 140 wpm). An experienced court reporter often recorded 200 or more words per minute. In 1922, a New York City courtroom stenographer named Nathan Behrin set a world record when he blazed through a speed contest at 350 words a minute, for two minutes, and made only two errors.[26]

Shorthand systems date back to the Greeks and Romans, but the ones most frequently used in twentieth-century American offices were those

Just You, Him, and a Steno Pad

Of all the secretary's duties, dictation was the most intimate. Perhaps it's one reason why the boss-secretary relationship was viewed with a certain amount of suspicion—it involved a man and a woman behind a closed door, after all. Dictation worked like this: The stenographer or secretary joined her boss in his office, closed the door behind her, flipped open her steno pad—and waited for him to say something. Some bosses spoke very rapidly, and heaven help the unseasoned girl who landed with one of these speed demons. Others paused frequently to think about what they were going to say. When that happened, the secretary was supposed to remain stock still, lest her pencil tapping or hair smoothing drive the great man's would-be brilliant idea right out of his mind. If he groped for the right word, she was not allowed to supply it, unless she was sure her interruption would not distract him. If he dictated with a pipe in his mouth, or with his back to her as he mused out the window, if his deodorant failed, or he was habitually drunk after lunch, she was simply supposed to do her best. One guidebook described a typical boss's dictation as follows: "Miss . . . take a letter to that company you know their man came in when I was at lunch one day—Gentlemen at least I hope you are—heh-heh—In reply to yours of the what was the date of their letter I think I must have it at home with some other papers—I beg to advise that ungk mump glik pop (that's how it sounds as he shifts his cigar to the left molars and bends over to tighten a shoelace)" and so on. (Speaking from experience—though I transcribed Dictaphone tapes—I consider this a spot on re-creation, minus the gum chewing and occasional burps.)*

* Marie L. Carney, *The Secretary and Her Job* (Charlottesville, Va.: Business Book House, 1939), 129.

The gum-chewing steno who couldn't read her own shorthand notes was immortalized in this "vinegar" valentine from the 1940s.

developed by Isaac Pitman (1813–1897) and John Robert Gregg (1867– 1948). Pitman, an Englishman, introduced what he called "Stenographic Sound-Hand" in his *Manual of Phonography* (1837; "phonography" was a generic term for the phonetic representation of words). In Pitman's system of shorthand, circular pen strokes and the sounds they represented were differentiated by "shading"—how hard or light the pen was pressed to paper—as well as whether they were situated on, above, or below the base line. Dots—

heavy or light—also helped distinguish vowel sounds from one another. But it was Isaac's brother, Benn, who became the Johnny Appleseed of the Pitman method of shorthand in the United States. Benn Pitman (trailblazing as well with his creatively spelled first name) emigrated to Cincinnati in 1852, where he introduced his brother's phonography to the local populace with free lectures and demonstrations. A major shot of publicity came thirteen years later, when Benn Pitman was appointed the chief stenographic reporter at the Lincoln assassination trial; by 1889, ninety-seven percent of American shorthand writers used the Pitman method.[27]

As a youngster growing up in a small Irish village, John Robert Gregg watched his older siblings struggle to learn Pitman shorthand (the Gregg family patriarch required all his children to learn the skill after he witnessed a journalist record a Sunday sermon verbatim—an excellent reminder of what passed for entertainment in the days before electricity). Rather than replicate their failure, ten-year-old John chose Odell's shorthand, which he taught himself with great success. From then on, and for the rest of his life, Gregg was obsessed with shorthand—and critical of Pitman's approach to it. He began work on the system that would bear his name while he was still in his teens and published his first pamphlet, *Light-Line Phonography* (1888), when he was twenty-one years old. Gregg based his method on cursive strokes that resembled longhand and were meant to flow more naturally from one to another, thus increasing the stenographer's speed. Consonants were represented by strokes that resembled elongated commas; vowels, by hooks and circles. Students of the Gregg system also memorized 184 "brief forms"—combined strokes that represented commonly used words and phrases. In 1893, Gregg moved to Boston with the intention of starting what his biographer called "a crusade for Gregg Shorthand in the New World."[28]

During the early years of the twentieth century, Pitman and Gregg were fierce competitors for the hearts and minds of America's stenographers. Which system was easiest to learn? Which produced the fastest writers? Claims and counterclaims of superiority filled the pages of *Typewriter and Phonographic World* and other industry publications. Practitioners steeled their pens against one another in time trials and speed demonstrations throughout the country, each competitor sponsored by the corporation whose method they used (world speed champion Nathan Behrin, for example, competed under Pitman's banner). Nonetheless, by the mid-twentieth century, Gregg occupied the throne of a shorthand empire (among its holdings were a textbook publishing company—still active today—and a college) that had made deep inroads into what had been Pitman's almost exclusive territory.[29]

But Gregg's success didn't eradicate the Pitman method. Until the combined forces of the stenotype machine used by court reporters, the Dictaphone, and the computer finally killed the regular use of shorthand in the 1970s, secretarial schools, business colleges, and high schools regularly taught one or the other method. The lack of a standardized system caused some problems, to be sure. Woe to the secretary trained in Pitman if she was called on to transcribe the notes of an absent coworker who took them in Gregg. Like the Word Perfect–trained temp of a later generation who found herself sent to an office using MS Word, she was up the proverbial creek without a paddle. Some offices got around potential snafus by hiring only Gregg- or Pitman-trained secretaries and stenographers.

Another drawback of shorthand was that of handwriting in general: everybody drew their "pothooks" a little bit differently, so notes taken by one practitioner might be completely illegible to another—or even to the note taker herself when it came time to read them back. Secretarial guides urged readers to practice their shorthand penmanship frequently, lest they lose valuable time trying to read inaccurate or illegible marks when transcribing their notes. "Doing your homework every other day or trying to catch up with it on the weekends is a surefire way not to pass," scolded the *Junior Secretary* in the 1960s.[30] Along with *Junior Secretary*, magazines like the *Gregg Writer* and *Today's Secretary* (all three titles were part of John Robert Gregg's publishing empire) usually included stories and essays printed in shorthand, in addition to exercises, games, and crossword puzzles that gave readers a fun way to practice their outlines. "Remember, a stenographer is like a piece of silverware, the more she is polished, the brighter she will be," advised the *Gregg Writer* in 1946.[31]

THE LIVING METHOD
SHORTHAND
COURSE
THE NEW, REINFORCED LEARNING METHOD
THAT HELPS YOU MASTER SHORTHAND QUICKLY AND EASILY
USE THE SYSTEM OF YOUR CHOICE: THE LIVING METHOD VERSION OF
ORIGINAL GREGG, PITMAN, RAPID WRITING—
ALL CONTAINED IN THE BASIC INSTRUCTION MANUAL

• Learn basic symbols in 7 days   • Achieve a rate of 120 words per minute
• Take dictation at controlled speeds • Master the never-fail read-back-system
• Refresh and improve your stenography • Qualify for legal, medical, engineering work

4 33 RPM RECORDS AND 2 COMPLETE INSTRUCTION MANUALS

by Lewis Robins and Reed Harris

The marvels of recording technology meant that a would-be stenographer could learn the tricks of the trade in her very own home, 1960.

A sloppy stenographer and her illegible notes were at the center of what might be taken as a cautionary tale told in the pages of the *New York Times* in 1928. On a June afternoon that year, Miss Hetty Dingle, a stenographer at the National Magazine Company in Manhattan, went missing. "Dull thuds and faint cries" from inside the company safe soon made her whereabouts known. An office boy carelessly had shut the vault's door, but no one had the combination—except Hetty. "It's on a slip of paper in my desk," she shouted to her would-be rescuers, who there turned up a scrap of paper covered with shorthand scribbles. Her sister stenographers tried in vain to decode them, but Hetty's outlines were legible only to herself. The police were called; a steel drill finally breached the door. The slip of paper was passed through the hole, and Hetty read the combination aloud to a detective waiting outside. If she pondered the error of her shorthand ways during the hour and a quarter she spent in the safe, she didn't tell the press, commenting only that it had been "kind of warm in there."[32]

Shorthand outlines (usually the Gregg method) even found their way into pop culture and consumer items aimed at or associated with female office workers. Faith Baldwin's 1930 bestseller *The Office Wife*, for example, repeated the title in shorthand on its hardbound cover. Thirty or so years later, toiletries manufacturer Paul Klein packaged an "executive" line for men in bottles printed with the Gregg shorthand symbol for "Very truly yours." The squiggle was a subliminal message to the women who formed 92 percent of the customers for the products (men presumably being too shy to buy cologne for themselves in the decades before the birth of the metrosexual). "Almost every girl who goes through school gets some brush with shorthand and the very first things they learn are 'Dear Sir' and 'Very truly yours,'" Klein explained to the *Los Angeles Times* in 1963. He clearly presumed that the siren song of her work life was strong enough to draw her to his product.[33]

Shorthand may have been "the written language of the profession," as *The Private Secretary's Manual* (1943) termed it, but typing perhaps best provided most girls and women with the employment insurance Lucy Mayo extolled. It was far easier to brush up on one's typing skills after a long absence from the keyboard than to pick up the steno pad and remember just what all those squiggles meant.[34]

Requirements varied by employer, but the threshold typing speed for an entry-level secretarial position was usually about 40 words per minute (80 wpm for shorthand). Skilled typists could whiz along at much higher speeds. Margaret B. Owen was a product demonstrator for the Underwood Typewriter Company and the "World Champion Typist" of 1915. Her winning speed of 137 words per minute is astounding even today, even more so when you consider Owen was typing on a heavy, manual machine. Brenda Cooper, who won the title World's Fastest Typist in a contest that took place

A fifteen-year-old typist earns her daily bread in the 1910s.

as part of Professional Secretaries Week 1982, used an electric typewriter—and typed 91.4 words per minute, adjusted for errors. On a good day back at the law firm word-processing department, I probably topped out around 100 words per minute, but that was on a computer keyboard—and my typos weren't being tabulated.[35]

Whether she was a speed demon or normal operator, once a woman was adequately trained in shorthand and typing, it was time to look for a job—and to do that, a girl had to look her best.

Looking Her Best

Writing in 1892, the president of the Business Education Association reflected on a delicate problem. Many of the young girls who came to study shorthand and typing at the commercial business schools did not "live in the best homes" nor were they "used to the best society." They were trying to pull themselves up by their bootstraps, to be sure, but sometimes their personal hygiene left something to be desired:

> How are you going to tell a girl to comb her hair; who is going to tell her that she is uncomely, uncleanly, that even the odor of her person and her garments are not pleasant, that persons do not like to sit at the same table with her? Shall we throw these girls out, or shall we take them and do a little for them?[36]

The humanitarian decision was to "do a little" for these socially inept students who didn't understand that wrinkled rags and a whiff of body odor weren't going to get them the job of their dreams; the result were the classes in what the *Independent Woman* (the publication of the National Federation of Business and Professional Women's Clubs) referred to in 1940 as "personal adequacy . . . dress, grooming, posture, carriage, voice, diction, business etiquette, [and] poise" that haunted the curricula of commercial high schools, business colleges, and secretarial schools for decades to follow.[37]

Part of the emphasis on looks was simple common sense: a well-groomed, nicely dressed job applicant was more likely to get hired. There was also a consensus that a disheveled exterior was indicative of a similarly disordered interior. "If her blouse is not absolutely fresh her chances are lessened," reflected an employment agency representative in 1931. "We take it as an indication of other slipshod qualities." A crisp collar and freshly pressed skirt were more than an instant introduction to a job candidate; an attractive appearance bespoke "an interested, fastidious, alert, and well-ordered mind," counseled the *Independent Woman* in 1940. "Any girl beginning her career, or any woman well in one, would do well to keep this fact always in mind. For given two candidates, the prize invariably goes to the girl who *looks* like a winner." The notion that appearance reflected aptitude sometimes even extended past clothing to body size; *Secretaries on the Spot* (1967), "a collection of actual secretarial problems and how they were solved" published by the National Secretaries Association, included a case study where supervisors protested hiring an overweight woman because they believed "generally speaking, an obese person is inclined to be untidy in her work."[38]

Wanted: Attractive Secty to Busy Exec

Fans of television's *Mad Men* (a drama set in the fictional Sterling Cooper Advertising Agency in the 1960s) may remember a scene from the first season wherein the voluptuous—and extremely competent—head secretary knowingly positions herself directly in front of the executives who are watching from behind a one-way mirror the focus group she is facilitating, then turns away from them, and bends over. The men, bourbon in hand, stand up and salute her upside-down heart of a derriere. The secretarial "caboose" was also a focal point of a song-and-dance number from 1962's hit musical *How to Succeed in Business Without Really Trying*. The version of "A Secretary Is Not a Toy" preserved in the 1967 film is a candy-colored extravaganza of firmly girdled secretaries, pipe-smoking junior executives, and office relations that would today land the perpetrator a pink slip, if not a court date. In the moments before the cast bursts into the song, a group of executives debate who has dibs on the pulchritudinous new "girl" in the office. (The joke's on them, however, because she's the big boss's mistress and thus strictly "hands-off" when it comes to the other men in the office.) Both *Mad Men* and *How to Succeed* may have exaggerated the gleeful lust with which the executives viewed the support staff—and the good-natured way in which the women were often shown responding—but the idea that part of the secretary's role was to serve as eye candy for the men around her was supported by all sorts of real-life evidence.

Perhaps you're not old enough to remember (or maybe you remember all too well) that prior to 1968, employment ads were divided into columns headed "Help Wanted—Male" and "Help Wanted—Female." Nor

were bosses afraid to ask, very specifically, for the qualities—physical as
well as professional—they were looking for when it came to hiring a new
secretary. The following ad appeared in the *Chicago Tribune* on Sunday,
March 14, 1943.

SCINTILLATING SECRETARY

Let her be lovely to look at, charming to talk to,
spirited and gay. A capable secretarial assistant to a
major executive, whose work and contacts have the
sparkle of fine champagne.
    Excellent salary for a lass under 30 with a good
education and all the cobwebs swept from her brain.

An ad from the May 22, 1951, edition of the *New York Times* took a less
chatty approach, using capital letters to specify the intangible qualifications
of its perfect applicant:

ALL AMERICAN GIRL

MUST BE EXTREMELY ATTRACTIVE
Exceptionally efficient worker,
five years experience as an executive secretary,
Age 24–30, Singl. Resident New Yorker
SALARY UNLIMITED

Today, we can pick out more than one politically incorrect if not downright illegal phrase in these two short ads, but before Title VII of the Civil
Rights Act made gender-based classified ads illegal, it was perfectly acceptable for the boss to order up his dream girl—and with specificity. In 1920,
the *San Francisco Chronicle* quoted a call to "a big employment agency"

from a would-be employer who preferred looks to skills: "This is a classy automobile sales concern. We sell a classy car. And we want a classy girl to take letters and perform general clerical work. One not over 25 years of age and none of your dowds, mind you. A swell dresser we want." (Not that he wanted to pay for such a jewel: "Salary? Oh, not more than $25 a week!" That's roughly equivalent to $6.75 an hour in 2010 dollars.)[39]

How did women react to such blatant appeals for youth and beauty? It's impossible to know definitively, but in 1943, with the nation hard at war and more middle-class women than ever working outside the home, the "Scintillating Secretary" ad caused a sensation. Over two hundred women sent application letters to a box at the *Tribune* (one sent four in a single day); two-thirds of the respondents had a college education. One applicant stated her qualifications in a twelve-stanza verse—then forgot to sign her name to it. Several applicants enclosed photographs of themselves, a considerable number (each no doubt thinking herself original) signed their notes "Scintilla," and one described herself as "the fairest of five daughters." Other replies were less enthusiastic. One woman read between the lines, or thought she did, and began her letter "Dear Wolf." Someone else wondered if the employer was "aging and losing his hair," hence his need for "some glamor [sic] in the office." Another woman simply sent back a copy of the ad with the age limit underlined along with the plaintive inquiry "Does this mean we can't scintillate after 30?"[40]

The ad even spawned imitators. A company seeking a Dictaphone operator a few weeks later began, "'Scintillating Secretaries' may be okay, but we will be satisfied with a capable, experienced girl."[41]

The *Chicago Tribune*'s "White Collar Girl" columnist Ruth McKay was alerted to the Scintillating Secretary ad when several of her readers sent her carbon copies of their application letters, and later reported that an "attractive . . . artistic . . . capable" Smith College graduate finally got the job.[42]

In *How to Be a Hero to Your Secretary: A Handbook for Bosses* (1941), perhaps the only guidebook for executives penned by a secretary, author Gladys Torson pleaded with men to be honest with themselves when it came to interviewing prospective hires. "If your ideal secretary is a girl five feet four with red hair and no freckles and no other type will make you happy, draw up your specifications before you send out for applicants. It is useless to waste your time and hers in interviewing a six-foot brunette." A boss was also within his rights to ask an applicant to remove her hat, the better to appraise her looks, though such a request might "prove a little disconcerting to the girl"—not least because, according to *Strictly for Secretaries* (1965), wearing a hat "would rate her a good notch above a hatless competitor."[43]

If the "girl" was following the rules given by the secretarial manuals, it was a very becoming hat indeed. "You will *look your very best* because you are well aware that before one word is spoken in this scene, *how you look* will have already created the all-important first impression," was how the proper job interview look was described in *You Can Be an Executive Secretary*. Dress, grooming, and makeup counted for as much as 75 percent when it came to getting hired, according to one expert. "One off-note in a girl's color scheme (such as bright-colored shoes), or an indication of a tendency to go to extremes (such as hoop earrings), or one major sin (such as red fingernails" was enough to label a girl "untouchable from an employment agency's standpoint." But even when a secretarial candidate was dressed in guidebook-approved quiet good taste, the hiring executive saw only one thing: a woman ripe for ogling.[44]

In fact, sizing up a potential new secretary from head to toe after the personnel director left her in an executive's office was not only acceptable, but expected—allegedly by the candidate herself. In *Survival in the Executive Jungle* (1964), a "practical straight-from-the-shoulder guide" to the "cutthroat competition" of executive life, Chester Burger explained the gender politics of the job interview man-to-man:

> You won't look upon her as you would a male job applicant. You'll quickly notice whether she's comely or homely. No detail of her figure, from neckline to ankle will escape you. The female applicant expects this. Having discovered the rules for survival in the male business world, she has carefully prepared for her interview with you. Her grooming is immaculate;

her dress is conservative; her smile is working overtime. She may lack experience in dealing with executives as such, but she is fully able to handle herself with men.

But the hiring executive should never let the well-groomed, cheerfully smiling female fool him. Her feminine wiles were already working overtime. The job interview thus turned into a game of cat and mouse:

> While outwardly, you may appear to be interviewing her with cold objectivity and businesslike manner, she knows this isn't so, and so do you. One perceptive professional secretary told me that male executives often acted as if they were sizing up an opportunity for subsequent dalliance.

But where the executive saw a potential conquest (and a "perceptive professional" saw a letch), many women were simply using the experts-approved rules of job interviewing. Burger understood that the eager-to-please attitude taught by secretarial schools and guidebooks might be confused for something else: "Sometimes a young executive, hiring a secretary for the first time, mistakes a girl's job-seeking charm as an invitation for an affair" (which he counseled against, citing "several promising careers that were halted in their tracks by hi-jinks after five").[45]

Assuming she passed the executive's once-over—not to mention the typing and shorthand tests—the newly hired secretary faced her next hurdle: getting to know her new coworkers.

You're in the Office Now, Miss Sec:
The Fine Arts of Charm, Etiquette,
and Getting Along with Others

It's a good idea to discover whether your boss has any color incompatibilities. . . . You don't want to sashay into the office in your lovely new lavender dress only to find that lavender is his pet aversion. If he's irritated by a color you wear, chances are your day will be far less pleasant.

> Helen Whitcomb and Rosalind Lang,
> *Charm: The Career Girl's Guide to Business*
> *and Personal Success* (1964)

I have a confession. When I started out, I was a bad secretary—and that's bad as in "incompetent," not bad as in "naughty." As I stated previously, my typing skills were negligible. But more than that, office procedure mystified me ("do I file this or throw it away?"), and I hated making phone calls to strangers (though, in an ironic twist, everybody agreed that I "gave good phone" as long as I was answering). Let's see how my work for a not-for-profit art gallery—my first secretarial job—measured up to the secretarial paradigm the head of a large temporary help agency described to the *Chicago Tribune* in 1946.

The Ideal Secretary	*Me*
Is attractive and personable, but she need not be beautiful.	So far so good. Who isn't attractive and personable in their mid-twenties?
Dresses neatly and conservatively, not ostentatiously.	My working wardrobe was composed of 1950s-era men's gabardine work shirts and jeans, occasionally interspersed with dresses I'd worn in high school. My boss's view was perhaps best summed up the day she slipped me a check on the kind-but-firm condition I would spend it on new clothing. I did—but I kept on wearing the baggy shirts and threadbare dresses too.
Protects her boss and conserves his time, but doesn't coddle him.	Anne was a savvy businesswoman who didn't need anybody to protect her—and if anybody was getting coddled, it was me.
Thinks for herself and expresses herself. Knows the business well and takes an interest in it. Knows her boss well and keeps her interest in him strictly professional.	Interested in the art business? Definitely. Knew the boss well but kept it professional? Yup. But crippled by shyness and self-doubt, I didn't think for or express myself until I was in my thirties. Some secretarial experts would bill that as an advantage.
Exhibits no superiority over other employees merely because she's the boss' secretary.	Exhibit superiority when I could barely bring myself to answer the phone? Uh, no.

Is alert, tactful, and, of course, thoroly [sic] competent in her professional skills.	Alert? After my morning coffee, yes. Tactful? Definitely. Competent in my professional skills? Not for many years to come.
Doesn't fall in love with the boss or permit him to fall in love with her. The "office wife" routine is for the movies.[1]	Given we were both heterosexual females, the "'office wife' routine" was mercifully not an issue.

All tolled, then, my rating was a wobbly four out of seven, depending on how you added it up—perhaps I was better office broken than I've given myself credit for, but I was decidedly less than stellar. Oh sure, I was reasonably personable (see item one above), but my dress and deportment left something to be desired (see item two above). Of course, I didn't have a secretarial school background. If I had, I would have been more well versed in that nebulous quality called charm.

Be Charming, Miss Secretary!

Charm combined elements of personality (charming women were generally submissive and deferential to others, i.e., men), dress and deportment (both ladylike), voice ("ever soft, gentle, and low, an excellent thing in a woman," to quote Shakespeare, as did many of the guidebooks), and daintiness (usually an advertising code word meaning one didn't burp, fart, or forget to wear deodorant in any one of several unusual places). The specter of charm was used to sell consumer goods as disparate as douches and mink coats. "You cannot define charm in a word," wrote the authors of the *Secrets of Charm* (1954); after almost four hundred pages, all they managed to conclude was that "we know when we are in its presence." According to *How to Be a Good Secretary* (1969), charm was a kind of "internal beauty" that erupted, almost uncontrollably, out of ordinary-looking people: "The reason is that Mother

Charming Girls Get Jobs!

Big business is charm conscious," wrote modeling-school mogul John Robert Powers and syndicated beauty columnist Mary Sue Miller in *Secrets of Charm* (1954). When "an industry head" asked the John Robert Powers School "to evolve a yardstick by which applicants in both its worker and executive ranks could be graded on charm . . . in and out of business," it came up with the following list, guaranteed to forecast the "merit" of the would-be employee "at the time of her interview"—even though it asked nothing about her skills.

1. Is the applicant's bearing graceful? Gracefulness indicates self-assurance and poise.
2. Does her figure reflect health and beauty routining [*sic*]? If so, she is self-disciplined and reliable.
3. Does her appearance attest to a sense of fitness? How tasteful, becoming and suitable is her dress?
4. Is her face neglected or carelessly made up? The careless person is seldom capable.
5. Is she well groomed from head to toe? Fine personal standards carry over into work.
6. By a pleasant voice and groomed speech, does she show the consideration needed for harmonious association with colleagues and clients?
7. Does her conversation indicate an awareness of the world around her? Wide interests stamp an enterprising, flexible person.*

* John Robert Powers and Mary Sue Miller, *Secrets of Charm* (Philadelphia: John C. Winston, 1954), 360–61.

Nature failed them in one way and is making up for the imperfection in another way. Therefore the *charm* which they exhibit so abundantly is what *makes them beautiful*. . . . Just as a volcano belches out from its depths, the rich minerals that are hidden beneath the earth's surface, Mother Nature generously pours forth *from her heart* all her warmth and sincere goodness."[2]

Charm was often equated with feminine success (in mid-twentieth-century America, this meant heterosexual marriage and motherhood). *Charm: The Career Girl's Guide to Business and Personal Success* (1964), a secretarial school textbook, made it clear that while "appearance, personality, sophistication, and thoughtfulness" often made the difference between "the girl in the private office with her name on the door and the back-office drone who is always bypassed at promotion time," there was more than a potential promotion at stake. Cultivating these qualities also meant "the difference between loneliness and a full and happy life" outside of the office.[3]

Behind her desk, it was important for the secretary to "look spotless, well pressed, neat, and scrubbed clean" at all times because, among other reasons, she, and the other women at the office, were responsible—at least subliminally—for the well-being of their coworkers. Attractive people had "the power to inspire those about them," even though the incentive they offered was "on the subconscious level." Training in beauty and charm thus added "up to the poise and graciousness" that not only won jobs but also kept "the boss, customers, and fellow workers happy," opined a reporter for the *Chicago Tribune* in a 1941 overview of "Miss Secretary . . . America's Golden Girl!" A dose of good grooming gave a "girl the self-confidence she needs to succeed" and did "a great deal toward counteracting fatigue." A favorite "outfit worn on gloomy-weather days" even perked up one's morale, at least according to *How to Be a Good Secretary*.[4]

But self-confidence and personal satisfaction paled in comparison to vocational duty. It was incumbent on the secretary to look good because her appearance reflected directly on her boss:

> Your good grooming is evidence that he knows how to pick a smart girl—
> that he's a pretty clever fellow. He may be only third assistant to the pur-

Your Personal Behavior: What to Avoid

I t didn't matter how well groomed and dressed a secretary was if she ruined the picture by "careless personal behavior." *The Successful Secretary* (1964) polled secretaries in a range of fields and asked them to list the most flagrant examples of office boorishness.

- Loud talking or loud laughing, in the office, the powder room, or the corridors
- Using language unbecoming a lady
- "Office hopping"
- Taking a lengthy coffee break, or lengthy lunch hour
- Sitting on desks
- Smoking in someone else's office, or while walking
- Posture or stance that smacks of Hollywood
- Undue familiarity with superiors
- Officiousness
- Lack of interest in one's job
- Discourteous behavior
- Strident unpleasant voice
- Chewing gum
- Nail biting
- Lack of humility, inability to make mistakes.

How many secretarial sins are you guilty of? I've chewed gum while sitting on a desk and swearing like a sailor—but I've done my best never to be discourteous.

chasing agent, but if he can choose an attractive and charming Girl Friday who's efficient as well, his prestige has leaped several notches. Needless to say, when he can take pride in you the benefits are sure to bounce back your way.[5]

A member of the Chrysler Corporation's steno pool takes a moment to powder her face in 1942. According to The Successful Secretary *(1964), the only time for such "primping" was during "lunch hours and after closing time."*

Could she expect candy and flowers? Comp time? A raise? Alas, the benefits—though tantalizing—remained unspecified. It was impossible to tell if a Chicago secretary who attended a "beauty-for-business" class sponsored by a local modeling school in the mid-1950s was pleased or dismayed by her boss's response to her makeover: "I was surprised to find that my boss has noticed me more since I started using some of the advice from the course." What exactly did she mean by the word "noticed"? Did a new haircut lead her boss to suddenly remember her very existence, as well as the pile of work he had for her to do? Or, as any number of sitcoms and B-movies would have us believe, did it cause him to lean over her desk and throatily whisper, "Why, Miss Jones, I never knew you had such beautiful eyes!"

The latter situation was to be avoided at all costs—according to the guidebooks. While it was important for the secretary to dress well and be well groomed, looking like a movie star could distract the men around her. "Regardless of how much an employer may admire bombshells in his social life, he doesn't want them in the office," opined *The Successful Secretary* (1951). Sexy outfits (those comprising "plunging necklines, black stockings, too-tight skirts, too-tight sweaters, sheer blouses and billowy skirts") were inappropriate for the office because they drew men's attention from their ever-so-important work: "No good businessman has time to spare for the distractions of a would-be siren."[6]

Dressing like a femme fatale was bad, but dressing "like a fashion model" wasn't much better—doing so implied that a woman "cared more about her appearance than her job." Just as a low-cut blouse distracted her boss, dressing in the latest designer clothing drew "too much attention to the secretary" and antagonized "the other girls in the office." It also intimidated men. In *The Secretary's Guide to Dealing with People* (1964), author Jean Vermes imagined a scene where an executive of a tool-and-die concern asked a long-time customer, George, why he seemed less friendly lately. The problem, it seemed, was neither the company's product nor its service; it was the "debutante in the outer office":

"She makes me feel as through she's doing me a favor by letting me sit in the same room with her. She wafts around so elegantly on those stilt heels, with that overstuffed hairdo, and fashion model profile, that the only man fit to associate with her would be a Cary Grant or a Tony Curtis."

Her boss laughed. "Little Millie O'Flannery!" he exclaimed. "Why she's no more a debutante than I am. I thought a good-looking girl would add a little class to the old firm."

"Oh, there's nothing wrong with good looks," said George. "But a secretary shouldn't give the impression that she is a creature from another world."[7]

Unspoken in the conversation is the suggestion that the comely creature from another world wouldn't give an old goat like George the time of day.

Along with "a little class," the successful secretary sold the illusion of the girl next door, friendly, fresh, and maybe, under the right circumstances, available for a little personal dictation.

Like Baby Bear's porridge, then, the just-right secretarial appearance was slightly titillating but not too hot. As advice manuals going back to the turn of the twentieth century painted her, the ideal secretary optimally blended into her office surroundings as naturally as yet another highly polished credenza. It was "but right and natural for a business man to want a good-looking, healthy secretary," opined *The Efficient Secretary* (1917), before it bored into the nitty-gritty of the reader's soul: "You know you would want the best-looking desk and the newest machine you could get, and to the business man his secretary is merely part of the office equipment." An employer expected his secretary to be "as attractive as possible, because, quite naturally, he doesn't want a frowsy frump in his office," explained columnist Helen Dare in 1912 (he did, however, worry about the amount of time she spent primping rather than "getting those urgent letters out").[8]

This sounded blunt, but as *Charm*, the secretarial textbook, explained it some fifty years later, the professional secretary knew that "in the business world," she was "not only under obligation to do a good, conscientious piece of work, but part of the bargain" was that she "look decorative" while she did it:

> Companies often spend large sums of money to make their reception rooms and offices into glamorous settings, and they expect their employees to help further the effect by always appearing perfectly and tastefully groomed. . . . Of what worth are the potted philodendrons, the lavish drapes, and the modern furnishings if the customer is confronted with the sleepyhead who staggers in, featuring curlers and kerchief, or the gumchewer in the grimy blouse with a button missing? The customer won't be taken in by the elegant props.[9]

Yet, the experts suggested again and again that the ideal secretary was herself an elegant prop, the black velvet background to her shining white pearl of a boss. *Her* looks might even affect *his* promotion, if the inventor of the speedwriting method of shorthand is to be believed. In 1961, Dr. Alexander L. Sheff told the "White Collar Girl" column that "just as top brass take a look at the wife of a junior executive before upgrading him, they may well take a look at his secretary. This is why voice, manners, and appearance are important accompaniments to skill." It was up to the secretary, he continued, "to retain and enhance the atmosphere" set by the boss. By doing so, she contributed "to his aura of success"—and that, by all accounts, was perhaps the major part of her job.[10]

Getting Along with Others

The boss may have sat alone at the top of the secretary's personal office hierarchy (he, of course, might have had other bosses above him), but he was hardly the only person in the office with whom she had to interact. In fact, as the secretary to an executive, it was up to her to promote "greater office courtesy" by setting an example to her coworkers. According to *The Secretary's Guide to Dealing with People*, some personnel directors actually requested "information about a secretary's popularity among the office force," not her efficiency or experience, "when checking her reference with a previous employer."[11]

Popularity was subjective, of course—and it was probably better that she didn't get *too* friendly with the rest of the office. "Discourage co-worker chit-chat about last night's date or the big football week end and this morning's resulting fatigue. Adroitly disengage yourself from conversational groups mournfully matching tales of their forlorn states of health or the depleted state of their wardrobes," wrote Lucy Mayo. "A cheerful smile and a brisk good morning with a diplomatic personal comment or inquiry here or there is generally adequate personal interchange to establish the day's camaraderie." Anything more, by Mayo's exacting standards, was "malingering."

A brand new secretary also had to remember that etiquette in the office was different from that practiced at home or on the street. For one thing, the ordinary courtesies she normally expected from the men she came in contact with would not be extended to her at work. This was a particular problem

Looking Beautiful over the Phone

It's always been important for a person dealing with the public via the telephone to enunciate clearly, but the amount of emphasis the experts placed on modulation and tone suggests there was more to the secretary's voice than simple communication. The secretary who learned to speak in a smooth, sexy manner became a sort of dream girl to the men who spoke to her, or so suggested *How to Be a Super-Secretary* (1951):

> Hundreds of men with plain secretaries [*the horror!*] have been startled to hear an outsider say: "Your secretary must be lovely . . . she certainly sounds beautiful over the phone." Isn't that a flattering way to have others speak about *you*?

Flattering? It was tantamount to hearing someone say, "Geez, I thought you'd be prettier in person." But beyond making the caller (women probably phoned too, but the booklet depicted the caller as male) think she was a knockout, the super-secretary's purr had to suggest untold possibilities:

> When you have to say "Mr. Smith is out," you add a note of explanation to the caller. And your voice implies "I'll do all that I possibly can to help."

The aural equivalent of a big dirty wink, "telephone charm" helped add "thousands of dollars" to an executive's business, mentally tucked into the fantasy secretary's imaginary g-string, perhaps. No wonder "one out of every two executives rated" it "high in their qualifications for a super-secretary."[*]

---

[*] *How to Be a Super-Secretary* (New York: Remington Rand, 1951), unpaginated.

for early generations of female office workers, who were used to a more formal system of etiquette; *The Ambitious Woman in Business* (1916) reminded secretaries not to be "offended if men failed to pick up the papers she dropt [*sic*], or to open doors for her." Nor was a secretary to expect any of the men in the office to rise when she entered the room.[12]

Almost all the guidebooks mentioned that inescapable annoyance of modern office life: the collection taken up in order to buy a gift for a coworker. In short, everybody has always had mixed feelings about being asked to contribute on behalf of someone they might not like too much— and yet they don't want to be seen as cheap or unfriendly by not chipping in. As *The Secretary and Her Job* (1939) noted, if "done within reason" it was easy to enjoy the giftee's "surprise and pleasure at being especially remembered." But if the hat was passed so frequently as to be "silly," it was time for a white lie: "Just say, 'I only wish I could, but I'm absolutely broke this week.' If that doesn't work you can add, cheerfully enough, 'I'll have to borrow car fare from you if I do.' That will work."[13]

"Touchy Types"

Some offices are diverse with regard to the racial, religious, and gender makeup of their staffs; others aren't. I've worked in both environments and definitely prefer an office atmosphere that more closely resembles the cosmopolitan city I live in—it's more interesting and realistic. Issues occasionally arise concerning our differences, but that also reflects the outside world.

Most of the secretarial manuals assumed a white, Christian, heterosexual workforce in which everybody was one big happy family—with the exception of a few shirkers and an office wolf or two. The biggest interpersonal issue seems to have been body odor, and how—or even if—one told a coworker she smelled bad. (Everybody has worked at one time or another with this person; the expert consensus seems to have been to tell her gently but frankly—heaven help the emissary chosen to do so.) Many offices were just like the ones the guidebooks imagined: before the advent of fair hiring legislation, an employer could legally bar African-Americans, Jews,

The Ladies' Room

All the guidebooks discussed the need for the secretary to be considerate to others in the office, but only *The Successful Secretary* (1964) bravely suggested taking that courtesy behind the restroom door:

> Women have a reputation—well-deserved, unfortunately—for being slovenly and even dirty in their use of public rest rooms. You can avoid this reputation by being considerate of those who use the ladies' room after you. Avoid combing your hair over the sink so that stray hairs fall into the basin. If you spill your face powder, take a minute to wipe out the sink with a paper towel. If you aim that paper towel at the wastebasket, and miss, pick it up; it's good for the figure.*

I sincerely doubt that women are any more "slovenly" and "dirty" than men when it comes to public restrooms, but other than that, amen, sister.

* Parker Publishing Editorial Staff, *The Successful Secretary* (West Nyack, N.Y.: Parker Publishing, 1964), 37.

---

or Catholics—or anybody else for that matter—from his workforce if he so wanted. He could simply find an excuse not to hire an otherwise qualified candidate after her stellar interview. Or he could keep the "wrong" sort of people from showing up in the first place by use of a carefully worded job listing, like this one from a 1923 issue of the *New York Times*: "Alert, intelligent girl . . . to grow with a successful young Christian firm." Likewise, the woman who placed a "Situation Wanted" ad that appeared on the same page and read "Stenographer, American" made it clear that she was different from those Italian, Irish, and Eastern European immigrants, no matter what their passports said about their citizenship.[14]

Beginning in the 1940s, states began implementing fair hiring laws that made such discrimination illegal (Title VII of the 1964 Civil Rights Act did the same nationwide). Nevertheless, biased employers found ways to circumvent these laws (and some still do). Employment agencies in six major cities (Los Angeles, San Francisco, Chicago, Boston, Detroit, and Philadelphia) were all too happy to comply with a request for a "white Protestant stenographer" made by investigators for the American Jewish Congress in 1963. Of the 385 agencies contacted, 90 percent agreed to accept the job order—despite the fact that antidiscrimination statutes were in effect in all the cities where the survey took place. Some of the agencies even admitted that advertising for an "all-American girl" or "someone to meet the public" helped them evade equal hiring laws.[15]

Long before she looked for a job, though, a young African-American woman might be turned away from her local secretarial school. Connecticut's State Interracial Commission noted in 1946 that while there were many job openings for stenographers "regardless of race, creed or color," the commission had a hard time finding qualified applicants—in part because some secretarial schools in the state "discouraged" the admission of black students. At the height of the civil rights era in 1963, *Jet* magazine reported that "at least five major private business and secretarial schools in the Washington area" refused to admit African-American students. In Kansas City later that year, members of the NAACP (National Association for the Advancement of Colored People) claimed victory when three local business schools, including the Dickinson Secretarial School, agreed to integrate its classes (the policy was "only a trial," noted the head of the Kansas City Business College).[16]

That fall, a course "designed as a springboard" for African-American women "seeking jobs with the larger corporations" was offered under the auspices of New York University, whose recently established Office Training Program was directed by a Katharine Gibbs alumna. The program was designed for women who already possessed skills learned in high school business courses or at nondiscriminatory secretarial schools but who would benefit from eleven weeks of "post-graduate drill in typing, stenography, and English," not to mention the "subtler skills of grooming and deportment." On

The segregated office: Aurelia Toyer and Torreceita E. Pinder, stenographers in the U.S. State Department, were assigned to the staff of the president of the Republic of Liberia during his stay in Washington, D.C., in 1943.

completion of the course, the women would be considered for jobs in the companies who backed the program—among them IBM and RCA—all of whom wanted "to improve their public image by hiring" nonwhites. Competition among corporations for qualified black stenographers and secretaries was "murderous," a Union Carbide personnel officer told the *New York Times*.[17]

Around this same time, the few secretarial guides to actually broach the subject of office diversity usually did so in a tone of high-minded condescension. "The people you come in contact with may be very different from you in education background, race, religion, politics, age, and general outlook on life," began *Strictly for Secretaries* (1965); what followed seemed more like a nonsequitur than advice. "You want the window up; Trudy wants it down. You want tea at 10 a.m.; Trudy wants borscht for lunch. And so it goes. Associating with these people can be a wonderfully rich and broadening experience." The image of the office as a melting pot was a lovely one—and perhaps Trudy's preference for borscht meant her ethnicity was something other than "all-American girl"—but *Strictly for Secretaries* left readers in the dark when it came to actually dealing with "these people," or one's attitude toward them.[18]

The Secretary's Guide to Dealing with People used a more concrete example. Agatha is asked by her boss to temporarily supervise the steno pool; when she gets there, she discovers some exotic workers. "A few of the employees were Negroes, who, because of their recent introduction into an integrated business world, were usually sensitive, and imagined slights where none existed." In the guise of Agatha's boss, who gives her a few tips on handling these and other "problems" in the steno pool, the guide schooled its readers about "The Touchy Type" of worker:

> There are a number of reasons why a person may be hypersensitive. It can be a highly personal problem, or, then again, it may be just a general feeling of inferiority and a desire to overcompensate. The latter is especially true among members of minority religious or racial groups, which have been victims of prejudice in the past. These people are usually capable and conscientious, but they feel that they must do better than everyone else in order to prove themselves. They are tense and keyed up, and anticipate slights. If girls in this category cause unrest in the office, they must be talked to confidentially, and have it explained to them that their sensitivity can hold them back from business success.[19]

That a coworker might have been "touchy" because she encountered racism or anti-Semitism in the office itself was not addressed. *Secretaries on the Spot* (1967) included an example where "nine girls in one department" of a company "drew up a petition to have a tenth transferred or fired because she was of a different religious faith from the others." Who could blame the odd girl out for feeling just a little touchy? The personnel department denied the petition, and the manager stated that employees were not hired, promoted, transferred, or terminated on the basis of petitions. How these individuals continued working together after the failed petition was not reported—nor was any information given on how to avoid such a situation arising in the first place.[20]

The Other Man in the Office

Though the majority of hands hovering over typewriter keyboards in twentieth-century offices belonged to women, the male secretary never entirely disappeared. Railroads, for example, traditionally hired men long after the majority of secretarial positions in other industries went to women, in part because rail executives frequently traveled with their secretaries. Doing so was much easier when both parties were male because there was no question as to the propriety of their traveling together. A woman secretary traveling with her boss had to make sure her hotel room was on a different floor from his and consult with her etiquette books before she decided whether or not she could have dinner with him in public. This was no joke. According to the 1943 edition of Emily Post's *Etiquette*, the reputation of the confidential private secretary going on a business trip with her male employer was "adequately protected by the circumstance of necessity," like that of "the trained nurse" who in the course of duty occasionally caught a glimpse or two of otherwise off-limits male anatomy—not that the professional secretary was going to see anything like that in the commission of her assignments. On the other hand, if the traveling secretary "by any chance" dropped her professional role for one that "could be described as glamorous, the impropriety of this change in her personality" affected "not only her own reputation but also that of the organization" her boss represented. "And now, having said that Miss Secretary may defy convention, it is necessary to add a fairly formidable array of qualifying exactions that the critical world expects her to follow," Post added by way of introduction to two and a half more pages of specific dos and don'ts. The secretary could indeed dine with her executive—even in his hotel room—but only for convenience, never for social pleasure (the "danger mark," according to Post). Her well-tailored traveling wardrobe was to be strictly inconspicuous: no "barebacked evening dress . . . no too obvious make-up . . . no strong perfume, and no champagne," Post added for good measure.

If, on arrival at the hotel, the secretary was shown to a room that adjoined her boss's (instead of on another floor as she had requested), she faced a quandary:

> Should she at once refuse the room and perhaps make an awkward scene that would annoy her employer, or worse yet, make it evident that she is thinking of herself as a young woman and not a piece of office furniture? Or should she for these reasons stay where she is and let Mrs. Grundy's spies make what account they can of those side-by-side numbers?

Post assured her readers it was "most likely" that the boss regarded his secretary "with complete unawareness of her personality other than as a dependable business aide," thus it was up to the secretary to come up with an excuse ("the elevator next door, a crying baby . . .") and ask for a new room. Making too big a fuss over the connecting door would merely "make him aware of her as a young woman," and presumably burst the bubble of professionalism that they both pretended protected her from his baser instincts.[21]

A male secretary faced none of these hurdles. He did, however, face a special one of his own: the suspicion that a man who wanted to work in a "women's profession" had to be a little light in the loafers. "Tragically enough, to most boys there is almost a stigma to the title 'secretary.' . . . It sounds sissy, I suppose—and that is probably because it is so basically a girl's job," wrote Rae Chatfield Ayer, hitting the nail square on the head. (As much as I hate to give credence to a stereotype, this echoes my own experience of male secretaries—I've only worked with a very few over the years, but most were gay.) The *Gregg Writer* magazine tried to quash rumors of effeminacy by emphasizing the machismo of male secretaries currently fighting their way across Europe and the Pacific in the Second World War. Writing shorthand "10,000 feet in the air over the Owen Stanley Mountain Range in New Guinea" or "huddled in a foxhole under a giant papaya tree," as did two company clerks profiled by the magazine in 1946, made secretarial work sound as rugged as carrying an M-16 on the frontlines of a firefight. A veteran paratrooper felt the need to separate what he did from that other type of male secretary when he told a reporter for the *Gregg Writer* in 1947, "I used to think

The Office Boy

(A) nother male coworker the secretary frequently came in contact with, besides her boss and, rarely, a male secretary, was the office boy. Like shorthand and carbon paper, the office boy has gone to that great filing system in the sky reserved for outmoded technologies. Up until the 1960s or so, the office boy picked up and delivered the mail and interoffice memos, and did go-fering the secretary was too busy to do. Like the office clerk of the previous century, there was always the possibility that an office boy could work his way to the top of the company—as the secretary watched from her permanent place behind her typewriter. In the event of that possibility, however far-fetched it seemed, the secretary needed to treat him with kid gloves. "Do not be 'snooty' with the office boy," suggested the author of *Kitty Unfoiled: An Informal Portrait of the American Secretary* (1952). "Someday he might be vice president."*

The secretary also had to watch her tongue lest she crush the office boy's fragile male ego in training. "Do not scream at these growing boys, for their impressionable minds retain your attitudes as an example of a person higher up on the business ladder," instructed *The Private Secretary's Manual* (1943). Nor could she ignore his feeble attempts at conversation. "Remember that your interest may inspire these boys to do bigger things; indifference may kill even a spark of ambition which another has kindled in him."†

---

* Anson Campbell, *Kitty Unfoiled: An Informal Portrait of the American Secretary* (Pittsburgh: Reuter and Bragdon, 1952), 40.
† Bernice C. Turner, *The Private Secretary's Manual*, rev. ed. (New York: Prentice Hall, 1943), 21.

stenography was a sissy's job. But the War has taught me the priceless value of shorthand and typing." Certainly there were no homosexuals in combat! Or, how about this rugged war story from *Today's Secretary* in 1953:

> It was a man's world. And again, shorthand was the jumping-off place into adventure. It was a week after the Nazi panzers retreated out of Athens, hounded by the Greek partisans and British liberation forces that had stormed ashore the previous September.
>
> Back in Cairo, where I'd been stationed with other U.S. troops, an OSS intelligence mission was formed. Its purpose: To fly into Greece. Orders came through that I was to go along as secretary to the Mission's chief, Marine Corps Major Gerald Else. [22]

A combination of shorthand skills (175 wpm) and fluency in Greek made Elias John Pepper the man for the job. Twenty years later, *Junior Secretary* alluded to the ways a "real man" used his office skills. Young men who enrolled in typing class might one day find such ability "useful during their years of military service." After he received his discharge, typing skills would help the small businessman at the start of his career, when he could not "afford to hire a secretary. . . . Without his typing skill, he would be lost." The article implied that the moment business picked up, he would of course hire a woman to do the sissy stuff.[23]

Despite the whispers about their sexuality, male secretaries were able to claim other privileges of their gender. There was the assumption that they were somehow more serious about their work than their female coworkers. "Can you imagine a man in your office sitting about filing his nails when there is work to be done? Or phoning the laundry about a lost shirt? Do you really believe men spend as much time primping as women, or that they waste their energies in silly, jealous quarrels?" asked a 1946 article in the *Gregg Writer* about lazy "working girls."[24]

Men unquestionably spent work hours shilly-shallying and wasted time with personal phone calls, but because they were executives, they often did it behind closed doors—a situation in which many young male secretaries imag-

The Private Secretary: His Duties and Opportunities (1916), by Edward Kilduff

T
he Private Secretary: His Duties and Opportunities was the last gasp of an earlier age, when an ambitious male stenographer was in the catbird seat to "take in many valuable bits of information concerning his employer's business" and benefited from "the personal contact with the trained mind and strong intellect of his employer." A "wide-awake stenographer" took advantage of this free education because he knew that the "direct line of advancement for the stenographer" was into the position of private secretary, and from there into the boss's chair. Indeed, The Private Secretary reads less as a guide to working as an assistant than as a blueprint of how to take over the office:

> The private secretary has a great advantage from being in proximity to those at the top, for he may learn a business thoroughly and directly without the delays and rebuffs that are unavoidable when one begins at the bottom. He is personally trained in the large problems of the business by the head of the business himself. . . . it is reasonable and likely that he should be placed in a good executive position when a man is demanded who is familiar with the intricacies of the business.*

Unlike later guidebooks for female executive secretaries that warned against becoming bossy, The Private Secretary suggested that men who wanted to get ahead plunge forward with the conviction of Teddy Roosevelt galloping up San Juan Hill. "Theoretically, the secretary is supposed to put down on paper just what is said and just as the dictator said it. As a matter of fact, he should do no such thing." Author Kilduff's assertion that the secretary go ahead and immediately correct any and

---

* Edward Jones Kilduff, The Private Secretary: His Duties and Opportunities (New York: Century, 1916), 8–9, 11.

all errors bucked the standard line in guidebooks aimed at women: the stenographer wrote down exactly what the boss said. Corrections might be made, but only the smallest and most obvious ones concerning grammar or word usage; otherwise she didn't correct or rewrite without her boss's explicit permission or tacit understanding. *The Private Secretary* was bolder yet: exemplar secretary Frank Campbell has a new letterhead engraved based on his own design without the chief's input or knowledge.[†]

That there were as yet very few women in business was confirmed in *The Private Secretary*'s discussion of letter-writing tone: "Letters to women—who for the most part are unused to the short, snappy letters of business—should be carefully watched for the fault of curtness. Women very easily take offense at any abruptness in tone."[‡]

[†] Ibid, 69, 112.
[‡] Ibid, 101.

ined themselves. The "young man taking secretarial work usually does so in order to open to himself the door to an executive position," noted a *Today's Secretary* advice columnist in 1953 in response to a reader question about "the best opportunities for male stenographers and secretaries." Indeed, the fact that men expected to move up was given as a reason why women made better secretaries. A boy wanted to "become a 'big shot,'" and dreamed of the day he would "have his boss's job and be dictating to a secretary of his own!" but an ambitious girl was merely "apt to bend all efforts to reach the top as an executive secretary."[25]

Bosses also hired female secretaries because they were a bigger status symbol in the outer office—a discreet reflection of his sexual prowess. A male legal secretary who worked during the 1960s and '70s noted that most men favored women secretaries because they preferred "to have their peers ask, 'Who is that sharp chick working for you?' rather than 'How did you ever find that efficient man?'" The same secretary hoped against hope that macho sex symbol Warren Beatty might "play a sexy male secretary" in a film some day, thus "end[ing] these sissy rumors forever" as well as encouraging a new wave of hetero men to pick up shorthand and typing skills.[26]

Perhaps one reason Beatty hasn't gotten around to that role (to date, anyway) is that Fred MacMurray beat him to it. In the movie *Take a Letter, Darling* (1942), MacMurray played Tom Verney, a "rugged, handsome male secretary," working for A. M. "Mac" MacGregor, Rosalind Russell's "beautiful but self-sufficient lady advertising executive." Perhaps to undermine the whispers about male secretaries (echoed in the film by a clerk who wonders aloud, "What kind of man does that kind of work?"), Tom is presented as "a sort of glorified gigolo," according to one contemporary reviewer, who escorts Mac to business dinners, where his job is to "distract the client's wife while she charms the husband into signing with her agency." Mac's got her own issues with gender role displacement, a problem not so subtly telegraphed by her male nickname. A woman working in a "male" career, her presence confuses the ad men who come to the office—aren't all women secretaries?—a problem summed up by her male senior business partner when he tells her, "There's no name for you." Luckily for the sanctity of traditional heterosexuality, Tom isn't really a secretary—he's a down-on-his-luck painter who happens to be doing secretarial work for quick money. After a suitable amount of role-reversal hijinks, boss and secretary predictably fall in love, but not before Tom drags hard-headed Mac into his car in a machismo-confirming, femininity-enforcing act. See, male secretaries weren't sissies after all![27]

The Boss's Wife

Perhaps the most important person the secretary had to deal with, besides the boss himself, was the boss's wife. The two of them were frequently lumped together in the public mind; after all, it was a generally accepted old saw that "next to a man's wife, his secretary was the most important person in his career." In theory, the two should have been great pals; they were "working for" the same man after all. "Normally, you and she will have the same objectives—to be as helpful as you can be in promoting his effectiveness," suggested *You Can Be an Executive Secretary* (1965). A legitimate grievance of many secretaries, however, was that the boss's wife often borrowed them to run errands or provide childcare services—at no additional charge, of course. This was even a plot point in Faith Baldwin's novel *The Office Wife* (1930): wife and secretary first meet when the latter shows up at the boss's house—on a Saturday, no less—to help the former with a charity mailing. In *The Art of Being a Successful Business Girl* (1943), Gladys Torson noted that some otherwise not-so-friendly women warmed right up to their husband's secretary when they needed "the annual report of the Women's Club typed for free" or their Christmas cards addressed ("You have such nice handwriting, my dear"). Torson was of the opinion that a secretary should be "glad to do all she can for a wife who treats her as an equal *always*," not just when she wanted a favor. "I think you are justified in feeling imposed upon if you have to stay after hours to do her work," Torson added sensibly. (She also advised bosses that "probably the safest way to avoid trouble" between secretary and spouse was to "keep your wife out of the office as much as possible.")[28]

Most wives wouldn't dream of asking their husband's secretary for personal favors, but those who did so could be appallingly shameless in their requests. An indignant secretary wrote to Abigail Van Buren in 1967 after her boss's wife "sent a girdle to the office for me to take back to the store for credit," wrapped only in torn tissue paper and without a receipt. More ominously, the wife had begun to bring her little boy to the office for the secretary to entertain while she went to the beauty parlor.[29] In fact, being asked to provide free childcare was a frequent complaint. A *Saturday Evening Post* article about a secretary shortage in 1961 was illustrated with a photograph of a secretary using her desk to change a baby's diaper. It was, naturally, the boss's baby; his wife, the caption explained, was at the doctor's. The practice of free secretarial childcare is alive and well in the San Francisco Bay Area as of the early twenty-first century. Most secretaries smile indulgently as their office supplies are plundered for art projects, but the smiles usually fade as the work piles up on their desks—watching the boss's kids doesn't supersede other tasks, of course.[30]

A secretary and her boss's wife may have gotten along famously—or per-

"Pressing Business! You Deceitful Wretch!" The boss's wife walks in on her husband's on-the-clock love-making, 1901.

haps they never even met—but pop culture nevertheless painted the two as mortal enemies, locked in combat over possession of the boss-husband. Long before the advent of electronic media, people in the late nineteenth and early twentieth centuries amused themselves with a simple home entertainment system called a stereoscope. This was a wood and metal contraption that allowed one to view a cardboard-backed photographic slide—known as a stereograph—in three dimensions. Stereographs depicted all sorts of subject matter: far away lands and the "exotic" people who lived there, American battlefields and national parks. Stereographs were also devoted to humorous— and sometimes slightly risqué—topics. A series of cards from 1907 purported to show what happened when a well-meaning wife dropped in on her hard-working husband at the office. "Pressing Business! You Deceitful Wretch!" is

"You Amorous Little Upstart! I'll Teach You Not to Hug Married Men!" The boss's wife takes her revenge, 1901.

the title of a stereograph showing a stylishly dressed young wife walking in on her husband, who is snuggling with his secretary on his lap. In the next card in the sequence, her husband drops the secretary like a hot potato, as his wife grabs her rival by the hair. "You Amorous Little Upstart! I'll Teach You Not To Hug Married Men!" it reads. It seems that even a century ago there was an audience for the proverbial catfight between pretty girls—and that husbands got off far too easy.

In 1912, journalist Helen Dare tried to ease the minds of "secretly tormented, uneasy, distrusting wives" by reminding them that the pretty girl down at the office in all likelihood was too "busy avoiding the mistakes her employer gets grouchy about" to notice him as a man, and if she did regard him personally, it was "not infrequently to wonder how he ever got a wife

Wife vs. Secretary (1936)

P ublishing mogul Van Stanhope (Clark Gable) and his wife, Linda (Myrna Loy), are a happy, frequently canoodling married couple with separate bedrooms in this filmed version of the Faith Baldwin story with the same title. Down at the office, Van has a cozy relationship with his secretary, Whitey Wilson (Jean Harlow), and while their bantering skates on the knife's edge ("Have you been true to me?" he teasingly asks her on his return from vacation; "Yes, dear," she replies), it remains tilted toward the side of professionalism. Wife Linda has nothing to worry about, until her mother-in-law, Mimi, sticks her nose where it doesn't belong. "I don't see any reason why he [Van] should come home at all," she tells Linda after meeting Whitey, evincing no great trust in either her son or his marriage. Suddenly, everybody's telling Linda that Whitey must be "one of *those* secretaries." Whitey, meanwhile, has a loving boyfriend named Dave (Jimmy Stewart). But she refuses to marry him because he wants her to quit her position with Stanhope Publishing, thus reinforcing Dave's belief that Whitey's job is "spoiling" her for housewifery.

After a wild office ice-skating party where Linda and Dave sit seething on the sidelines while Van and Whitey cozily glide arm in arm around the rink, both couples are at the breaking point. Indeed, Whitey returns Dave's ring when he pitches a fit of jealousy after watching the chummy way Van and Whitey fall on top of one another on the ice.

Linda's suspicions get the best of her too when Van heads to Havana for a secret business meeting, with Whitey in tow. By now, his wife's outspoken distrust of his motives has caused Van to notice Whitey's pulchritude, so when they celebrate the successful purchase of a rival newsweekly with a night of drinking, Van invites her into his room. Whitey enters and goes so far as to remove Van's shoes, then decides she'd better leave. On her way out, she answers the phone. Alas, it's Linda—and it's 2:00 A.M.

Convinced now that husband and secretary are having an affair, Linda moves to her mother-in-law's house. After earlier telling Linda that

Van cannot be trusted, Mimi now exhorts Linda not to leave him. Men, after all, are like "naughty children," says Mimi. "You wouldn't blame a little boy for stealing a piece of candy if left alone in a room with a whole boxful, would you?" (With in-laws like Mimi, who needs enemies?)

Van and Linda are headed for the divorce court when Whitey saves the day, telling Linda that should the divorce go through, Whitey will eventually marry Van, even though she knows she won't make him as happy as Linda does. Linda skedaddles back to lovesick Van; ditto Dave to Whitey, just in time for him to deliver the movie's moral: "Don't look for trouble where there isn't any; because if you don't find it, you'll make it."

who'd stand him." This was a rule that held true unless the boss was a "libertine" and the secretary a "hussy."[31]

Familiarity undoubtedly bred disinterest where most real-life secretaries were concerned, but pop culture was much more interested in the libertines and hussies. Novels like John R. Coryell's *Wife or Stenographer—Which?* (1928), published by tabloid publisher and health-nut Bernarr Macfadden, made the most of clandestine office relationships. Coryell's book might better have been titled *Wife and Stenographer—Both*, as the boss and steno actually sleep together before returning to their respective spouses—a racy plot line at the time. The movie *Wife vs. Secretary* (1936; Faith Baldwin wrote the scenario on which it was based in the wake of her successful novel, *The Office Wife*) starred Jean Harlow as the secretary, Myrna Loy as the wife, and Clark Gable as the lucky man between them. Granted, nothing much happens for the wife to be worried about (when Harlow visits Gable in his hotel room during the wee hours of the morning, they share nothing more than some lust-filled glances), but the type was cast in stone: when it came to feminine wiles, the secretary was not to be trusted around the boss.

By setting her up as the secretary's often unsuccessful rival, the nudge-nudge, wink-wink stereotypes about the relationship between boss and secretary hurt Mrs. Boss too. After all, many of the jokes starting with "Didja hear the one about the boss and his steno?" shared an underlying assumption: that the executive's spouse was somehow wanting in the sex-appeal department. Illustrations in newspapers and general-interest magazines, cartoons on cocktail napkins and in men's magazines—even on bowler's crying towels—and other pop-culture portrayals usually showed her as middle-aged or older, overweight, and shrewish. Sometimes the spouse was accompanied by a passel of unruly children, the better to contrast her matronly state with her husband's curvaceous, young, accommodating—and single—secretary.

How accommodating? *Laughing Stock* (1945), a compendium edited by publisher and humor-collector Bennett Cerf, included a joke that purported to show the progression of an affair between a boss and his "pretty secretary":

Extract from a Wall Street broker's petty cash book:

April 1.	Advertisement for a pretty secretary	$1.60
3.	Violets .75	
4.	Candy 1.25	
8.	Secretary's salary 30.00	
10.	Flowers 3.00	
11.	Candy for wife 7.50	
15.	Secretary's salary 40.00	
18.	Hand-bag 12.50	
19.	Candy for wife 3.00	
22.	Gloria's salary 60.00	
24.	Theatre and dinner, Gloria and self 55.00	
25.	Chocolates for wife .90	
28.	Fur coat for wife 1800.00	
29.	Advertisement for male secretary 1.60[32]	

This was considered amusing enough that a similar "Expense Statement" made an appearance on a novelty ceramic mug from the same era. One side of the mug showed a topless woman—in 3-D, no less—making explicit the nature of the relationship between boss and employee. And just above an entry for a "Mink Stole for wife" is:

10/25   Doctor for stupid stenographer   375.00

That's right—it's a reference to an abortion, still illegal at the time, and not generally a laughing matter. The mug was perhaps a gift best given from one philandering executive to another as a desktop trophy—and perhaps as a subtle reminder to pick up a pack of condoms lest his indiscretions destroy his career.

Given the steady stream of jokes at their expense, perhaps it's no wonder that a group of women married to "top-level" and "other-than-top-level" executives listed a sense of humor high on the list of qualities they deemed important for the "ideal executive wife." The social-science journal *Marriage*

"Say, J. B. What became of that dumb red headed stenog you used to have?" The boss's wife (and former secretary) portrayed as a ball-busting matron. From an early-1950s ink blotter.

and Family Living analyzed the wives' responses to a questionnaire concerning "The Generalized Role of the Executive's Wife" in 1961:

> An executive's wife may be the object of jokes concerning "the other woman," "the office wife," or she may be referred to as "a golf widow." To be able to laugh at these jokes and not take them seriously is deemed useful in such instances.

Laughing—however feebly—at jokes of which she was the butt could not have been easy, especially if her husband's secretary was an attractive woman. Being a "good egg" in the presence of sexist humor was just one way in which an executive's wife was caught in the mid-twentieth-century web of pink think. The wives who responded to the *Marriage and Family Living* questionnaire included their thoughts on proper behavior for women of their station in life: "The wife of an executive must not talk too much, drink too much, be too friendly or overdress; she must not be too ambitious or 'too nice.'" The latter was explained as being "so perfect as to make others uncomfortable or feel inferior" in her presence. "Too ambitious" needed no explanation: good wives neither pushed their husbands up the ladder, at least not too hard, nor competed with them in the workplace.[33]

Notably lacking from these executive wives' list of dos and don'ts was the suggestion that an ideal spouse dropped everything the moment her husband asked her to do something for him. Yet this is exactly what *Los Angeles Times* advice writers Hubbard Hoover and Isabelle Macrae Hoover advocated in a 1948 installment of their "Pursuit of Happiness" column, headlined "Wife Can Easily Out-Wife Her Office Rival." According to the Hoovers, the wife versus secretary "problem" might be solved in the wife's favor if she started acting a bit more like her husband's geisha instead of his spouse. "Isabelle," wrote Hubbard in the back-and-forth style he and his cowriter wife employed, "you can hardly imagine what a heady experience it is for a man when for the first time in his life he has a private secretary":

> He gives her $10 and tells her to go out and buy a wedding present for his old classmate. She puts on her hat and does it right away. . . . How does

this compare with the situation on the home front? Jack [the husband] asks Delia [his wife] to do something for him. She says "uh-huh" and three weeks later it is not done.[34]

It didn't matter that Delia had household and childrearing duties of her own. It didn't matter that the secretary was paid to cater to her boss. All Jack wanted was the "novel experience of having a woman around who does what he wants when he wants it," whether he was at home or the office. Thus, the answer to Delia's problem was simple: "If she would just listen attentively to all of Jack's requests, and for a while put them at the top of her list, she would soon have no worry about a possible rival."[35]

The women who gathered in Washington, D.C., for a regional meeting of the National Secretaries Association in October 1949 supported the theory that

a good secretary "anticipates" her boss's home life so he will be happy at least in the office if he isn't at home.

"If his wife nags at the boss's shirttail," one secretary put it, "you have to be tactful and know what to do about it."

A pretty secretary getting passed from lap to lap, steno pad on floor, was the boss's wife's worst nightmare—and the secretary's, too. Novelty postcard, circa 1930s.

3's a Crowd

(T)he 1979 game show 3's a Crowd dared to ask "one of the most visceral questions of the times: Who knows the husband best . . . his wife or his secretary?" A threesome of contestants (a man, his wife, and his secretary) each answered a series of questions, some silly ("What about your secretary most reminds you of a tarantula?") and many risqué ("What is the funniest or most unusual place you and your wife ever made whoopee?"). Host Jim Peck "egged-on" contestants to "divulge infidelities or just plain fight" (in the pilot show, two women reputedly bickered until the wife grabbed the secretary by the hair). Points were awarded to the wife or secretary whose answer coincided with that given by her husband/boss. At the end of the half-hour show, $1,000 was split by the "team" with the most correct answers: the wives or the secretaries. If 3's a Crowd sounds reminiscent of The Dating Game or The Newlywed Game, it's because legendary game-show producer Chuck Barris was behind all three.[*]

Even though 3's a Crowd would seem right at home next to many of today's reality programs, the show's unspoken but heavily hinted-at suggestion that secretaries slept with their bosses was profoundly uncomfortable to the viewing audience of thirty years ago. TV Guide called it "an arena of jolly sadism" and "despicable"; "crotch humor" was the assessment of the Los Angeles Times. Not surprisingly, a clerical workers' organization, Los Angeles Working Women, targeted the show for "perpetuating outrageous myths about working women." In response, almost a thousand women sent in letters of protest.[†]

Nor did contestants enjoy appearing on the show. According to Chuck Barris's 1993 biography, The Game Show King, the couples on 3's a Crowd "left the studio humped-back and devastated. Except the

---

[*] Chuck Barris, The Game Show King (New York: Carroll and Graf, 1993), 160; Lee Margulies, "The Fall Season," Los Angeles Times, March 15, 1979, F1; Barbara Isenberg, "Chuck Barris . . . Going . . . Going . . . Gong!" Los Angeles Times, April 6, 1980, L5.
[†] Isenberg, "Chuck Barris," L5; Margulies, "The Fall Season," F1.

secretaries" who "seemed to love playing" and usually won. Barris also claimed that its abrupt cancellation in the spring of 1980, along with that of several other game shows, was due to "public backlash," as was his year-long retreat to his Malibu beach house.‡

‡ Barris, *Game Show King*, 162, 163.

This did not translate to dirty dictation and naked romps in the file room, however. One woman spoke for many when she told a reporter that "most secretaries are glad to leave their boss after eight hours." Indeed, "familiarity breeds contempt" is perhaps the best description of many secretary-boss relationships. A secretary's blunt words from 1941 have the ring of absolute truth, even today: "The only thing the [boss's] wife need worry about . . . is that some day, in a fit of rage, the overworked secretary may slay the dear man."[36]

Break Time!

By the time she finally parsed her relationship with the boss's wife or figured out the fine lines of office etiquette, the poor secretary cannot be blamed for needing a good, strong cup of coffee, maybe even a cigarette. The coffee break as we know it didn't exist prior to the Second World War, when the federal government began to encourage organized midmorning and mid-afternoon breaks as a morale booster for defense workers. Garden-variety office workers, meanwhile, did what they always did—snuck out for a cup when they could. *The Private Secretary's Manual* (1943) had a less-than-morale-boosting opinion of the practice, as did many bosses: "The secretary who spends fifteen minutes in smoking or otherwise dissipating her firm's time can scarcely be said to have a proper attitude toward work."[37]

By the mid-1950s, the coffee break was a well-entrenched facet of office life for all workers. Despite the occasionally justified fear that their wily employees would not return promptly to their desks after the allotted ten or fifteen minutes, management by and large believed that caffeinated workers were not only happier but also more productive—at least that was the conclusion of a mid-twentieth-century survey of coffee-drinking habits in 1,160 offices in forty-five states (commissioned, of course, by the Pan American Coffee Bureau). Around the same time, firms began installing coffee-dispensing vending machines or having a service deliver brewed coffee and pastries to the office.[38]

Having these snacks in the office created a whole new problem for the secretarial advice mavens to weigh in on. Although *The Successful Secretary* (1964) acknowledged that a woman was "certainly entitled" to take a coffee break (as long as she was back in reasonable time), it counseled against taking it at her desk. What if she spilled coffee all over the stacks of correspondence and files waiting for her attention? (I admit I'm guilty of this misdemeanor—and gauging by the number of stained documents I've seen, so are many others.) Nor was it "a very businesslike sight" for visitors to see her "munching on a cruller" when they stopped by her desk. Most important, though, an "executive should never be asked to wait" until his secretary finished her coffee break if he had "a rush telegram" or other important dictation to give.[39] "It will come as no surprise that executives look with high favor upon employees not addicted to the pernicious coffee-break habit," reported *You Can Be an Executive Secretary*.[40]

Depending on where she worked, a nicotine-addicted secretary might not have to wait for a coffee break to get her fix. Prior to the 1990s, it was legal to smoke in many office buildings—and some companies allowed workers to smoke at their desks. But cigarettes were a trickier proposition than coffee, not because a careless flick might cause a nearby stack of papers to start smoldering (though that was always a possibility), but because the relationship between "ladies" and smoking was historically a complicated one. Prior to the First World War, the vast majority of American women avoided tobacco altogether. When the flapper generation—already reviled for its love of short skirts, bobbed hair, and liquor flasks—started smoking with alarming frequency (the number of cigarettes women consumed doubled between

1923 and 1929), the older generation was appalled. Women who smoked challenged the nineteenth-century ideal that women were morally superior to men. In the words of historian Paula Fass, smoking "implied a promiscuous equality between men and women and was an indication that women could enjoy the same vulgar habits and ultimately also the same vices as men." It didn't help that the women who took up smoking early in the century were considered "disreputable or defiant," hence the habit's association with immorality.[41]

Smoking—even decades later—didn't jibe with the secretary's idealized femininity. "Suppose, after investigation, you have found that the company permits smoking at your desk and that there is no prejudice against women smoking," began *The Successful Secretary*'s section on smoking; a page and a half of rules followed. Most of them concerned commonsense good manners regarding a habit that not all her coworkers shared (don't smoke while others are eating, air out your office frequently, and so on), but many addressed what "ladies" did and did not do. The secretary was not to smoke while acting as receptionist: "Many people still consider smoking unladylike, and most companies do not want the first woman visitors see to be smoking." She was to put her cigarette out if her boss stopped at her desk "for any length of time" (if he stopped by "for just a moment," it was okay to leave it burning in an ashtray). Smoking during dictation was forbidden. She was not to smoke while walking around the office, in the hallways, or at the cafeteria. "A lady does not smoke while walking on the street, either," it added parenthetically. Nor was the secretary to let her cigarette dangle from her lips, for this gave her "a 'tough' and unladylike appearance." Looking like a gun moll, with a cigarette hanging from the corner of her mouth, would never do; it simply wasn't charming. But every secretary, be she caffeine fiend, nicotine addict, or teetotaler, needed a certain mental toughness when it came to dealing with the boss. Her treatment of him, after all, could make or break her career.[42]

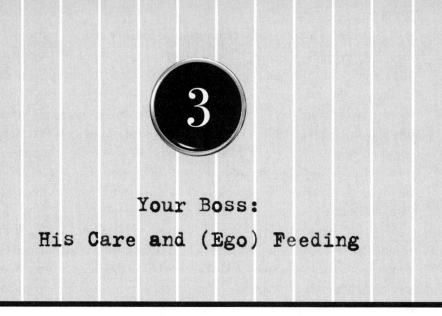

3

Your Boss:
His Care and (Ego) Feeding

Men are naturally lazy creatures and don't want any responsibility
if there is some capable female around to take care of it, so take
advantage of that weakness and your progress [as a secretary] won't
be slow.

> Lorene Bolt, Secretary of the Year, 1951[1]

• • •

In a way, getting along with an executive is like getting along with a
husband, only more so.

> Jean Vermes, *The Secretary's Guide to Dealing
> with People* (1964)

I may not always be an ideal secretary, but I'm a lucky one. I've always
had good bosses. My boss at the art gallery, for example, was long-
suffering and mostly understanding where my rookie shortcomings were
concerned. Better yet, she kept cases of excellent champagne in the garage

(we worked in a converted typewriter repair shop) for openings and other work-related causes. Every couple of months she would come in on the day the gallery was closed, declare it "Party Monday," and break out the bubbly at 11:00 A.M. Yes, it was hard to get work done with a champagne headache at two in the afternoon, but on those days morale—as well as the workers—could not have been higher. One beautiful summery Monday we even closed up shop entirely, piled into her VW convertible, and drove down the northern California coast to Pescadero, a little town known for its olallieberry pie. In short, any faults Anne may have had as a boss—not that she had any!—were more than balanced by her terrific joie de vivre as a human being.

Not surprisingly, then, if I was forced to choose which of the ten executive types listed in *How to Be a Good Secretary* (1969) best described my former boss, it would have to be *"The dynamic type, with seemingly inexhaustible energy."* She definitely possessed a "terrific driving force" that demanded "every ounce" of my twenty-five-year-old vitality—in truth, I had a hard time keeping up with her ("Oh, loosen your girdle, Lynner!"). I think she would have liked me to "show initiative and . . . assume considerable responsibility," as *How to Be a Good Secretary* suggested to secretaries of dynamic-type bosses, instead of watching quietly from the corners as I often did, but all in all, we got along pretty well. I'm very grateful that I've never worked for the *contrary type*, who had "a weakness for *always being right*, even about a subject he does not know too thoroughly" (though I've met plenty of attorneys along the way who fill this bill) or the *aggressive type*: "In order to exercise any initiative, with a man of this type, you must *first* find out if he approves."[2]

While few secretarial guidebooks shared *How to Be a Good Secretary's* flair for italics and creatively placed commas, many recommended observing one's executive with an attention to detail reminiscent of Jane Goodall studying the wild chimpanzees at Gombe. In *You Can Be an Executive Secretary* (1965), Lucy Mayo suggested making a "character study" of one's executive in the proverbial little black book:

Include notes about his work habits, his reactions to various circumstances and people, his pet peeves, his directions or suggestions for your own conduct in functioning with him in tandem. You may also wish to add facts about members of his family if you are to have contact with them or for no other reason than to be able to exhibit a courteous and knowledgeable interest of them.

Just in case the secretary didn't realize the potential dynamite these "highly personal observations" represented, Mayo recommended keeping the little black book "under lock and key in the drawer of your desk that is PRIVATE" (the same one in which she recommended the secretary keep her "purse, an extra pair of nylons, [and] hand cream"; this was also the place where former secretary Helen Gurley Brown suggested a female executive— but not her secretary—could stash a fifth of her favorite liquor, for either impromptu celebrations or the drowning of sorrows).[3]

Studying her employer to ascertain his personality and management style was important because these observations and conclusions helped the secretary help her boss get ahead—and that was the core of her job. Beyond the basics of typing and filing, the secretary acted as a buffer between the boss and the public: screening calls and visitors, performing triage on the mail, organizing small projects. By taking care of correspondence and calls that didn't require his specialized knowledge, the secretary conserved the boss's time for "more important" matters. The secretary's work was of equal, if not greater, value when it came to getting the day's work done; simply put, a skilled secretary increased executive efficiency. But whereas her ability to calmly juggle visitors, phones, and letters while the boss was in the boardroom was important, it paled before the ideal secretary's foremost talent: massaging the executive psyche.

Sometimes this was easy. Simply walking past his secretary's desk each morning was a daily affirmation that he had climbed the ladder to a certain point. "'Miss Amy, please take a letter,' are words which have inwardly thrilled every young executive with a sense of his own importance. As the opening scene in a Hollywood movie, they symbolize executive power and status," wrote Chester Burger in *Survival in the Executive Jungle* (1964).[4]

Call Him Mister

Not only was Miss Amy herself a living, breathing status symbol, but there was the comforting way in which she said, "Yes, Mr. Boss." For it was generally understood in most offices that while the boss was free to call his secretary by her first name, under no circumstances (at least during business hours) was she to call him anything other than Mr. Whatever-his-name-was, regardless of how he was addressed by others in the office.

Addressing the boss as Mr. Blank "maintain[ed] the dignity of *his* position" and allegedly emphasized an "atmosphere of *mutual* respect." The italics are mine, because while his secretary was busy maintaining his dignity, Mr. Boss reserved the right to call her whatever he darn well pleased: from Miss Green to Betty to "girlie," "sweetie," "hon," or any number of less-than-respectful diminutives. A secretary who wrote to *Los Angeles Times* columnist E. V. Durling in 1938 showed more than a flash of anger describing her two biggest workplace annoyances, both of which continued to irritate secretaries in the decades that followed: "Hear the plea of an office wife and campaign for office peace. . . . Start in by suggesting bosses do not start fifteen minutes before closing time dictating letters that 'must be mailed tonight, girlie.' And tell the damn fools not to call their secretaries, girlie." Even worse, consciously or subconsciously refusing to remember a secretary's name—tantamount to refusing to acknowledge her presence as a human being—was a habit that often extended past secretaries to include all women in the office. "It doesn't matter what my name is," a switchboard operator attending a meeting of the advocacy group Women Office Workers (WOW) told the *New York Times* in 1975, ". . . because I'm commonly known at work as 'Doll,' 'Sweetie,' 'Cookie,' or 'the Girl.'"[5]

Whether the "damn fool" personally demanded it or the company rule book required it, calling the boss "mister" was an exercise of power that subtly but sharply reminded everybody just who was in charge: "Calling the vice-president by his first name will prove to him that he . . . made a mistake by mixing socially with the help," explained *The Secretary's Guide to Dealing with People* (1964). That her use of his first name might be seen for more than simple collegiality was another reason why the boss didn't like it when his secretary forgot to use his title "the day after the [office] bowling match when they got pally" or after the holiday party—when they got to be more than just pals.[6]

Even in situations where the boss-secretary relationship was without question a professional one, calling the big man "Bob" (even at his request) when everybody else in the office called her boss "mister" might lead to unpleasant interoffice gossip. *The Successful Secretary* (1964) warned that the "only time" it was permissible for a secretary to call her employer by his first name was "when you and he are alone in the office" (to work on a legitimate project, of course!) and only if he had previously asked her to dispense with the "mister" treatment. (The same book also suggested that the secretary "never use the casual pronoun 'he' when speaking about your executive to others," coworkers included, because to do so revealed "a casual, even careless attitude" toward him—advice which seems excessive, even for the time.)[7]

In some offices, such extreme formality meant that men and women who worked side by side for decades might rarely address each other except as "Mr. Brown" and "Miss Green." A Chicago-area secretary who married her millionaire boss in the 1950s admitted that she didn't "think he even knew my first name for years." (She got her revenge: "I sometimes forget and call him Mr. Crown," she told a reporter, years after their marriage.)[8]

What the successful secretary never forgot was that her executive's delicate sense of self-importance required more than her regular use of the word "mister" if it was to flourish under the constant strains of the workaday world. As the author of *The Secretary's Guide to Dealing with People* frankly put it, a secretary had "the power to inflate or deflate an executive's ego."[9]

Massaging the Executive Psyche

The experts had been telling women for years that a man's psyche was as fragile as a butterfly wing, and might collapse altogether if his wife worked outside the home, so imagine the secretary's surprise when she realized that her slightest misstep might cause the titan of American business for whom she worked to similarly disintegrate. Luckily, the prophylactic for such a fiasco was already at her fingertips—and it didn't involve typing. An executive who had "employed secretaries and stenographers from coast to coast" advised readers of the *Chicago Tribune* in 1941 that "practically all girls sense that to succeed socially with men they must contribute to a man's ego." The successful secretary merely realized that the "same principle" applied at the office as well as on a date. Nor was her boss the only one to benefit from this arrangement; when a man found a "sympathetically understanding" secretary who enhanced his "feeling of competence," she became "invaluable" to him, and her job became secure.[10]

Perhaps the best way for the secretary to shore up the boss's ego was to simply forget she had one of her own. A good secretary, according to *Vocations for the Trained Woman* (1910), understood "the power of losing one's self in the interest of another and finding pleasure in the act and art of service." Writing in *The Private Secretary: His Duties and Opportunities* (1916), author Edward Jones Kilduff listed "self-abnegation or unselfishness" as one of the two "moral qualities . . . essential to the private secretary" (the other was trustworthiness). The secretary (presumably male in Kilduff's book) was the employer's "other self," who "submerge[d] his own individuality and interest" to "be part of the chief." Kilduff was careful to point out that this did not mean the secretary should treat the boss with "fawning humbleness," merely that the secretary should carry out the big man's orders as asked, remembering always that the chief was "the one in command."[11]

"Hey, Girlie, Pick Up a Pair of Socks for Me on Your Lunch Hour."

Keeping her employer's calendar and making sure he got to off-site meetings on time were services she was paid to provide, but the "little extras" she might be asked to do often crossed the line into servility, especially if she had

So You Think Your Boss Is Bad

In 1977, Women Office Workers (WOW), a New York–based organization devoted to improving "the professional image and job conditions of clerical workers," sponsored a contest (its slogan was "An Office Worker Is Trained. Not Maid") asking secretaries to share the "most ridiculous personal errand" they'd run. The entries made picking up an occasional bag of dry cleaning look like a prize in and of itself: there was the man who required his secretary to deliver stolen office supplies to his home address, for example, or the one who asked his girl Friday to clean his false teeth. It's hard to believe the latter didn't take first place, but the winner (who took home only "bragging" rights) was a woman whose boss had her photograph him before, during, and after shaving off his moustache—at the office, of course. The secretary who had to pick up her boss's wife and newborn baby at the hospital was a close runner-up.*

* Edith Evans Asbury, "Women Office Workers Rally to Give Their Dos and Don'ts to Bosses," *New York Times*, April 28, 1977, 31; Janice Mall, "About Women," *Los Angeles Times*, June 26, 1977, H15.

to run the boss's personal errands on her own time—which she frequently did. "In all justice you should be allowed the time taken for errands in addition to your lunch hour, but by the time you add an hour or more to your lunch hour the afternoon is practically gone, and when are you going to type that bookful of notes?" Trying to balance company time with her own was a "vicious circle" that caused "many a girl" to go "down struggling," noted Gladys Torson in *The Art of Being a Successful Business Girl* (1943). (Writing on the topic of personal errands in *How to Be a Hero to Your Secretary* (1941), Torson snapped, "Don't ask your secretary to stop at the bank, pick up your golf club that you left to be taped and match a piece of material for your wife's new dress and then expect her to be back from lunch in an hour. That lunch hour belongs to her and not to you or your wife!")[12]

The "sub rosa" nature of these "extra duties" is what made them the secretary's "biggest legitimate gripe," in the words of *Esquire Etiquette: A Guide to Business, Sports, and Social Conduct* (1953). Some executives were truly so busy on the job that they needed an assistant to handle their personal affairs. When a secretary was hired for such a position, it was with the foreknowledge that she would be paid to run hither and yon when she wasn't working at her desk. When interviewing a potential secretary, most men said nothing about unpaid work "as a nurse-maid, shopper, personal bookkeeper, errand-girl, maid and social secretary" because to ask the secretary to perform such unpaid personal services didn't fall within the realm of her job description; asking her to perform these tasks was an exercise of executive power, pure and simple, yet one that left him in an uneasy indebtedness to the secretary who agreed to perform such favors. (*Esquire Etiquette* was on the secretary's side when it came to the matter of personal errands: "She . . . may take it upon herself to hang up your hat and coat and trot out for your coffee—but she'll hate you if you take these services for granted. You had better share the 'dirty jobs,' to protect her self-respect and your own." Alas, the chance that an office tyrant who needed to be reminded of such a basic tenant of humanity would recognize himself in such a description in the unlikely event he was reading an etiquette book in the first place was probably slim to none.)[13]

Not all bosses required their secretaries to take care of their personal business, but the willingness to do so marked the super-secretary from the rest of the pack. In addition to being judged on experience, education, appearance, and "poised personality," the woman chosen as Secretary of the Year in 1954 underwent a "mock interview with a personnel director." Her winning answers to his questions included that she would be "happy" not only to do personal errands for the boss but also to "work extra hours on his outside organizational interests." Evelyn G. Day, president of the National Secretaries Association in 1961, "like many top level secretaries," practically managed her boss's "whole household, hiring the servants, paying the bills, buying presents, handling his investments and taxes." *Charm: The Career Girl's Guide to Business and Personal Success* (1964) tried to invest these tasks with the gloss of celebrity glamour, as it urged its readers to accept errand running with an eager-to-please attitude: "Many secretaries to famous personalities think nothing of preparing lunch for their bosses, taking suits to the dry cleaner's, walking the dog, or even baby-sitting with the children. No matter what comes your way, accept it with good grace."[14]

The idea of the girl Friday as a present-buying gofer was so ingrained in the popular psyche that secretaries were among the only women admitted to an otherwise stag Christmas shop. Every holiday season from the late 1930s until the shop went coed in 1971 (after a little nudging from New York City's Human Rights Commission), Manhattan luxury goods department store Bonwit Teller opened the stag "721 Club," named for the store's Fifth Avenue address. Here, men could "shop in peace and quiet for presents for women." Afternoon cocktails were available. The only woman allowed in the 721 Club, other than sales associates and models, was the "secretary shopping at her boss's behest." To gain entrance, a secretary first had to show proof that she was indeed on such a present-buying mission for the boss (rather than just wanting a peek at the boys' fort, one assumes). She was then required to slip into "a pink smock so that she will not look like an ordinary customer" who stumbled by accident into this bastion of male camaraderie.[15]

The Office Housekeeper

While running errands often amounted to a personal compact between the secretary and her boss, cleaning up behind him was an expected part of the deal. As "an office housekeeper," the secretary was expected to keep the boss's inner sanctum tidy, make sure that his desk was dusted, his plants watered, and his pencils sharpened.[16] In her account of women office workers from 1870 to 1930, historian Margery W. Davies quoted "a remarkable set of parallels" between office wife and housewife, compiled by a secretary during the first quarter of the twentieth century. The list made an explicit connection between secretarial work and housewifery.

TO PRODUCE SATISFACTORY RESULTS, THE SECRETARY AS WELL AS THE HOUSEKEEPER HAS TO COMBINE SKILL AND KNOWLEDGE WITH HER PERSONAL TRAITS.

The Housekeeper Must	*The Secretary Must*
Understand and take efficient care of kitchen equipment	Understand and take efficient care of office equipment
Understand varied domestic skills	Understand varied secretarial skills
Know how to follow a detailed recipe in the right order	Know how to follow detailed instructions in the right order
Give attention to her work—often to several tasks at once	Give attention to her work—often to several tasks at once[17]

Another eleven points drove home the fact that the secretary and the housewife were virtually interchangeable. Keeping the office at a white-glove-test standard of cleanliness was a badge of secretarial honor; only a "careless and indifferent" secretary ignored the dust bunnies piling up on the credenza in the boss's office. Pride also meant she used the proper tool for the proper job. "A dusting mitt or a piece of clean cheesecloth is much more appropriate for emergency use in the presence of a caller than a piece of worn-out underwear brought from home, even though the latter may make a better dust cloth," noted *The Private Secretary's Manual* (1943).[18]

Keeping the office cobwebs at bay might reap a reward larger than money. When a woman complained of work duties that turned her into "a combination office boy and janitor," columnist Ruth McKay reminded her that not only did most stenographers keep a dust cloth handy "for use the first thing every morning," but "at least one girl with her eye on the bachelor boss got her man by her office housekeeping."[19]

The experts agreed that a single woman benefited from using the office as a training ground to practice her domestic skills. "In fact," wrote Jean Vermes in *The Secretary's Guide to Dealing with People*, "the better a job you do as a secretary, the better a job you are apt to do as a wife, and eventually a mother and homemaker." A "responsible job," according to a former secretary who married her boss, was "fine training for marriage" because a woman who had supported herself was "less likely to be extravagant or go berserk on her husband's money." Even Helen Gurley Brown, in the pages of *Sex and the Single Girl* (1962) no less, called a career "the greatest preparation for marriage." Secretaries-turned-wives were "better organized, better able to cope with checkbooks, investments, insurance premiums, tradesmen, dinner parties and the mixing of a really dry manhattan." The secretary who did all these things for her boss really knew "how to please men," including her future husband.[20]

If you imagine that an hourly wage at least made such drudge work bearable, think again. A mid-1960s guidebook described not only how to squeeze these humdrum tasks into a busy schedule but also the proper attitude to be taken toward them:

> Once the working day has begun, you will have no time to dust desks and water plants. Even if you did, it does not look appropriate for a secretary to busy herself with such chores on company time. . . . It is assumed that you care enough to come in a few minutes early in the morning to prepare your executive's office for him before he arrives.[21]

In this way, office chores fell into the same category as those performed at home by housewives: real labor, but unpaid and undervalued. Evidence suggests that secretaries did not enjoy doing these tasks—which they in all likelihood performed at home too. During the International Secretary of the Year competition in 1970, held at the National Secretaries Association convention in front of some sixteen hundred onlookers, finalists were asked which phase of their work they found most irksome. When the winning entrant replied that she most disliked the "dishwasher type of thing that all secretaries have to do and enjoy the least," a "roar of appreciation went up around the room."[22]

Service with A Smile

But no matter how much she hated being the office housekeeper, an award-winning secretary made sure she kept a smile plastered on her face even as she clasped the hated dust rag in her hand. For, in addition to keeping the boss's office spic-and-span, the secretary was also expected to meet and greet visiting executives with the same verve the wife offered guests to her home. "Liken such 'housekeeping' tasks to your hostess duties in your own home, where your objective is to make your guests comfortable, relaxed, and in a mood to enjoy your hospitality," wrote Lucy Mayo in *The Exec-*

"Her employer wants someone pleasing to look at. As long as he's paying for it why shouldn't he have an attractive girl . . . instead of one who needs a thorough overhauling?" The Secretary and Her Job, *1939.*

utive Secretary. The ideal hostess and successful secretary shared many qualities: the ability to command a situation without seeming to; to "keep everybody happy and to keep things moving along smoothly; and to see that everybody interacted "in such a way that pleasant relations naturally develop."[23]

This meant that the secretary cultivated "a pleasant manner and a friendly smile . . . for everyone, regardless of rank." When spoken to, her face showed that she was "interested, alert and alive" by the "gleam in . . . [her] eye or a slight smile." *The Secretary's Guide to Dealing with People* exhorted readers to remember that "cheerfulness and enthusiasm are infectious, and a happy, vigorous secretary contributes to the production of a happy, vigorous boss." Her disposition also set the tone for the workplace at large. In 1962, anthropologist Dr. Ashley Montagu told readers of *Ladies' Home Journal* that women exercised a "great humanizing and civilizing influence" in "offices, factories, and around conference tables." When a secretary joined an all-male office, her soothing feminine presence meant the "men start[ed] wearing their jackets at their desks, rough swearing" stopped, and "snarling males" were soon "smiling and saying good morning to one another. Without women," Montagu concluded, "men revert[ed] to the jungle."[24]

The office was undoubtedly a very different place in 1962 than it is today, but even close to fifty years ago Montagu's suggestion that it took only a bit of womanly warmth from the secretary to calm her boss's inner savage beast was a bunch of hooey—or else why did those secretarial manuals devote so many pages to dealing with grouchy, dictatorial, or otherwise snarling executives? Indeed, it was the boss's "privilege" to "give rein to his prima donna instincts" whenever he felt like it, warned one guidebook. It was important for the secretary to remember on these occasions that he didn't mean it personally; in fact, he was "probably entirely unconscious" that he was taking it out on her. The executive was a busy man, after all. If he was irritable and snappish, it was because he had "many problems on his mind"—big important ones. "Perhaps the toast had been burned that morning, or the wife had admitted to running a large bill at the jeweler's," suggested Elizabeth Gregg MacGibbon in *Manners in Business* (1936). But regardless, it was best if the secretary simply "ignore[d] his mood and act[ed] as pleasant as ever." In the face of a boss who "indulged his mean disposition by yelling and swearing," a "tactful" secretary "smilingly said, 'Yes, Mr. Smith,'" even when he shouted for her in "much the same tone he would have used in calling a dog."[25]

On the other hand, the secretary's "own emotional problems, whether of joy or sorrow," were to be kept out of the office at all times, lest the employer's concern for her feelings "consume too much of his time and dissipate the attention he needs for his own efficient accomplishment." If she was depressed or sad, office etiquette required that "one be as cheerful as possible," noted *The Successful Secretary* (1951). She never sulked while the boss ranted and raged because, between the hours of nine and five at least, she had "just one mood . . . fair and sunny . . . [and] you wear it no matter how you feel." No matter how abusive her boss became, no matter how many ballpoint pens or unprintable curses he hurled in her direction, she needed to remain calm. Not only was crying unprofessional, but it paid heed to the frequently laid charge that women were "too emotional" at work. A boss who screamed at his underlings was just as disruptive of office routine as a weepy secretary, but such behavior was rarely considered a fault in a man; indeed it might be considered indicative of his testosterone-fueled deal-making prowess. Tears, on the other hand, were a sure sign of femininity and weakness, which is quite possibly why they allegedly made men so very uncomfortable. A crying secretary "embarrass[ed]" and "unnerved" her boss. "Weeping just doesn't belong in business," wrote Elizabeth Mac-Gibbon. "Men hate it there as much as anywhere else—probably more." It was best, she suggested, to "parcel-check" one's emotions outside the office door, keep business relationships friendly but impersonal, and develop a social life outside the office, where she could blow off steam without compromising her job.[26]

To help control one's emotions during the workday, *How to Be a Good Secretary* suggested memorizing the following device:

C—is for cheerfulness
A—is for amiable
L—is for likable
M—is for magnetic[27]

Presumably, repeating this mantra under her breath helped the secretary maintain "the right impression" in the face of an executive meltdown. (Maybe now is a good time to mention that at least one of the reasons why such an incantation was needed was because the general advice concerning

An ideal secretary demonstrates her loyalty to the boss—
and the need for the advertised soundproof tiles, 1942.

amartinis at lunch was that they were to be indulged in rarely, if at all—at least by the secretary. The boss was another story.)

Perhaps most important (from her employer's standpoint anyway), the secretary's C-A-L-M smile displayed her "subtle deference" to the boss, an "indication that good as she is, she knows he's even better," in the words of writer Mary Kathleen Benét. Writing in the early 1970s, Benét meant her words as criticism of antiquated gender roles in the office, even though taken out of context they sound like something from a contemporary secretarial manual. Indeed, the secretary was supposed to display a blind allegiance and rah-rah boosterism usually associated with the propaganda mills in small third-world dictatorships. When discussion turned to the boss, for example, loyalty demanded that nothing but words of praise passed the secretary's lips. If he was "difficult to work with" (in other words, a jerk to her and everybody else he came in contact with), the loyal secretary defended his reputation. "Does your executive seem stern or unpleasant to others in the office?" asked a guidebook from the 1960s. "Perhaps he is so busy he does not have time to practice some of the ordinary courtesies. . . . Help his image by letting others know you find him easy to work for." When a secretary and her coworkers gathered for a cocktail after work and engaged in that time-honored (though one guidebook called it "insidious") "pastime of let's-pick-the-boss apart," the loyal secretary was supposed to "deftly change the subject."[28]

His Number-One Fan and Fall Girl

Few bosses were tantrum-throwing ogres, and fewer still were the saintly capitalists described in the most jingoistic of the secretarial guidebooks, like *How to Be a Super-Secretary* (1949), which indulged in straight fantasy: "The more important an executive, the more gracious, considerate, and democratic he is." Most executives (then and now) resembled the average boss described in *Manners in Business*: "alternately cross and amiable, unreasonable and considerate, hard-working and lazy, wrapped up in business and indifferent to it." But no matter which way the boss's emotional wind blew on a given day, the secretary was supposed to behave as if she

Rose Mary Woods: The Loyalist

If there was ever a shining example of secretarial devotion, Rose Mary Woods was it. Born in Sebring, Ohio, in 1917, Woods began her secretarial career at age seventeen. Seven years later, she moved to Washington, D.C., where in 1947 she met freshman representative Richard Nixon when he served on the congressional committee for which she was staff secretary. Impressed by the orderly expense accounts he turned in after a European junket, Woods joined Senator-elect Nixon's staff in 1951. When "The Boss," as Woods called him (she urged others to as well), narrowly lost the 1960 presidential election to John F. Kennedy, she followed him into exile in California. After his election in 1968, President Nixon rewarded what he once called her "unquestioning loyalty and absolute discretion" by making Rose Woods his first staff appointment.[*]

These qualities were put to the ultimate test beginning on October 1, 1973. On that fateful day, Woods was hard at work transcribing one of the tapes Nixon secretly made while he occupied the Oval Office, this one a telephone conversation between the Boss and presidential aide H. R. Haldeman. The phone rang. Woods removed her earphones and "reached for the stop button with her right hand but by mistake must have hit the record button," all the while keeping her left foot on the Dictaphone's pedal, a gymnastic feat later known in less-than-sympathetic quarters as the "Rose Mary stretch." ("That's a badly set up office if you have to go though all those contortions," was the opinion of an attendee at the National Secretaries Association convention the following year.) When she returned to the tape after talking on the phone for 4½ to 6 minutes (her estimates varied), to her horror she discovered a loud buzz or hum had replaced the conversation. "I've made a terrible mistake," she immediately confessed to Nixon. "Don't worry about it," he assured her. "It's not a subpoenaed tape." Except that it was in fact one of the tapes requested by Congress—and the

---

[*] "Rose Woods, The Fifth Nixon," *Time*, November 19, 1973, 22; Nixon quoted in "The Secretary and the Tapes Tangle," *Time*, December 10, 1973, 15.

gap turned out to be 18½ minutes long, obliterating what investigators suspected was a crucial conversation that took place just days after the break-
in at Democratic headquarters at the Watergate Hotel.[†]

Whether Woods erased the tape, inadvertently or on purpose, or otherwise took the fall for the Boss is a question that has never been fully
answered. Woods took credit only for approximately 5 minutes of the
famous gap, though expert investigation of the tape later revealed that it
consisted of five to nine separate erasures—gaps that weren't caused by
improper use of the foot pedal.

Whatever the answer, Nixon and Woods retained their loyalty toward
one another. When the Boss decided to resign the presidency in 1974, he
asked Rose Woods to tell his wife and daughters.[‡] After Nixon left the
White House, Woods allegedly kept "his half-smoked cigar in the ashtray, his glasses on the desk and his wastebasket half-filled" in her office
at the Executive Office Building, until the Ford administration made her
take down the erstwhile shrine to her old boss.[§]

Rose Mary Woods died in 2005. She maintained what Nixon biographer Jonathan Aitkin called her "clamlike" discretion until the end.[**]

[†] Angela Taylor, "Out from behind the Desk and into the Spotlight—Temporarily," *New
York Times*, April 26, 1974, 32.
[‡] Philip Shenon, "Rose Mary Woods, 87, Nixon Loyalist for Decades, Dies," *New York
Times*, January 24, 2005, B7.
[§] Patricia Sullivan, "Rose Mary Woods Dies; Loyal Nixon Secretary," *Washington Post*,
January 24, 2005, B04.
[**] Quoted in ibid.

were a starry-eyed teen and her boss a member of the latest and cutest
boy band. "Are you so much a fan of your boss that no one would criticize
him in front of you?" was the first of the thirty questions comprising a quiz
called "Do You Act Like a Good Secretary?" that appeared in the April 1953
issue of *Today's Secretary*. (Answering "yes" was worth three points; "so-so"
["*somewhat* or *sometimes*"] netted a single point; a firm "no" earned negative
two points.)[29]

The Secretary's Guide to Dealing with People went a step further and suggested that the secretary "imagine her boss as the product" and "herself as his personal advertising medium" when introducing him to office visitors. In this way, the secretary burnished the big guy's image by appropriating the techniques of Madison Avenue:

And how is the product always presented in the television commercials?

1.   With a smile.
2.   With an offer of service.
3.   Conveniently accessible.
4.   With an invitation to repeat the experience.[30]

Defending her executive during employee bitch sessions and praising him in front of clients were easy tasks compared to the times she was expected to act as a patsy when he needed a convenient excuse for his own shortcomings. Everybody understood that lying—on the part of both boss and secretary—came with the territory, and that it should be done with finesse. The time-honored phrase "I'm sorry, he seems to have stepped out for a moment" not only allowed the boss to catch up with his workload without being interrupted by phone calls, but also allowed him to hide in his office when an irate client dropped by. And therein lay the rub.

There were times when it was "expedient to place the blame" on the secretary's shoulders. "A customer who would be annoyed or insulted by your failure will be more inclined to accept the inconvenience if it is explained as a secretary's mistake," wrote Chester Burger in his guidebook for executives; or, as business manners expert Elizabeth MacGibbon put it in her handbook for secretaries, "What man would voluntarily appear dumb or unobliging to customers, friends or family when the blame can so easily be shifted?" It was all right for people to think that the secretary was bad at her job, as long as the executive didn't lose face and the company didn't lose a client. Burger did counsel, however, that when such a scenario occurred, it was "best to be completely candid" with the secretary, and explain that the executive only

passed the buck in order to "pacify a customer who would otherwise be irritated" if he knew the truth. Company loyalty meant that keeping a client
happy was more important than collateral damage done to the secretary's
reputation. It simply wasn't a big deal. "From an ethical viewpoint, no one
was hurt by your 'white lie' and it does not, for that reason, seem important
to me," concluded Burger.[31]

Such "white lies" may not have seemed important to the executive whose
rear-end they protected, but they definitely were a sore spot for the secretary who prided herself on efficiency and professionalism. "A girl does not
mind being the office scapegoat," wrote MacGibbon in 1936, but make no
mistake: taking the fall for her employer was right up there on the secretarial hate list with bosses who started dictation at a quarter to five in the
afternoon. Among a list of "New Year's Resolutions I Wish My Boss Would
Make!" that appeared in *Today's Secretary* in the early 1950s was "that I will
cut by 50 per cent the number of times I blame my secretary for my over-
sights. (*All too often he hides behind me when he forgets an appointment,
doesn't want to take time to see someone, or waits too long to answer a letter.*)"
Even MacGibbon conceded that it was "something else" when a boss blamed
the secretary for his mistakes when there were "no outsiders to be considered." Few of today's administrative assistants would disagree.[32]

Now, a reasonable person might think that when a boss found a paragon
of secretarial virtues the guidebooks described—skilled in shorthand and typing, willing to fall on her sword for him, and so forth—he thanked his lucky
stars and they lived happily ever after. There was a point, however, where the
"one-woman publicity campaign" the secretary was supposed to wage for her
boss slid past mere unctuousness to something more sinister. Even the best
secretary, warned *Esquire Etiquette*, could at any moment "begin to plump
you [her boss] up out of all proportion to your actual importance. . . . Watch
out lest she put on airs that will reflect on *your* manners and good taste."
Daily close proximity to a powerful man like himself might lead to a kind of
hero worship, as if she actually started to believe the propaganda she spread
about him. *The Successful Secretary* (1951) warned against something called
"*Big-shot-itis*," which caused the secretary of a high-status executive, a firm's

Karen Simms, Private Secretary (1963), by Bernard and Marjorie Palmer

(P) oor Mr. Burnham. All he wanted was a new secretary. Instead, he got Karen Simms, who, though highly recommended by the local business college and skilled in the secretarial arts, regarded the office as a "mission field as pagan as any spot in the South American jungles or the fleshpots of the Orient." People in the office smoked and told off-color stories. Some of them even dyed their hair. It was up to Karen to convert them to the fundamental religion practiced by the Simms family, the kind that considered theater-going and dancing evil and required attendance at three separate church services on Sunday.*

Karen is just one of the girls who was pulled out of the typing pool at the Burnham Manufacturing Company to temporarily substitute for Mr. Burnham's secretary while she prepares for her wedding. But the secretary's vacation is extended after she is felled by a virus, and Burnham asks Karen to stay on. Karen's heart soars—her dream of becoming a private secretary is within her grasp. But then Mr. Burnham asks her to hold all his incoming calls so he can catch up on some work. "When I get calls, just tell them that I'm not in the office and that I'll be gone for the balance of the day"—a flat-out lie! How can she perform her job duties without compromising her faith? By getting her heathen coworker, Marti, to answer the phone, that's how. One day, when Marti isn't available, Karen sends an annoying phone call through to a busy Mr. Burnham, and the manna hits the fan.†

Karen's kindness to an eccentric but important client saves her job, and before you can say "in a pig's eye," she's converted Marti. As the book ends, Karen is angling to save Mr. Burnham's soul too. Alas, the reader

---

* Bernard and Marjorie Palmer, *Karen Simms, Private Secretary* (Chicago: Moody Press, 1963), 31, 32, 29, 43.
† Ibid., 70.

never finds out just how Burnham Manufacturing Company operates when neither of the boss's secretaries is willing to utter the words, "I'm sorry, he's stepped away from his desk"—unless he had, in fact, stepped away from his desk.

vice president, for example, to get a swelled head just because she was his gal Friday. Should she be lucky enough to find herself in such a position, she was to remain cordial to everybody in the office, from the lowliest office boy or gofer to the big boss himself.[33]

A similar, but far worse, situation arose when the secretary to whom a big muckety-muck entrusted so many important tasks suffered a sort of psychological transference with her boss. "Such a woman," Chester Burger warned, might "try to establish an unhealthy emotional relationship with the executive." Not a romance, but "a possessive relationship":

> She may come to look upon you as "her man" in the office, her personal property and responsibility. And if you allow it to happen, your secretary will soon act as if she held your job.
>
> If you don't stop her, she may soon be telling you, pleasantly but firmly, what to do next, whom you should see, and "if I were you, Mr. Soderholm. . . ." She'll push more and more strongly to dominate you unless you ring the bell and call a halt."[34]

Mr. Soderholm's secretary had fallen prey to the scourge of "officiousness."

Officiousness—and How to Avoid It

In the teen career novel *Wendy Scott, Secretary* (1961), Wendy's dad gives his secretarial school–bound daughter a bit of advice. Mr. Scott knows from his own work as an accountant that though the executive secretary is trained to become her "boss's alter ego," there was "a big difference between the gal

The secretary as the woman behind the man. Business letters were the boss's "personal representatives," but they were also "letters your secretary will be proud to write . . . letters you will be proud to sign," 1952.

who thinks she's 'executive' and the gal who really is. The nasty name for the former is *officious*. Remember that, Wendy, if you ever become a secretary." Even today the word is sometimes associated with a certain kind of meddlesome and intrusive female. "She was an officious busybody who made trouble for everyone" is the sample sentence given by one online dictionary; another suggests "an interfering old woman." The word showed up again and again in secretary manuals. *How to Be a Successful Secretary* (1937) explained how one secretary's "officious manner" made her "quite generally disliked" by her coworkers and boss, even though her technical skills were excellent. *The*

Bosses' Pet Peeves

 ere's a roundup of what qualities bosses didn't like to see in their secretaries, according to *How to Be a Super-Secretary* (1949):

- Argues
- Too bossy
- Too emotional in attitude
- Gloats when she changes phrases . . . thinks knowledge of grammar more important than knowledge of business
- Tactless in correcting others . . . even the boss
- Brags about being secretary to a "big shot"
- A trouble-maker among co-workers
- Swears . . . (this should be the boss's privilege)
- Not lady-like enough
- Egotistical . . . smart but not smart enough to hide it*

*How to Be a Super-Secretary (New York: Remington Rand, 1949), unpaginated.

Successful Secretary (1964) listed officiousness as one of "the most common examples of inappropriate personal behavior" exhibited by secretaries.[35]

The officious secretary forgot, perhaps conveniently, that the "secretary's reward as often as not" came in "the form of reflected glory" instead of direct recognition for her contributions. A secretary was constantly told to remember her place vis-à-vis the executive she worked for: she was there to anticipate his needs, but not to overpower or compete with him. Yet when she really did man the laboring oar on a particular project—or perhaps on a daily basis—it was hard to pretend otherwise. "The able secretary often acquires a belief that it is she who is handling the big job, when, as a matter of fact, she is merely the vehicle for carrying out instructions," warned *The Ambitious Woman in Business* (1916).[36]

Thus, when it came to initiative, the secretary walked a narrow tightrope. The manuals suggested that one of the perks a woman who worked up to the position of private or executive secretary could look forward to was the level of responsibility with which her boss entrusted her. But even though she handled confidential business transactions with little supervision and much aplomb, wrote letters over her boss's name as well as her own, not to mention balanced his personal checkbook, she was supposed to remain humble to the point of invisibility. "Are you *modest*—willing to *prove* your worth, to perform without constant acclaim or focus of spotlight?" asked Lucy Mayo. "Are your manners those of a lady? Will your conduct reflect the prestige of your executive, your company?" Nobody liked an "overaggressive secretary" who gave "the impression that she is the real boss of the office":

> Eventually . . . he may feel like a stranger in his own office, as Miss Efficiency handles more and more of his phone calls, correspondence, and visitors, making decisions and submitting them for his approval only after they have become accomplished facts.[37]

The fact that she could quite often perform much, if not all, of the boss's job as well or even better than he could needed to remain a deep, dark secret— as did the true depth of her intelligence. "Don't let your brains show too much," advised the author of *So—You Want to Be a Private Secretary* (1943):

> A woman was offered a job as a typist. During the interview, the man who was hiring her mentioned that he was taking a course in a nearby college. She was on the verge of divulging that she had taken this course herself and could help him with the homework. She wisely kept still.[38]

Keeping silent was more important than keeping still when it came to undoing executive errors. If a secretary found a mistake in the boss's grammar when typing up his letters or if he asked her to make an appointment to see Salesman X at the same time he was already scheduled to meet with Vice President Y, it was best to keep her mouth shut. "If you are tempted to try to prove to your chief that he has made an error, let reason and good judgment conquer the impulse—and don't do it." If she could "quietly and tactfully" put the situation right—making subject and verb agree, for example—there was no reason to alert the boss to his mistake. Still more tact was necessary if the secretary had no choice but to ask the boss to rectify his error. "You might say, for instance, 'Somehow the figures given you for this report were for June instead of July, Mr. Exec,'" instead of directly pointing out that he obviously inserted the wrong figures from the file only he had access to. It was all about subtlety. An executive told the author of *You Can Be an Executive Secretary* that when his secretary heard him say something bone-headed (or, in his words, something "perhaps . . . not consistent with the standards she knows we wish to maintain") while dictating, she fixed him with "a mother-to-bad boy look" that stopped him dead in his tracks.[39]

His Office Mother

The ability to channel the boss's mom came in handy throughout the day, not just when she needed to telegraph her disapproval. *Good Jobs for Good Girls* (1949) opened its chapter on secretarial work with the following jingle: "Recollect / this helpful verse: / he's a Baby, / you're his Nurse!"

There was the matter of his physical well-being. "Busy men sometimes need a secretary who makes them look after their health," counseled *The Private Secretary's Manual*. She could help by "bringing in a well-balanced meal each noon" (the same book suggested the secretary herself eat "a hearty breakfast" the better to "stand an occasional postponing" of her own lunch). She also kept an eye on his appearance: a good secretary saw "when you need a haircut," noted businessman W. H. Kiplinger in his "Salute to Secretaries" given at the National Secretaries Association convention in 1967, then she made an appointment with his barber and put it on his calendar. One of the "faithful super-secretaries" profiled in a 1979 *Fortune* article was a veritable whirlwind of maternal solicitude to her two bosses: "Nancy handles their investments, helps out their wives and children, pays their servants as well as their grocery bills, picks their luncheon spots, and

A *sexy-but-maternal spinster secretary babies her boss. "Vinegar" valentine, 1940s.*

tries to run their lives so, as she says, 'each man will have as much time as possible to do the things he wants to do and is good at.'"[40]

If her boss was a "born procrastinator" and acted like a teenager with a term-paper deadline every time a report was due, it was the secretary's duty to ride herd on his progress and "exhaust every possibility of forcing him to do his work on time." She could do this by bringing him some recent correspondence and asking—in a not-too-leading manner—if he wanted her to answer it. She could thus "bring his mind back to his work" in a way that made him think that doing so was his own idea.[41]

Pity the secretary who thought she left her toddler at home. Her boss's "fits of temper, sulkiness, sarcasm, and similar qualities" were "hangovers from a maladjusted childhood" that could be overcome only "by sympathetic understanding" from his secretary-mom. Evidencing her disapproval of such behavior "in an objectionable manner" (the rolling of her eyes, for example) would only undermine her employer-child's confidence.[42]

Perhaps she could quell the boss's tantrums by resorting to arts and crafts. In 1952, *Today's Secretary* described how one secretary helped her boss greet "every day with a chuckle—sometimes a downright hearty laugh" by clipping out "funny pictures, jokes, or gags" from magazines and newspapers and pasting them to his daily to-do list along with "cheerful words" like "ALL SET TO 'BOWL' 'EM OVER?" (next to a cartoon of a man rolling a ball down the lane, of course) or "Good Morning—we'll get a lot done today—you sure look full of ambition." There's no doubt that having his daily agenda ready and waiting each morning was an aid to the boss's efficiency, and it's also likely that some secretaries enjoyed expressing their creativity when decorating his list of things to do. But was pasting cartoons on the chief's daily calendar really one of the "extras . . . that help[ed] make certain secretaries indispensable" as suggested by *Today's Secretary?*[43]

It's National Secretaries Day!

So what could the secretary expect in return for all that typing, dusting, and executive ego-stroking? There were few secretarial guidebooks as forthright as *The Art of Being a Successful Business Girl* when it came to the discussion of wages, which tended to be small: "Remember that if you are worth keeping on the payroll, you are worth a raise now and then. If your boss holds out no hopes for one, better get busy right now . . . looking for a better position." Many of the secretarial advice-givers followed the rules of ladylike decorum and didn't bring up the delicate subject of money at all. *Charm: The Career Girl's Guide to Business and Personal Success* suggested that the ambitious secretary would get noticed by the dint of hard work alone: "The cream naturally rises to the top. The girl who plays it smart by doing her best on every job will soon be accepted as an important member of the team, capable of handling more responsible work." The authors said nothing, however, about what to do in the likely event that the squeaky wheel—or the man—in the next cubicle got the recognition instead of the hard-working but silent girl. Nor did they say anything about getting a bump in pay to accompany those new responsibilities. Perhaps no counsel was worse than that given by an executive secretary who, speaking to a student gathering at a career day sponsored by a Los Angeles secretaries organization, warned the audience never to ask for a raise: "If you're good," she said, "you don't have to ask. You'll get one," a claim that any number of hard-working secretaries could have told her was dubious at best.[44]

Even if her reward didn't come in the form of currency, after 1952 there was one day a year when her boss was urged to spring for a card, a bouquet, or lunch—or any combination thereof. The National Secretaries Association was formed in 1942 to "provide a professional network and educational resources for secretarial staff" throughout the United States. Not a trade union, the association sought to raise the secretary's status by offering education and networking opportunities—and by making sure the public knew that any secretary worthy of the title was a cut above a mere stenographer.

Beginning in 1951, it offered a "Certified Professional Secretary" credential to those who passed a twelve-hour examination that tested their "education, experience, appearance, and poise." A certified professional secretary was supposed to earn more than her run-of-the-mill coworkers, the credential occasionally appearing in both "Help Wanted" and "Situation Wanted" ads. (Personally, I have never actually worked with anyone who confessed to having a CPS certificate.) Then, in 1952, Mary Barrett, president of the National Secretaries Association, C. King Woodbridge, president of the Dictaphone Corporation, and Harry Klemfuss, an account executive at advertising giant Young & Rubicam, joined forces to create National Secretaries Week. "I got sore because everybody paid tribute to Rosie the Riveter. Why not our secretaries, those wonderful gals?" Klemfuss told the *Wall Street Journal* in 1952.[45]

The iconography surrounding the first Secretaries Day on June 4, 1952 (the midpoint of the first Secretaries Week—it's hard to know why both a

designated day and a week were needed, unless it was to give a busy executive an extra four days to remember to do something nice for his "girl"),
drew deeply on the secretary's maternal and wifely caretaking duties. An
ad in *Time* magazine showed a corsage-bedecked young woman, and the
copy read, "In every male there's a silent voice that tells him *he* is Lord and
Master. It's high time I broke down and thanked you for not undermining my
little illusion." The boss then proceeded to thank his secretary for a litany of
personal errands and favors, among other things, "the buttons you've sewn on
my coat, the wedding presents you've bought, the reminders of birthdays I
was about to forget . . . the time you took the children to the circus . . . and
my wife to the matinee I couldn't make . . ." and "for smiling when I need a
smile and listening when I want an audience."[46]

But try as it might, the National Secretaries Association couldn't raise a
woman's status in the mind of her employer or the public at large by promoting the profession as one of substitute wives and mothers who took care of
men, no matter how competently they ran the office for them. In announc-
ing the first observance of National Secretaries Week, the *New York Times*
expressed nothing so much as disdain for the newly manufactured holiday
and by extension the women to whom it paid tribute. "It had to come. . . .
There are 1,500,000 blond, brunette, and red-haired typists, stenographers
and secretaries in business today and not all of them chew gum when they
hold telephone conversations. . . . Many a harassed vice president, after
glancing at his freshly typed letter to an important customer, wishes for a
national 'Be Kind to the Boss' week." The paper was still obsessed with gum
chewing the following year, when it called the holiday a time for "harried
executives" to "pay homage to the girl who keeps an office running even if
she chews gum once in a while and infrequently sends letters to people for
whom they are not intended when her mind is on her latest flame."[47]

Moving out of the steno or secretarial pool to work one on one as a private secretary to a junior or senior executive was considered the pinnacle of
secretarial success, but along with additional job responsibilities came a big
liability. Given the wifely attentions the successful secretary was supposed to

lavish on her boss, not to mention what one writer in 1905 called the "Dangerous Intimacy of the Office," it only followed that a smirking assumption formed in the minds of the public at large. "What goes on after office hours when a dynamic boss, bored with his wife, has a warm-hearted, beautiful secretary who wants marriage, but will settle for love?" asked the back cover of yet another pulp paperback devoted to the phenomenon of the *Office Wife* (1957). This was perhaps the most enduring secretarial stereotype: that of the hot-to-trot babe who serviced her boss with sex as well as stenography.[48]

Single Secs, Married Secs, and the Looming Shadow of the Office Wife

In offices all over the country you will find them. Undoubtedly, they would prefer home and marriage—or marriage plus a career—to a career alone. But when a normal life is denied them, their offices and jobs become the compensating factors in their lives.

> Anonymous, "My Husband Had an 'Office Wife'"
> (1949)

• • •

For all of woman's advance into man's world of business, industry or the professions, basically things are the same. A man is just a man, but a woman is a wife—potentially or actually. The number one question still is "Is she married or isn't she?"

> Clara Kirkwood, secretary,
> "White Collar Girl" (1954)

The excessive devotion with which the super-secretary was supposed to treat her boss burned an everlasting image into the mind of the public at large—that of the office wife. At its most benign (it was never a compliment), the term was a convenient shorthand for the woman who did what sociologist C. Wright Mills called the "housework of his [the boss's] business." A more sinister version of the office wife was an unmarried woman who substituted her boss for a husband. She was either a pitiable old maid or spinster who sacrificed a life outside the office in favor of her love (often unrequited) for her charismatic boss, or a seductress who lusted for, and possibly seduced, her married boss. Tied up in stereotype were anxieties about women who remained single (an "abnormal" state for a female) and the titillation factor provided by the thought of young bachelorettes working alongside married men.[1]

Married to Her Job

The stereotype of the bachelor-girl office wife may have had some basis in reality. At the turn of the twentieth century, some professional women hinted that business success came to women who were willing to put aside their personal lives—including a future husband and children—in service of the greater good of the office. "Another thing that will help you very much if you really mean to get ahead is to take a long view of things," advised Elizabeth Cook, a Wall Street bond seller who spoke to a group of women at the New York University School of Business in 1916. "If you have in mind that you are . . . going to do it [work] for years, perhaps all your life, you will be more likely to succeed . . . and then if the lover crosses your path and you go off with him, that is your affair, if you have done your best while you were there." Cook didn't specifically say that working women shouldn't marry, but, as historian Sharon Hart Strom noted, she clearly suspected that women who did were "turncoats" to the cause of female employment. A woman business teacher told an interviewer from the Bureau of Vocational Information in 1919 that "women should accept vocations with permanent intention. There will be less and less marriage as we grow less and less materially minded." (The idea that once women were economically independent traditional marriage would change utterly or fall by the wayside was popular with some late-nineteenth-century feminists, Charlotte Perkins Gilman among them. But even former president William Howard Taft, no feminist, shared the notion: he told a newspaper that he believed every girl should be "trained to some occupation," which would "make her independent of marriage as a means of support. Then she need not marry except in obedience to the dictates of her heart.")[2]

In fact, the advice offered to working women in the 1910s frequently "promised money and independence to any girl who would concentrate on her work eighteen hours out of twenty-four," wrote Elizabeth MacGibbon, in *Manners in Business*, from the sophisticated vantage point of the 1930s. According to *Vocations for the Trained Woman* (1910), the ideal secretary did "not substitute personal convenience and privilege for the work which she has promised to fulfil." She could not "succeed if her first desire is to be 'let out' when the clock strikes five." This may sound familiar to anyone who has felt their boss's steely-eyed gaze burning a hole in her back as she hurries out of the office at five o'clock, whether it's to get home on time to fix a family dinner or meet up with friends for cocktails. These early-twentieth-century advocates of working women demanded a deeper commitment to her job. "Your understanding of your right to stop work at a certain hour each day may prove a serious handicap to . . . your opportunity for advancement," warned *The Efficient Secretary* (1917). Rather than recommending that one cultivate a willingness to be flexible on occasion, *The Efficient Secretary* suggested that it was better to simply keep one's personal calendar free lest something come up at the office. To have her evenings "so filled up with outside interests" that it was always necessary to leave on time was not only "foolish" but indicative of an "unwarranted devotion to pleasure that crowds out a proper devotion to business."[3]

But such absolutism was short-lived. Just a few years after *The Efficient Secretary* was published, an editorial in the *Smith College Weekly* took to task the idea that a woman could be either a wife or a businesswoman, but not some combination of the two: "we cannot believe it is fixed in the nature of things that a woman must choose between a home and her work, when a man may have both." The task of finding "a way out" of the conundrum was "the problem of our generation," declared the editorialist. She and her cohort could declare at least a partial victory (today's working mother—busy juggling job and home—knows that the problem still hasn't been solved). By the time *Manners in Business* was published, in 1936, MacGibbon was able to point to the "outstanding success of scores of women" who combined marriage and business in the face of the "frequent failure of those who forsook home, family and friends." She urged her readers to "do as men do and forget the job when they are off it." Others weren't so lenient. The authors of *Secretarial Efficiency* (1939) suggested that since the secretary spent "more than two-thirds of her time away from the office," she needed to plan those hours "intelligently to serve her secretarial efficiency as a whole." Spending "all her free time reading magazines or attending the movies, or taking hard exercise" meant that "her expenditure of time" was "as poorly balanced as if she spent all her money on clothes. . . . As to friends, amusements, sports—choose whatever will combine to make you worth the most to your employer." I'm surprised the authors didn't go ahead and suggest a recreational shorthand league.[4]

Enter the Office Wife

Writing a series on American girls and women for the *San Francisco Chronicle* in 1922, English romance author May Christie (her novels *At Cupid's Call* and *Love's Gamble* were published the preceding year) noted the existence of a "new and interesting type of girl in America—namely, the young woman to whom marriage makes no real appeal." While Christie attributed part of the reason for this lack of interest in matrimony to a misguided belief that Americans did not look down on "old maids" as "life's failures," nor subject them to "impertinent and humiliating jokes," she more correctly understood that the major reason had to do with work: a job meant that a woman didn't "have to marry to improve herself financially" as did her sisters in so many other countries. But behind this financial and social freedom Christie detected an obsession—with the boss. "'I'm my boss' office wife,' I've heard many a clever secretary say, half-laughing and yet earnest. 'That man simply couldn't get along without me.'"

> And it's true. She knows it. The normal mother urge in her heart is filled by her protective attitude toward her "chief." In the strict interpretation of the form, there is no actual "love" between them, but the knowledge that she is tremendously essential to one man satisfies her. She makes his problems hers in a way the real wife—full of social and home duties—seldom does.

Christie herself seemed fascinated, in a positive way, by these new and exciting women of the future, who occupied "high positions" and had "real and much appreciated work to do." In her opinion, the secretary who gave her "brains and energy and time" to the boss shared with him a kind of "higher marriage."[5]

The perky, modern young secretaries she described owed much to the bold and cheeky flapper, with their brazen manners and morals. Curator and historian Ellen Lupton has pointed out that in popular fiction and film, the flapper often worked as a typist, stenographer, or secretary. The heroine of "Ruth and Peter," a serialized story that ran in the *Washington Post* in 1926, was clearly flapper material. Ruth Welles is the "young, pretty and very ambitious" secretary to Peter Barton, a "distinguished" attorney. They work in a Manhattan office building filled "with bobbed-haired girls whose skirts . . . were too high at the knee and [blouses] too low at the neck." Ruth herself wears lipstick (most "nice" women considered cosmetic use the purview of actresses and prostitutes for at least another decade), and when she visits her friends for dinner, she is happy to accept a cocktail ("First class gin! From my bootlegger!" announces the host)—both strong indications that Ruth has modern ideas about womanhood. She's no madcap flapper, however. Ruth has ambitions beyond a home, husband, "and maybe a couple of kiddies": she studies law at night in hopes of becoming an attorney herself—at least until she falls in love with her boss. "There she sat, in her little office; the secretary—the office wife!—tapping out meaningless words on her machine," in a jealous snit while he meets with a female client.[6]

What really fixed the type—and the phrase—in the public imagination, however, was *The Office Wife*, a 1930 novel by the highly successful romance author (and in the 1960s, doyenne of the Famous Writers School correspondence course) Faith Baldwin. My copy carries the tongue-in-cheek (I hope) flyleaf inscription, "After reading this book you will always want to select your husband's secretary—in fact you will insist on it."

When the novel was published, the phrase "office wife" was still new enough to cause one of its characters to react with glee when she hears it for the first time:

"Is that what you call them?" asked Linda, delighted.
    "Not original with me. I assure you. It's as current a term as T.B.M.," Jameson told her.[7]

T.B.M., or "Tired Business Man," was a slangy term popular in the 1920s and '30s—but clearly one without the staying power of "office wife." Like Sinclair Lewis's *Babbitt*, the T.B.M. suffered from ennui and often turned to "a cocktail or a vaudeville performance, in an effort to escape from the boredom which is the natural result of his highly specialized life," according to a 1925 sociological journal.[8]

The Office Wife's heroine is Anne Murdock, who works as a secretary to a junior executive in the copy-writing department of the Fellowes Advertising Agency. Her cropped hair, silk stockings, and lipstick mark her as a modern woman, the opposite of the serge suit–wearing Janet Andrews, a forty-year-old virgin who, after "starving her maternal instinct" at the office, becomes too lovesick for agency head Lawrence Fellowes to function effectively as his secretary. Luckily, Anne has learned "the great man's secretarial requirements" from Andrews, just in case such an opportunity might arise.[9]

Fellowes is pleased with the efficiency of his new secretary and recognizes her beauty, which he considers a liability: "No sooner were they ["the good-looking ones"] trained to satisfaction than they exchanged the typewriter for the mixing spoon." But Anne insists she won't exchange her career or her independence "for any man living," a point she makes clear when her boyfriend and coworker Ted O'Hara proposes marriage:

> "If you'd marry me—I swear, Anne, with you beside me I'd get to the top."
> But after a moment she answered, low:
> "But—I want to get to the top—myself!"
> All Ted's masculinity, all his sex pride came to the surface then. He forgot that he loved her—and wanted her, remembered only for the moment that they were man and woman in business, and, in a sense, competitors.
> "You'll get no further," he said. "A woman!"[10]

Nor does Anne's mother understand what "the world [was] coming to when healthy pretty girls preferred typewriters to babies." Her daughter has no plans of giving up either her career or her independence "for any man living!"

Anne's business ambitions go out the window when she falls in love with the dynamic but unhappily married Fellowes. She's briefly willing to become his mistress, but because she's a good secretary, she worries how it will affect his reputation: "She knew that . . . she would be harming him, exposing him to rumor, to gossip, and hurting him through his business, through his friends. She could imagine the raw, scornful comments . . . 'another Big Business Man gone goofy over his steno—!'" Not that she's mentioned her feelings to him; that doesn't happen until after he proposes marriage to her on page 274 of the 279-page novel. She will be a virgin on her wedding night. In the interim, there's a Reno divorce, the threat of a tabloid scandal ("BEAUTIFUL SECRETARY STEALS RICH HUSBAND FROM SOCIETY WOMAN"), a broken engagement, and a subplot involving Anne's younger sister and a gigolo.[11]

A movie version of *The Office Wife*, starring Dorothy Mackaill as the secretary in love with boss Lewis Stone, was rushed into production and appeared in theaters the same year that the book was published. It didn't really matter that, as in the novel, the secretary couldn't bring herself to commit adultery. The film was still what *Variety* called "sure fire," even if its mix of "11 o'clock night office hours with room keys and moonlight on the beach" was "so clean that no censor can censor it."[12]

Baldwin's work popularized the idea that proximity to the boss could spoil a secretary for the merely mortal young men of her acquaintance, measuring them as she did by "the yardstick of the man who has already arrived." In the wake of *The Office Wife*'s success, writers of all stripes were quick to offer their own take on what Baldwin termed a "modern problem." The heroine of a short story published in the *Washington Post Magazine* in 1931 (titled, of all things, "The Office Wife") found her boyfriends wanting by comparison with her executive: "They didn't read the right books. They didn't say the right things. Even their tastes in neckwear and clothes were terrible!" A year later, advice columnist Doris Blake opined that the "tragedy of women in business today" was that so many of them chose a "synthetic love life" at the office instead of marriage to a flesh-and-blood man. In an ideal world, young, single secretaries would keep "an eye open for conquest" during their hours behind the typewriter. "Where better are they likely to meet men?" Blake wondered. But no regular young man could measure up to a business dynamo like her boss. As a result she chose to live "in the shadow of a big man's success."[13]

Professional secretaries deplored the stereotype, which appeared with regularity in books, magazine and newspaper articles, as well as the movies. It didn't help that if a woman whose spouse was cheating on her with his secretary wrote into an advice column for help, the columnist or headline writer immediately tagged "the other woman" as an office wife. A woman named Ynez S. sprang to the defense of "self-supporting women, the so-called office wives" in 1939 after *Los Angeles Times* columnist Alma Whitaker published a letter from a wife worried about the "pretty clerks" who worked with her husband. "It hardly seems cricket for her to classify the office-wife and gold-digger as synonymous," wrote Ynez, ". . . Anyway, speaking for my ilk, I cannot let this challenge pass without saying we resent it." Asked by a reporter what professional secretaries thought of the label at the National Secretaries Association convention in 1949, an attendee simply said, "We have to live it down."[14]

Killers, Cons, and Abnormal Spinsters

By the mid-twentieth century, there was even more for working secretaries to resent about the office wife, as stories about her took on a distinctly film-noir tone. These were also the years when suspicions about women who remained single reached a frenzied peak in the popular press. "Psychiatrists agree," wrote the authors of *How to Pick a Mate* (1946), "that except in

In this mid-twentieth-century comic book's title story, young Kim Garland arrives in New York City with big plans. "I'll join your stenographers' pool, Miss Lee," she tells the head steno at the large advertising agency where she is hired. "But not for long. I intend to become a private secretary— and soon!" She sleeps her way to a spot as a television production assistant—or so it's implied—but loses her feminine charm in the process. "You've become a bitter witch, Kim!" a former boyfriend-boss tells her. "There isn't a person at the agency who doesn't thoroughly dislike you! Take a good look at yourself! You won't like what you see!" Private Secretary, *no. 1, 1963.*

unusual cases women who live alone will become neurotic and frustrated." Living alone, they and other experts concluded, was "an abnormal state for a woman." By this standard, the office wife, who spurned perfectly good neighborhood boys in favor of her perhaps unrequited love for the boss, was perhaps mentally unhinged.[15]

The two little words "office" and "wife" added a titillating frisson to a news story that otherwise had little secretarial connection. In the fall of 1938, a woman named Fern Dull shot and killed her common-law husband, William Holbrook, in front of the Benton Harbor, Michigan, police station. Reporters from the *Chicago Tribune* jumped on the fact that Dull worked in Holbrook's law office. "JILTED 'OFFICE WIFE' TELLS OF KILLING LAWYER" was just one of many similarly worded headlines during the weeks leading up to her trial; articles focused on "the silver blonde office wife" and "the quick trigger office wife," while downplaying other spicy details such as the fact that at the time of the murder Dull was sporting a black eye from one of Holbrook's regularly administered beatings. (The jury saw shades of gray the newspapers didn't; they convicted Dull, who had been indicted for murder, on a lesser charge of manslaughter and sentenced her to fourteen to fifteen years in prison.)[16]

A similar dollop of detective-novel spiciness was attributed to the office wife in "Could *You* Be Blackmailed?" a story that ran in *Los Angeles Times*'s weekly magazine supplement in 1951. Among the various extortion rackets the article described was "the common 'office wife' method":

> A girl takes a job as private secretary and sets about captivating her boss. She watches for her opportunity and eventually "her husband" confronts the pair—usually after hours when they are alone in the office or at late dinner when business has piled up.[17]

The article left it to the reader to imagine just what kind of shenanigans "the husband" walked in on that allowed the pair of con artists to squeeze the unwitting boss for a large sum of money. Readers understood it had to be sexual.

Stories with titles like "My Husband Had an 'Office Wife'" appeared in both women's and general-interest magazines and newspapers, and frequently blurred the line between fiction and nonfiction. "Wanted: A Husband!" appeared in the *Chicago Tribune* in 1952—but it was tabloid fodder all the way. "Miriam" was a "slim, attractive, . . . charming" secretary in an advertising agency who, despite "her aloofness with men," was infatuated with her boss. "She fell for his line about his unhappy marriage" and upcoming divorce. In the meantime, she enjoyed "flying week-end trips with him." But all that was ten years ago. Now, even though Miriam was a "successful career woman, with a high paid job as a private secretary," she was "still in love with her [still-married] boss, still single, and as bitter and lonely as most office wives." Her affair was long over,

> but instead of trying to meet other men, Miriam has gone intellectual, cultivated her eastern accent, donned horn rimmed specs and British walkers, and resigned herself to futility.
>
> She speeds the way with her intellectual superiority and sarcasm towards men in the presence of men, and tries to convince herself that marriage is for morons only.[18]

In private, Miriam slings back martinis "under her thickening waistline" and contemplates suicide, while admitting it "would be nice to have someone to come home to, for a change." Pathetic as she is, Miriam is considered luckier than "Janet," who after a three-year affair becomes pregnant with the boss's child. He ends their affair; Janet goes to a home for unwed mothers. After giving up the child for adoption, Janet lives "in a bachelor girl apartment, owns a mink coat, and plays the races." How does she accomplish this on a secretary's notoriously low salary? "Instead of trying to regain her self-respect, she took the easy way out. Now she's a secretary by day, a party girl by night."[19]

The irony, however, is that while pop culture portrayed the office wife as bitter, neurotic, or worse, many women lied about their marital status at work—because no matter how awkward it was for the secretary to be married to her job, it was much more problematic if she was married to a man.

The Marriage Bar

Some companies guarded themselves from the start by screening out married—even engaged—job applicants in what economists call "the marriage bar" ("the firing of women upon marriage or denial of promotions and more responsible positions to them because they might marry and have children"). However, few employers were as obsessive in this regard as Edward S. Black, a Newark, New Jersey, lawyer who, fed up by the number of stenographers who left his office to get married "just about the time" they were "becoming useful" to him, advertised in 1911 for a "young woman stenographer who will sign contract not to get married; life position." Black's contract specified that "the party of the second part," in addition to remaining single, would

> not attend dances; . . . refrain from entertaining the company of gentle-men and not accompany gentlemen friends to any place of amusement or recreation; . . . not go to theatres or places of amusement or recreation by herself or with girl friends more than once a week; . . . [would] in all ways discourage marriageable men from seeking her company by absenting her-self from places where she is likely to meet them; . . . not listen to girl friends if they try to dissuade her from living a girl-bachelor life; . . . shall not affect puffs, rats [these were horsehair forms upon which fashionable Gibson Girls built their enormous hairdos], powder, paint, or in any other way make herself attractive to look upon.[20]

For committing herself to the secular nunnery of Mr. Black's office, the right candidate could expect to receive the lordly sum of $20 per five-day workweek (roughly $400 in 2008 currency).

Edward Black was a crackpot, or possibly the invention of a *New York Times* editor with a column to fill and a deadline bearing down, but the marriage bar was very real indeed. In the late 1930s, Louise Hollister Scott inter-viewed the personnel directors and hiring managers of several corporations in the course of researching *How to Be a Successful Secretary* (1937). One of these explained that her company does not employ a girl whose engagement has been announced, or who is married, and requires a girl who marries while she is employed to resign six months after her marriage. They feel that, in all probability, the engaged girl will not stay on the job long enough to pay for the expense of training her; and that, in most cases, the married girl does not need the job as much as does her unmarried sister, nor is her interest in the job likely to be so dominant.[21]

In addition to a space marked "single," this company's job application probably had one for a woman to indicate whether or not she was engaged. Other choices, of course, were married, widowed, divorced, and separated, each carrying its own weight when it came to the hiring process (as did an applicant's race when she marked anything other than "white" in the space asking for her race). The practice was neither unusual nor illegal at the time. The marriage bar not only codified the cultural convention that all "normal" women wanted to get married, and once they did, they would stay at home and raise children, but also made such behavior a self-fulfilling prophecy. Newly married women "always quit"; therefore, the company was justified in firing them.

This is my career goal. Color it soon!

According to popular belief, most secretaries were just marking time until marriage. From The Secretary's Coloring Book, *1962.*

"I'm Glad I Lost My Job"

The question of whether or not wives should work outside the home had been a hot-button issue since at least the 1920s, with much of the "anti" argument based on the concept that marriage was a job in and of itself. In 1933, as state legislatures considered taking married women's jobs away from them, the *Los Angeles Times* published an article by "An Ex-'Office Wife.'" "I'm Glad I Lost My Job" told the story of Connie, a secretary who called her two-year-old marriage a "failure." Oh, sure, she and husband Jerry have "every evidence of success and security": a fancy apartment, with a dreamy orchid and green kitchen—but who had time to cook? She and Jerry are a working couple, and both suffer from "badly frazzled" nerves. Then, after months of rumors, it is announced that Connie's office will close in two weeks. "I began to grow panicky. . . . All of the things we had become accustomed to meant two paychecks." But her coworker Jimmy has it worse. After all, he's a breadwinner. "Somehow I couldn't drive the picture of Mrs. Jimmy and Jimmy, Jr. from my mind. What would he do?"*

Connie looks for a new job but quickly runs into a problem. "Married women were definitely out, preference being given to single girls." But when Jerry picks her up after her last day of work, he is wearing "a grin which took me back two years that seemed like a million." During her first jobless week, she learns to cook, and they move to a smaller, less fashionable apartment that has the fireplace they've always wanted. Snuggled up before it, she pretends to be asleep, while Jerry muses aloud: "Guess I had everything figured out wrong. . . . Somehow it seemed all right for Connie to work. . . . I didn't know what a great feeling it was to have someone depending on you for things. Gee, she was working all day long for things I should have been giving her. . . . I've really got something to work for now."†

---

* Ex-"Office Wife," "I'm Glad I Lost My Job," *Los Angeles Times*, June 18, 1933, H11.
† Ibid., 20.

Suddenly, Connie sees the light of traditional gender roles. She realizes that "the most successful marriages" are those "where the girls remained at home" and "gave their husbands a sense of superiority." She remains unemployed. Within a month, Jerry has been promoted. "One may learn office routine in a few weeks, or a few months at most," Connie concludes. "But to be a good wife, one must devote a lifetime to it. It is no part-time occupation and evidently was never meant to be. . . . I have found a career!"

It didn't help the cause of the working wife that many young women fully intended to quit their jobs the moment they married. "Sure, we want a career if necessary," one of a group of young women "preparing for secretarial work" told the *Chicago Tribune* in 1941. "But the goal of all of us is to get married." (She charitably added that while she personally didn't believe that "married women ought to work, . . . they should be able to if necessary.")[22]

The marriage bar also worked in tandem with what organized labor called the "family wage," which paid married men enough money for them to support a stay-at-home wife and growing family. A working wife, therefore, "didn't need" her job. The latter argument was especially loud during the Great Depression in the 1930s, as both individual states and the federal government attempted to legislate against married women working outside the home. A female reporter recapped the situation for the *New York Times* in 1939. "There aren't enough jobs," she wrote, "and the newest and brightest solution advanced by an astonishing number" of elected officials was "to forbid married women to work if their husbands have jobs." Legislators believed that by firing working wives they could effect a "cure-all and end-all of the depression," in the words of the *Times*'s snarky reporter. "There was much quoting, in stentorian tones," she continued, of an economist's assertion that "unemployment would drop by a full million tomorrow" if all married women were booted from their jobs.[23]

In 1939 alone, twenty-six states introduced legislation to do just that.

Most of the bills were aimed at married women in government jobs and teaching. Many would have prevented both wife and husband from working for the same employer if their joint income was over a certain amount, or would have required a wife to prove that her husband earned less than a certain amount, or that she was living apart from him "for justifiable causes" (in the words of California's proposed bill), in order to keep her job. Though the majority of the legislation failed or was later rescinded, many working women were justifiably outraged by these proposed laws. In Massachusetts, a woman representative submitted her own satiric bill to the state legislature that would have kept "married men whose wives have sufficient income to look after them" from being hired for public service jobs. "We are opposed to the attack upon the status of women as adult human beings, which is made under the mask of humanitarianism [i.e., putting male breadwinners back to work]. We are opposed to the attempt to thrust married women back to a position of economic dependence," said former suffragist and chairperson of the National Women's Party, Florence Bayard Hilles, in 1933.[24]

Even where there were no legal bars to keep married women from working, neither were there laws to prevent individual employers from discriminating against them. A survey carried out by the National Federation of Business and Professional Women's Clubs in 1940 discovered that of 485 businesses polled, 40 percent had "definite restrictions" against married women workers. Some industries were more prejudiced against working wives than others: 80 percent of the insurance companies on the Federation's list turned "thumbs down," as did "more than 30 per cent of the banks and the same number of public utilities." Manufacturers, hungry for cheap labor, were mostly happy to hire working wives; only 10 percent of them reported that they said "no" when a female applicant wrote "'married' on the dotted line."[25]

In turn, when it came to listing their marital status on a job application, many working wives chose to write "single." In 1941, "White Collar Girl" columnist Ruth McKay of the *Chicago Tribune* estimated there were approximately two million female office workers concealing their marriages from their employers. Writing a month before the attack on Pearl Harbor, McKay believed that the bias against married women was "fast disappearing under the stress of the rearmament program." As American men were swallowed up with the draft, the arguments that married women were keeping bread-winners from gainful employment fell by the wayside. But while the country's entry into the Second World War and the resultant need for women war workers ended the attempts to legislate married women out of the workplace, individual businesses continued to discriminate against them.[26]

"Should you or shouldn't you?" asked Patricia Flynn, the author of *So You Want to Be an Executive Secretary* (1963). But though her language echoed Clairol's popular and provocative "Does she or doesn't she?" ad campaign for its line of at-home hair dyes, Flynn was very serious about the subject she so coyly broached: "How do you feel about putting your marital status on your resume? Or listing the number and ages of your children?" She was convinced women should do neither. "I have watched while employers looked over resumes of applicants," she wrote. "Which ones do you think go into that bigger pile which lands in the wastebasket? Of course! Those that too prominently mention husbands and children."[27]

Boss versus Husband

In addition to the widespread belief that newlywed women "always quit," there was an equally prevalent conviction that wives who remained on the job were less attentive to the work at hand than their single sisters. Elizabeth MacGib-bon was all for the "modern trend" of married women keeping their jobs where they could, but sympathized "with any business which puts up with girls whose minds are on their homes rather than their work." She gave the example of a secretary in her office who arose at five each morning, "either washed, ironed, scrubbed floors, or baked before she got breakfast" and went to work. She did her "household shopping" on her lunch hour, and when guests were coming to dinner, she left early, whether or not her work for the day was completed. "When, from weariness and absent-mindedness, she began to make mistakes in her work, I had no compunction about replacing her with a less encumbered person, for I knew her husband could support her."[28]

This is a career girl in our office. She wants to get married.

I think this is a married girl. She hasn't been here long enough to get Blue Cross and Blue Shield benefits.

Single women just wanted to get married; married women couldn't concentrate on work. From The Secretary's Coloring Book, *1962.*

Almost thirty-five years later, in *The Secretary's Guide to Dealing with People* (1969) Jean Vermes told the story of Ada, a working wife whose constant worry about her children made her "jumpy and inattentive" at the office. "Finally Ada's boss suggested that she consult the company doctor. This gentleman prescribed tranquilizers and recommended that she take a week off to rest her nerves." Instead of suggesting "she quit her job, as some men might have," Ada's husband sits her down for a talk. They agree that she can't "act unbusinesslike with frantic haphazard calls" to the housekeeper, because that is "the sort of thing that makes executives wary of married secretaries." After Ada resolves to call the housekeeper daily at noon, and perhaps again at five, her nerves are restored, and soon "her executive was boasting that 'Married secretaries are the best.'"[29]

Married women, especially those with children, did have responsibilities outside of the office that single women didn't, but there was an unstated theme running through the scenarios of working wives losing their concentration at work. If the secretary was an executive's office wife, what happened when she had a real husband to divert her attention from her boss? "One employer's unveiled threat" from the mid-1960s sounded like nothing so much as the outraged bellow of a jealous man: "If she comes in late once more because she has to take her husband's shirts to the laundry en route to work, there are going to be some changes made around here!" The merest implication that her boss "was of secondary importance" to his secretary's husband was unacceptable. "On the job the boss is KING, and the smart secretary knows that nothing in her behavior should suggest otherwise," advised Lucy Mayo.[30]

On-the-job sexual dynamics also changed if the secretary was married. According to an employment service manager in the 1920s, a man wanted "an unmarried woman of attractive appearance" to "add to the general attractiveness of the office. . . . a married woman's attitude toward men who come to the office is not the same as that of an unmarried woman," who was "more casual" toward male visitors. "A warm reception from an executive" could not "offset the effects of a frigid one from a secretary," according to a 1951 handbook, using a word frequently associated with wives who suffered from what one marital guide of the era called "sexual indifference" and a failure to orgasm. The employer, too, usually preferred "the attitude of the unmarried [and presumably less frigid] woman toward himself."[31]

Husband versus Job

Opinion differed as to whether a wife's working outside the home hurt her marriage. Pop psychologist Clifford R. Adams, author of the *Ladies' Home Journal*'s "Making Marriage Work" column, argued strongly against wives working after marriage. A young bride-to-be who confessed she "never liked housework" and planned to continue in her secretarial position after the wedding, even though her husband opposed it, didn't really want a career in Adams's opinion, but merely wanted to "avoid irksome household tasks." Perhaps, he continued ominously, she was "unconsciously seeking to evade other responsibilities of marriage as well." Adams didn't specify what these were, but his advice seemed to echo the idea that a woman could pledge her allegiance to either home or office, not both. No wonder *Independent Woman* urged its readers to compartmentalize their home and work lives. "Don't become all-absorbed in your job to the detriment and neglect of a husband or home," it advised in a 1940 article with the foreboding title "Empty Cradles." "Learn to concentrate on work at the office and on the family and husband after working hours."

Adams was also critical of husbands who allowed their wives to work outside the home. He warned single girls against the "pathological male parasite" whose main goal in life was to find a wife or "series of wives" to support him. Clues to this dangerous man included a mediocre job record and taking it "for granted that you [his soon-to-be wife] would continue working after marriage." Needless to say, a young woman "would be wise to disregard" this type as a possible husband. A "good husband," according to Adams, did "not want his wife to work after they marry" because he saw her as "a full-time homemaker and mother of their children."[32]

Women who were "successful in coordinating marriage and work" (and thus, the article in *Independent Woman* implied, avoided those empty cradles) followed a few simple rules for bolstering the male ego: "In no way assume that you are superior to your husband. Strive to encourage him and make him believe in himself." These rules, of course, would have been familiar to any reader of secretarial advice books if one simply substituted the word "boss" for "husband." (While the title *Independent Woman* sounds like the broadest irony in this context, the publication was in fact the journal of the National Federation of Business and Professional Women's Clubs, a staunch supporter of the Equal Rights Amendment and other progressive legislation throughout the twentieth century.)[33]

Jean Vermes best summed up the awkward situation the working wife faced: "Man still believes, deep down, that woman's place is at home, and the married secretary may have to contend with both a husband and a boss who are glad to make use of her talents, but quick to deprecate her ability to lead a double life."[34]

Around the Desk We Go: The Murky World of Love and Sex in the Office

For the matrimonially inclined, secretarial work is about the best bet. Thousands of employers have married their secretaries. For the girl whose employer is already married or doesn't appeal to her . . . there are plenty of consolation prizes in the junior executives and various and sundry sub and sub-sub personnel.

> Marie L. Carney,
> *The Secretary and Her Job* (1939)

• • •

There is the crude one, usually the boss in a small office where there is no one to chide him for his activities. He is the pincher, the fanny-slapper, the squeezer, the nudger, the brusher-againster. The only thing to do about him is either develop quick reflexes for dodging and ducking, or slap his face and quit.

> Jean Vermes, *The Secretary's Guide
> to Dealing with People* (1964)

L et's make it clear right from the start: I've never dipped my pen in the company ink. Even long ago before I was married, the mere thought of the leering faces and gossip run amok that attend an intra-office romance kept me looking for love outside the office—that and the fact that I never worked with anybody who made me want to spend seven minutes in the supply closet with them. On the other hand, if you've worked in an office at anytime during the previous century, you, like me, have had at least one experience, hopefully not too disturbing, wherein a boss or coworker has tiptoed up to or even crossed the line of propriety. Most secretaries have at least one on-the-job horror story to tell: a demotion after she refused to go drinking with out-of-town executives; how the new "girl" didn't listen to advice warning her to avoid the attorney with grabby hands when he visited from the out-of-town office; or how everyone whispered after a consensual relationship with a superior went awry. Others share tales of romantic success: how they met their adored spouse while working overtime on a big account, or the forbidden fling they had with an unmarried higher-up—fun, sexy, and utterly without repercussions. Depending on where you work, you may one day be taken past a particular copy machine or conference table and told in secretive yet reverential tones about who did what to whom there, after the Christmas party the year before last.

At the same time, you probably have to attend a once-every-so-many years sexual harassment training (or, as one office I worked in called it, "prohibited behavior training"). This consists of spending an hour or two sitting around a conference table—quite possibly the legendary one—while an overpaid consultant discusses proper office behavior, then administers a multiple-choice test that is impossible to fail. In technologically advanced offices, this is done online. In either case, as soon as everybody signs the paper saying they've had the training, all the usual suspects immediately start acting like idiots again. Just be grateful they don't know about "scuttle."

Off to the Secretary Races!

Writing in the *Wall Street Journal* during the height of the Clarence Thomas Supreme Court confirmation controversy in 1991, Helen Gurley Brown—*Cosmopolitan* editor, author of *Sex and the Single Girl* (1962), and self-described feminist—said she "lined up firmly" behind Anita Hill, the assistant attorney who accused her former boss Thomas of sexual harassment. But at the same time she supported Hill in her claim, Brown fondly remembered the "dandy game" played by her office mates at a Los Angeles radio station in 1940, which she first wrote about in *Sex and the Office* (1964):

> Rules: All announcers and engineers who weren't busy would select a secretary, chase her down the halls, through the music library and back to the announcing booths, catch and take her panties off. Once the panties were off, the girl could then put them back on again. Nothing wicked ever happened. Depantying was the sole object of the game.
>
> While all this was going on, the girl herself usually shrieked, screamed, flailed, blushed, threatened and pretended to faint, but to my knowledge, no scuttler was ever reported to the front office. Au contraire, the girls wore their prettiest panties to work.[1]

"Alas," Brown wrote with seeming dismay, "I was never scuttled." Still working her way through secretarial school at the time, Brown imagined herself "too young, too pale, too flat-chested" to be of interest to the office marauders. She swore her "sweet, normal" sister secretaries "enjoyed it." As evidence of their complicity, Brown told the story of how four secretaries banded together to depants the head scuttler one afternoon while he was on air in the radio booth—a rather tepid turnabout, given that taking a man's trousers off one time is not the same thing as leaving him naked from the waist down on multiple occasions.[2]

Brown herself clearly yearned to be scuttled, but we have only her word as to what the other secretaries thought. Were they really only pretending to be outraged, as she suggested? Did they, like Brown, think scuttle was "dandy" fun—or did they play along because they didn't want to be labeled a stick in the mud or, worse, fired for reporting male higher-ups to the front office? Were the four secretaries who banded together to depants their antagonist just kidding around in kind—or sending him a message about his unacceptable behavior?

If scuttle sounds less like acceptable office hijinks and more like on-the-clock sexual assault, perhaps you would prefer to partake in a "Secretary Race." Described in a 1949 *Good Housekeeping* article as an appropriate game to play at the office Christmas party, secretary racing seemed designed to encourage flirtations. The requirements were as follows: "Three secretaries, 3 bosses, 3 roll chairs. At given signal, boss sits in chair, with secretary on lap, then rolls across the floor at word 'Go.'" *Good Housekeeping*'s suggested refreshments included eggnog and punch, albeit both of the virgin variety. But add a little booze—as I'm sure many people did—and one can imagine how the secretary race might devolve into the murky water of confused feelings, and awkwardness throughout the following workday—if not worse.[3]

Around the same time that *Good Housekeeping* bestowed its seal of approval on this far tamer version of today's lap dance as a fun yet proper interaction between coworkers of the opposite sex, and Brown wistfully watched as her officemates scuttled, *Manners in Business* (1936) advised women on how best to deal with "the undercurrent of sex" that ran through the office, variously "upsetting, repelling, [and] attracting individuals." Since most businesses frowned on "any outward manifestation of attraction between the sexes," it was best for men and women working side by side to sublimate "their primary urges and become almost unconscious of each other's sex," thus keeping "the dynamite . . . in the cellar, so to speak." *How to Be a Successful Secretary* (1937) concurred. While a "happy social relationship" might develop between coworkers of the opposite sex (as far as the authors of mid-century guidebooks were concerned, there was no such thing as homosexuality), a secretary needed to be careful "not to let such an interest affect the business relation between" herself and the rest of the office crew lest she lose their "high regard." But in case her "good breeding and sound common sense" failed her when it came to ignoring the flirtatious glances of that junior executive down the hall, author Louise Hollister Scott mentioned a Massachusetts law firm that barred "its girls from accepting social invitations" from their male coworkers. If an infringement of the rule was discovered, the woman involved was "summarily dismissed." Scott noted that while the rule may have seemed harsh, the company believed that the office as a whole was more efficient if there were no "social relations." Finally, she noted (recognizing, perhaps, that some of her readers were going to view the office as a dating service no matter what she said) that she, along with many of the executives and secretaries she interviewed for her book, believed that it proved "to be disappointing in almost every case" when "a girl" became "interested socially" in a man who was her superior at the office.

This is where rubber met the road when it came to office relationships: where men, women, and the dynamics of power are brought together, the partner on the lower end of the office totem pole was most likely to suffer if and when things cooled down. "If you allow anything to start, when it peters out you will be the one to lose your job, not your boss," advised *The Art of Being a Successful Business Girl* (1943) in a section called "The Woman Always Pays"—and that was when the relationship was consensual. The venerable Emily Post was blunt: "Sex is one thing that has no place in business." The woman who went into office work because she hoped to "meet romance in the form of her employer or at least to rise quickly because of her physical charm" had mixed up "clerkship and chorus work."[4]

A Smorgasbord of Men?

It was in fact very easy to get the two confused. For in addition to the secretarial handbooks and authorities that counseled the secretary to keep her on-the-clock relationships strictly professional, a strain of popular wisdom suggested she'd better do exactly the opposite if she ever wanted to land a husband—and get out of the office. "Do our girls ever marry their employers?" the *New York Times* quoted the manager of an employment bureau in 1904. "Well, now, perhaps I ought not to tell of their love ventures; but it is not a rare thing for a boss who is paying his female amanuensis $25 or $30 a week to make her his wife and then hire another girl for half that pay to do her work." In many cases, he noted, the newly married former secretary was "shrewd" enough to "contrive" to find something for herself to do at the office, "so that she may keep an eye on the old man."[5]

Writing in 1906, Mary Mortimer Maxwell (the pseudonym of journalist Elizabeth Banks) explained why she encouraged a "well bred, well read, nice mannered" but single young woman acquaintance of hers to learn stenography and typewriting, then apply for a position in a New York office. Here her young friend could meet "real men, men of brain, men of worth, men able properly to provide for her," among them her boss, "his partners . . . their clients and business associates." Mere proximity would do the rest. "Day in and day out she meets them, talks with them. Later she lunches with them, walks with them, invites them to her home, marries them." Or one of them at least, though Maxwell's prose made it sound like there would be multiple grooms awaiting the lucky bride at the altar. (It should be noted that while Elizabeth Banks had plenty of office experience—she began her working life as a typist and later worked as a secretary both before and after she broke into journalism with her article "All about Typewriter Girls"—she never married.)[6]

Stories like this, plus occasional news items about, for example, a banker who married his stenographer, an executive who wed his typist, or, on one occasion in 1927 that must have launched a million daydreams, an English lord who married a secretary, reinforced the idea that romance was waiting in the corner office—not only in a novel or movie but also in real life. *The Efficient Secretary* (1917) warned against getting carried away with matrimonial daydreams: "In reading business romances and applying them to one's own life, it is well to remember that business romances that are published are interesting only because they are exceptional, and the law of averages governs the careers and lives of most of us."

The Efficient Secretary was swimming against the tide, along with other guidebooks that warned secretaries to keep business and romance widely separated. More common by far was the belief that the office was a "happy

A *"pretty typewriter girl" displays what looks like an engagement ring, circa early 1918.*

hunting ground for the two-legged dear," as a secretarial textbook from the 1960s colorfully described it. "Probably more romances begin in a business office than at any summer resort," wrote columnist Alma Archer in *Your Power as a Woman* (1957). In a chapter devoted to "Finding Love and Marriage," Archer suggested women evaluate their workplaces for man-finding potential. "If you find yourself stagnating in an organization filled with women, look for another job." If, on the other hand, one's office provided a satisfactory number of available male coworkers, Archer offered specific rules concerning their pursuit:

5. Don't park on his desk, gazing adoringly into his eyes as you make the small talk. His sly grin doesn't mean he likes the desk polish job, but that he catches on to your trick and will treat you accordingly.

6. Don't totter among the files and desks on super-spike heels. You'll maybe not only fall *for* him, but in front of him.

7. Don't be afraid to compliment the man in your office life, but do it when he's by himself. A swoon over his tie in front of the payroll spinster might be embarrassing.[7]

Above all, Archer counseled discretion—not because management might look askance at a budding office romance and possibly fire the woman so involved, but because men disliked "female aggression." Archer wrote beauty advice for a general audience, but mid-twentieth-century secretarial guidebooks weren't shy about advertising the office as a place to meet men. The authors of *Charm: The Career Girl's Guide to Business and Personal Success* (1964) also counseled restrained pursuit: "This is one case where success goes not to the fearless hunter. Subtle allure is the best female weapon, and it is the charming trapper who, most likely, brings home her man."[8]

Not surprisingly, given her easygoing attitude toward forcible panty removal, Helen Gurley Brown recommended a more aggressive approach to secretaries on the make in *Sex and the Office*. Brown even chided Elizabeth MacGibbon for advising readers of *Manners in Business* to make themselves "as inconspicuous as possible," before she shot down the oft-repeated line that executives were distracted by a secretary's too sexy appearance: "If a striking appearance really disturbed him, a girl with large mammary glands would have to wear a suit of armor, and you *know* any boss with a secretary who did that would shoot himself—or spend his entire day keeping track of his can-opener." In her opinion, "a bit of lace [slip] peeking out below a slender sheath skirt" during dictation was "fascinating."[9]

Contrary, too, to guidebook authors who suggested a secretary hide her brains lest they intimidate her boss, Brown urged her readers to value intelligence as well as competency. True, she couched her advice in man-getting

Dear Sob Sister: I'm in Love with My Boss

Laura Jean Libbey's advice column ran in the *Chicago Tribune* during the early part of the twentieth century and frequently contained anguished letters from office workers. A young woman identified only as "D" wrote to Libbey in November 1910. "I am a stenographer in a large office and am desperately in love with my employer, who is a married man," her letter began. "I know he loves me, for he is going to free himself from his wife to marry me, even though he loses all his friends, his position, and becomes hated by goody-goody people—all for my sake. I am 20 years old and he is between 45 and 50." Libbey's response was blunt. Leave your job immediately, she told the starry-eyed steno, because a "man who deserts his wife for no cause . . . would probably tire more quickly of you than he did of her."

A week later, Libbey's column carried a classic missive from another stenographer contemplating a relationship with her boss. It was, Libbey noted, "The Same Old Heartbreaking Query." "I am 19 and he is 39," the letter began. "He is married . . . but his wife is hopelessly insane, and he is asking me to marry him, saying he can get a divorce from her at any time." Libbey must have recognized the earmarks of a practiced seducer at work: a big age difference between the parties—check; an inaccessible wife—check ("insanity" was a nice, heart-rendering touch); a pending divorce—check. Her response was forthright and to the point. "You will spell out the most heartbreaking misery for yourself that can come to a woman. Don't do it!" she implored the letter writer, though as anyone who has tried to talk a friend out of dating the wrong person can attest, once someone makes up her mind, there's nothing anyone can say to stop her.*

As Libbey's column demonstrated, there was no shortage of love-

---

* Laura Jean Libbey, "Woman and Her Interests," *Chicago Tribune*, November 8, 1910, 8; and November 17, 1910, 8.

struck stenos. These are just two of many letters from young women seeking to navigate the rocky waters of office relationships. "I'm in love with my boss" remained a constant theme in advice columns throughout the twentieth century (also the twenty-first, and probably the twenty-second and beyond too).

terms—but at least part of her message was refreshingly different in an era that valued female submissiveness across the board. "Being great at a terrific job is sexy. You are far more intriguing than a drone or a slug," she told readers.[10]

Brown's *Sex and the Single Girl* made the earth-shattering announcement that it was possible for unmarried women to experience "unadulterated, cliffhanging sex" without remorse—*Sex and the Office* brought the idea into a business setting. The "romances and affairs" that started in the workplace could provide "some of the most . . . satisfying, memorable episodes in any two persons' lives" but rarely ended at the altar—especially since the parties may have been already married to others. Nobody ever got hurt in Brown's sexy playground of an office—she even mentioned birth control, albeit in passing ("Girls know about diaphragms"), but at the time a real rarity in books aimed at single women. A story about a young office worker ("a child" in Brown's estimation) who made a lunch date with a typewriter salesman only to find herself "in a boarded-up beach house" ended with: "Nothing happened. They tussled, she flew back to the car and demanded lunch." Brown labeled the salesman "a genuine creep," but only because he didn't choose for his trysting partner "a grown-up girl [who] might have enjoyed hunting for mythical papers in a beach house."[11]

A person who could eat after such an encounter, let alone with its perpetrator, was indeed a person who might enjoy a game of scuttle. When a New York newspaper called Brown in 1991 to see if there was "any sexual harassment" in the offices of *Cosmopolitan* magazine, she replied, "I certainly hope so. . . . The problem is that we don't have enough men . . . to go around for the harassing." It was, she admitted as she recalled the conversation in the pages of the *Wall Street Journal*, a "wantonly facetious" comment, one that garnered lots of negative press, especially since she went on to share her very positive memories of scuttle as an example of sexual harassment. In Brown's viewpoint, it was important to "come down hard on the bullies and the creeps but not go stamping out sexual chemistry at work." Bullies and creeps, she explained, were men who kept women from getting or keeping jobs, denied them promotions, or made them uncomfortable at work with an oafish "approach to sex." Sexual chemistry, on the other hand, led to "the best creative work" as men and women showed off for one another. Implied or "even stated sexual interest" between coworkers was therefore not a bad thing, as long as it didn't "fall in the category of tasteless or unwanted"—to my mind exactly where scuttle should have been consigned.[12]

Freezing Out the Office Wolf

There was plenty of evidence to suggest that long before the phrase "sexual harassment" gave nightmares to certain echelons of upper management (a group of women at a consciousness-raising session in Ithaca, New York, claimed to be the first to use the term in the 1970s), offices were populated with bullies and creeps aplenty—and that the "sexual chemistry" Brown extolled often left something to be desired. Whether he was called an office wolf, a Don Juan, or, as one man mentioned in *Manners in Business*, "Felix the Feeler," he took an unwanted romantic or sexual interest in his female coworkers. Sometimes he was ranked on a similar rung of the corporate ladder as the secretary—and that was bad enough—but sometimes he was the boss. At best, he was easily brushed aside as a pest; at worst, he was a sexual predator.[13]

A young stenographer narrowly averted disaster after meeting one of the latter in 1888. That fall, a man who claimed his name was W. W. Findlay appeared at Miss Campbell's school of stenography in Cincinnati, Ohio. He introduced himself as the "Third Vice-President of the Union Pacific

Railroad," and he wanted to hire a "lady typewriter." He was "referred to an attractive young woman of good standing," who accepted his job offer on the spot. She was to join Findlay in Omaha, then, "as he traveled a great deal," she would work with him "in his private [railway] car." But before she headed to Nebraska, her friends, perhaps smelling a rat, checked out Findlay's story. No one by that name was employed by Union Pacific. The company did, however, confirm that the man had in his possession "numerous railroad passes in the name of W.W. Findlay."[14]

A man named William Whittle placed an advertisement for a stenographer in one of New York City's many newspapers in 1924. Then, when an applicant showed up, he subjected her to one more little test in addition to the ones that checked her speed and competency at shorthand and typing. "Before I hire a girl I always test her morals by putting my arms around her and patting her arms," he told the magistrate, having been arrested after one would-be stenographer's mother complained. "If she don't resent it, I know she is used to it and not the kind of girl I want in my office."[15]

Few harassers wound up, as Whittle did, in the magistrate's office, because prior to the advent of sexual harassment legislation in the late 1970s (again as part of Title VII of the Civil Rights Act of 1964), a woman had little recourse when she found herself on the receiving end of a wolf's attention: she either put up with it or quit. In the early 1920s, the Boise Business Women's Club announced a campaign "to protect the office girl from the flirty employer." To that end, the club intended to keep a list of all offices in which flirtatious bosses were a problem—but such community policing was rare. Instead, the secretarial experts repeated the same formula again and again over the decades—and it wasn't a particularly helpful one. A secretary should avoid awkward situations with male coworkers, but if despite her best efforts something untoward occurred, she should ignore it—he probably didn't mean anything by it anyway. As historian Julie Berebitsky has pointed out, by representing unwanted encounters as "inconsequential, denying men's sexual interest [in their female coworkers], and warning women against office intrigue," the advice presented to secretaries made them "fully responsible" for the wolf-like behavior of their bosses and other men in the office. This echoed the standard advice given to young women of dating age throughout most of the twentieth century: that she had better not let things progress "too far" on a date, because she was responsible for her boyfriend's sexuality. ("Boys by nature, facts and statistics prove it, are a lot less aggressive than girls. They don't get 'fresh' unless a girl provokes a 'pass,'" wrote Lois Pemberton in *The Stork Didn't Bring You* (1948). Boys had "an inherent respect for womankind and motherhood," yet girls who indulged in petting ran the risk of unleashing "one of the most powerful forces in Nature": the hurricane in his pants.)[16]

If her employer dared to "use familiarity in manner or language," Mrs. Hester M. Poole suggested in 1898, the secretary was to fix upon him "a

"Business Should Not Interfere with Pleasure." How long before she wrote to the advice columnists because she was in love with her boss? 1907.

look of surprise and distance." If that didn't work, she was to say something along the lines of "I am not here for that purpose, sir!" (One here imagines her boss twirling his long, black mustache before slinking away in shame.) Luckily, such situations were rare and occurred in "exceptional cases only, among persons of low development." Women were generally "treated as ladies should be," unless the secretary lowered herself, in which case she "may expect a certain class to take advantage of it."[17]

What Poole suggested was often referred to as "freezing"—ignoring or otherwise sending a glacial chill toward the instigator of unwanted behavior. The "average woman of intelligence," opined Eleanor Gilbert in *The Ambitious Woman in Business* (1916), was "quite capable of freezing an undesired admirer into a state of respectful good sense, without even losing her job in the process." And if the cold shoulder didn't work, there was always the door. If it was "a case where she can not get rid of the attentions, she can, as a last resort get rid of the job. . . . She need never be kissed twice against her will."[18]

If a secretary was invited to work late after having a little dinner with an employer, and had "reason to suspect she should refuse, she should not hesitate to do so even though she may realize that it is likely to mean the loss of her job," wrote Louise Hollister Scott in *How to Be a Successful Secretary*. Scott didn't advocate blowing the whistle on a lascivious or leering boss, but her advice, like that given twenty-one years earlier by Eleanor Gilbert, was both proactive and integrity saving. But however satisfying it was to tell an inappropriate boss to take his job and shove it, quitting was simply not an option for most women. A secretary who depended on her paycheck to pay the rent and put groceries on the table was not about to walk out the door. Nor could she risk a retaliatory firing if she reported an incident to her higher-ups. The consensus opinion of most guidebook writers was thus to "act natural and pay no attention to personal remarks, pats or other approaches. Pass them off and keep quiet," as Gladys Torson expressed it in *The Art of Being a Successful Business Girl.*

In Torson's opinion, married men were the easiest to brush off. "The mere fact" that one's boss had a wife made him "easy to control, because he is obviously not in a position to pursue the same course of action a bachelor could follow." A mid-1960s textbook for secretarial students also suggested that an office wolf could be dealt with by "bringing the conversation around to a subject that tied him to domesticity," asking him about his wife or children, for example. Yet surely the authors knew that wedding vows, his own or anybody else's, were no match for a determined wolf. *Manners in Business* even suggested that "his wife's picture on his desk" was the first "ill omen" when it came to an office Don Juan—the photo was often there, author Elizabeth MacGibbon thought, "as a perpetual reminder [for him] to go home nights."[19]

Some guidebooks offered "helpful" examples of how to passively deal with office wolves so ludicrous that they would be laughable, if they weren't actually presented as workable solutions. "The boss' son kept inviting me to go out with him," began one of the "true experiences of office employees" presented in *The Secretary and Her Job* (1939). "I didn't like the fellow a bit, but I didn't know what unpleasantness I might cause myself if I persisted in refusing him. Finally I did go, wearing my sister's clothes that were too big for me and looked frumpish, and acting so dull and boorish that he never had the least desire to ask me out again."[20]

Secretaries on the Spot (1967) included a case where a young woman's boss "had a habit of leaning over her desk" and placing "his arm around her shoulder. Although she felt he meant no harm, she disliked this habit. She didn't wish to embarrass him or make him angry, but she wanted to discourage such habits." In this case, the book reported that the secretary moved her desk "so that no one could approach it except from one side," then, as an additional barrier, kept the slide-out work surface pulled open with correspondence piled on it. As a result, he couldn't reach her, and the problem ended.[21]

In both circumstances, the advice given by a Chicago secretary on the cusp of World War II—that if an office wolf got "fresh, a good, stinging slap may be called for"—may have been more useful. But even she added a tempering proviso: "Don't make it public. Most men will respect a girl if she demands it, but they're very vengeful if their vanity is hurt."[22]

Underlying the guidebooks' descriptions of troublesome situations was often the suggestion that the male involved "didn't mean anything" by the fact that his hand was on her bottom, and that she was overreacting. A "wise" young woman recognized that "some men" were "on the make" but didn't let "this useful bit of knowledge" turn her "into an overly suspicious or overly prudent prig":

> Even if you are convinced that you are a desirable young female, don't *imagine* things. If the boss asks you to dinner with him and to work late, don't jump to reel four. When he says dinner and work, he probably means dinner and work.[23]

But it wasn't always easy to gauge a man's intentions—especially if he was in a position of power and you were dependent on him for your job. And while there may have been men who respected a girl if she "demanded it," any number of them believed that a woman who found herself in a questionable situation must have been "asking for it" in the first place.

Unfortunately, what worked for the women described in these materials—ignoring or laughing off an improper glance, touch, or word, rearranging the office furniture, or wearing frumpy clothing—wasn't always helpful in real life. "I've always believed a girl got what she asked for but right now that doesn't help much," wrote the married recipient of too much attention, including phone calls at home, from one of her male coworkers, to *Los Angeles Times* advice columnist Amy Abbott in 1958. "I know of nothing wrong in my behavior. I dress, smile and talk as well as I can because I want to be liked, but see no reason why it should be taken as a come-on." Abbott assured the woman that if she kept on "being pleasant, courteous and unavailable," she would "eventually discourage" her harasser. If he kept on being obnoxious, well, then, it had to be her fault. Abbott's final words made it clear where she suspected responsibility for the whole ugly episode lay: "That IS what you want, isn't it?"[24]

Of the four hundred respondents to a questionnaire distributed at the annual meeting of the National Secretaries Association in 1970, not one said she would report a boss who made a pass at her. Instead, the majority reported they would "try to straighten him out and then forget it." Again, the secretary's own behavior set the pace for the men's in the office. "If you act like a lady," said one of the convention goers, "they treat you like one. There's no problem."[25]

But there were problems with this line of thinking. If you're female, you know that there are situations where you can "act like a lady" until the cows come home and yet there will be a guy out there who misinterprets your pleasant courtesy for barely controlled lust. There are also psychopaths. Sometimes these people are your coworkers and sometimes they are the men who sit in the corner offices. But why would a secretary in 1970, when there was little-to-no legislation to protect her, come forward about a superior making a pass? It would come down to her word against his—and he held her career in the palm of his hand. In her book for bosses, Gladys Torson told them, "You are really being very unsportsmanlike if you pursue your secretary since it is more difficult for her to turn down the boss than it is for her to say no to someone on whom she is not dependent for a living."[26]

Even *The Mademoiselle Handbook* (1946) departed from its usually sensible tone and started to sound like all the rest when it advised the woman interviewing for a new job that it wasn't "diplomatic" to tell the interviewer she was leaving her old position because "Mr. Dingle pinches you and tries to kiss you every time you go to the files in the back office." This advice was not meant to protect the job applicant lest she be labeled, however unfairly, as a troublemaker, but to protect the lecherous Mr. Dingle (a name I could not have made up on my own).[27]

The Office Party

The vast majority of workers understood the lines of demarcation necessitated by office decorum during the workday. But those lines became tangled at events that took place outside of work hours. Was it permissible to call the boss "Johnny" at the office Christmas party, or was he still "Mr. Bartlett"? What if he asked you to slow dance? What if you said yes? And what if you'd both had a couple of drinks?

The office party is the stuff of legends, at least pop-cultural ones: none of the ones I attended ever quite attained the boozed-up heights of, say, those depicted in the movies *Desk Set* (1957) and *The Apartment* (1960), let alone television's *Mad Men* (2007). An episode of *Mad Men* set in 1960 graphically showed the gory morning after an election night soiree in the offices of the fictional Sterling Cooper Advertising Agency: wastepaper baskets filled with vomit, partially dressed secretaries sneaking out of private offices, account executives wracked with hangovers and guilt.

The first office holiday parties consisted of probably little more than a quick toast with the boss before everyone headed out at the end of the day on Christmas Eve, possibly a couple of hours early if he was a soft touch—think of Scrooge's boss Fezziwig in Dickens's *A Christmas Carol*. However, starting sometime in the 1940s, the bacchanalian mix of management, staff, and booze portrayed in films and on television seems to have become an annual ritual—at least in Manhattan. Certainly, "the notorious stereotype of hilarity and secretary pinching" was well in place by the early 1950s. A cartoon depicting the "Office Party (Yule)" appeared in the *New York Times Magazine* in 1952; in it, the "office lush" pulled out his flask, the boss wished "he really could captivate the new blond typist, the way bosses do in cartoons," while other workers sang off-key and later passed out. "I remember the year the bookkeeper was chasing a stenographer from the top of one desk to another, and he fell off and broke a leg," recalled an "old-timer" who, already in 1952, was decrying a trend toward "tamer" office parties. "We used to gather around the water cooler and sing and then have a fist fight or two." In 1958, the *Los Angeles Times* reported a divorce granted to nineteen-year-old Phyllis Craig after her husband came back from the office party smeared with lipstick after kissing all twelve of his female coworkers—and then dragged her to their door when she refused to kiss him. A husband who attended an office party stag, then arrived home with the incriminating cosmetic plastered on his face, collar, necktie, and hair, was also at the center of a 1957 installment of the *Ladies' Home Journal*'s "Can This Marriage Be Saved?" column (presumably *Journal* readers who didn't heed the magazine's concurrently running "Making Marriage Work" column turned here as a last

Party Punch!

In *Sex and the Office* (1964), Helen Gurley Brown not only endorsed the impromptu office party, thrown for any "reason you can get away with, from the birth of new kittens to Bolivar's birthday," but also passed along a recipe for a simple punch to be mixed up in "a *large* container," perhaps "a plastic wastebasket from the dime store." To swing your next office party HGB-style, simply mix a gallon of white wine with three or more bottles of vodka ("an inexpensive brand will do"), along with fruit punch and maraschino cherries "to pretty it up." My head and stomach ache just thinking about it.*

* Helen Gurley Brown, *Sex and the Office* (New York: Bernard Geis Associates, 1964), 137.

resort). "Back then, boy, people really let their hair down," businessman Norman Spizz told the *New York Times* in 2000, when asked about office parties of fifty years ago. Workers "set out to drink and have fun, and they very often succeeded."[28]

No wonder the *Los Angeles Times* called the drunken office party "A Growing Christmas Scandal" in a 1953 exposé. "It's time we all woke up to the danger and disgrace of a custom that too often brings an aftermath of embarrassment—or worse—in both home and office." The article went on to describe parties where "secretaries, switchboard operators and file clerks tilted paper-cup highballs with executives and salesmen" before the lights were turned off at five o'clock "and the doors of some of the private offices were . . . discreetly closed." Fist fights followed, and "some of the girls who didn't want to go into the private offices were pushed around." Sometimes the parties went all night; there were cases where executive daddies didn't get home in time to open presents the following morning. The answer, according to the *Times*, was what would now be called a "family-friendly" holiday party where children, "wives and boy friends" were welcome. (There was no mention of husbands because it was assumed that women quit after they got married, and no mention of girlfriends because men on the executive track proved their steadfastness by being married, no matter how many secretarial bottoms they pinched.)

Predictably, some blamed the wives for taking "much of the mad, bad, gladness" out of the office party. "Today mamma insists on going right along to the office Christmas party, too—and if papa gets out of hand she's right there to take him back in tow" was the opinion of a syndicated newspaper reporter in 1952. Helen Gurley Brown complained in 1964 that "wives and the local police department, who complained that husbands were driving home intoxicated," had killed the free-for-all office party ("as crowded as Churchill Downs on Derby Day and so noisy you can't hear a cry for help"). But ultimately what led to the demise of the mad, bad, drunken office party was not wifely interlopers but liability. "Boss Pays for Actions of Office Party-goer" read a *BusinessWeek* headline in 1954; three years later the magazine asked "Why Office Parties Go Wrong." Booze, it seemed, was the real problem. In the mid-1960s, the National Advisory Commission on Alcoholism warned against drinking at late-afternoon office Christmas parties, where the combination of booze and an empty stomach might lead to a tragedy if a drunken worker were to slide behind the wheel to drive home. In 1974, the California Supreme Court ruled that the family of a man killed in a car accident after he got drunk at an office party was entitled to workman's compensation benefits.[29]

Secretarial guides generally suggested that the "discreet secretary" curtail her alcohol intake. According to *Manners in Business*, it was permissible to have a drink at the office Christmas party—but just one, lest things slide out of control. "I have seen unsophisticated stenographers exclaim 'How good this punch is!' and take more, not dreaming what it would do to them until they were almost out," wrote author Elizabeth MacGibbon. To drive home her point, she told the stories of Mary B——, whose tipsy, indiscreet babbling cost her a promotion to an "important and confidential position"; Amy H——, who never lived down her drunken pass (unsuccessful) at the head bookkeeper; and Marjorie L——, who, after a few drinks at the Christmas party, went back to her desk to type up a few things and wound up handing in "letters that looked like so much Czecho-Slovakian."[30]

It was hard to "remember to be ladylike at all times" if one had too much to drink. "Does your head become fuzzy after three drinks? Then take only two," advised *The Successful Secretary* (1964). Even if she drank nothing stronger than ginger ale, should a secretary be "too loud, too bright, or too gay" at the party, she might be whispered about the next day. Under no circumstances was she to call the president of the company by his first name, or discuss her personal problems with him or anybody else. If people were becoming "rowdy," it was best to "leave early (but pleasantly and without recriminations)." A bigwig in his cups might be "loosened up sufficiently to make surprisingly friendly overtures," but if the secretary "tactfully" forgot such "lapses," she would "win many appreciative friends." It practically went without saying that it was best to wear "something suitable for the office," dressed up with a piece of costume jewelry rather than a slinky party dress.[31]

These days, planning an office party is all about avoiding liability. Mistletoe is considered a "provocative decoration," while slow dances invite "prohibited behavior." Other suggestions from a labor lawyer to keep a party from devolving into a bacchanal (quoted in a 2000 *New York Times* article asking "Did the Grinch Steal the Office Party, Too?"): hold it away from the office, hire professional bartenders, don't serve salty snacks that encourage people to drink more. Better yet, don't serve booze at all. A 2007 survey showed that over half the companies polled planned a dry office party, the better to avoid drunken drives home and complaints of sexual harassment, which tended to spike during the office party season.[32]

But take my word for it, an office party without booze is like a meatloaf without salt: bland and oh so familiar. Back at the art gallery, drinking was an accepted part of doing business, and a blind eye was often turned to post-opening hangover-related absences (though the victim would indeed be teased for his or her weakness the following day). At the law office where I worked, colleagues still remembered full-on bacchanals in the late 1980s, when staff members passed out in the partners' offices, and an associate allegedly cashed his client's settlement check at a liquor store (though that one always sounded too good to be true). Money was tighter by the time I took my place behind the computer, and parties tended to curdle into separate groups of attorneys and staff. A drink or two often led to cautious intermingling, and though I was definitely on the receiving end of some questionable "compliments" from soused higher-ups, the wildest I ever got was to stagger straight from the party to the Macy's cosmetics counter, where I dramatically overspent on a French eye shadow compact—black! the most useful color—that remained in my makeup bag, unused, for many years to come.

Stepping Stone or Millstone?
Up the Ladder and out
of the Steno Pool

Now, let's get this clear. Women have always worked. And the men have always warmly approved. And the harder and grubbier and dirtier the work, and the longer the hours, and the lower the pay, and the grimier the environment—the more warmly and heartily have the men approved. It is only since some of the girls began to climb . . . into the Chanel and Dior suits and onto the five-figure payroll and into the corner office with the broadloomed floor that the boys have gone in for headshakings and mutterings and hues and cries and anguished plaints . . . about women's place being in the home.

Bernice Fitz-Gibbon, "Woman in the *Gay* Flannel Suit,"
New York Times Magazine, January 29, 1956

One of my favorite memories of growing up in Milwaukee in the late 1960s and early 1970s is visiting my Aunt Norma at work. My mother and I would drive downtown, park the car, and walk to the brass-fronted elevators in the marble-floored lobby of a turn-of-the-twentieth-century office building located on Wisconsin Avenue, just east of the Milwaukee River. From there we'd ascend to the insurance company where Norma worked. She'd introduce me to the other secretaries and staff members (there were no cubicles isolating the staff from one another, just glass-enclosed private offices for the higher-ups). If I was lucky, I got to play with somebody's typewriter. Then we'd ride back down to the lobby, cut across the alley behind the building, and walk through the back door of a darkly lit restaurant, where we'd sit in a leather-upholstered booth, I'd have a hamburger, and the waitresses would fuss over me. It was, I thought, the epitome of glamour.

As soon as I was old enough to understand, my mother was careful to point out that Norma wasn't a secretary like all the other women busy clickety-clacking away on their Selectrics. Norma was the company's corporate secretary (she later became vice president of one of its subsidiaries), which is probably why she had the time to spend a leisurely lunch with us in the first place.

Her story was exactly the kind the secretarial advice manuals loved to tell: that of a plucky Horatio Algerette, who, armed only with a steno pad and a typewriter ribbon, ascended to the high echelons of management. As a girl, Norma dreamed of going to the local women's college and becoming a physical therapist. But when she was thirteen, her father died, and her postgraduation plans drastically changed. Four years of college was out—she needed to get a job to help support her family. Instead of the green suburban campus of her dreams, Norma found herself at the local secretarial college, thanks to what she described as a "hard case" scholarship. A couple of semesters later, her ability to use both a typewriter and a wax-cylinder Dictaphone (her shorthand was still a little shaky) helped her get hired at an entry-level job—and from there she began her rise to the top.

Up by Her Bootstraps

She was not alone. Jane J. Martin, a "pioneer woman in the advertising field" during the second and third decades of the twentieth century, "entered business" as a sixteen-year-old stenographer at a drug company. She became a secretary to one of its partners and wrote advertising copy when he was out of town. By 1921, she reputedly made $25,000 a year (just over $300,000 in today's dollars) as advertising manager of the Sperry & Hutchinson Company, manufacturer of trading stamps. May G. Schaefer "began her business career as a secretary" and, in 1931, became the first woman to be elected as a bank officer in Bronx County, New York. [1]

And then there was Helen Gurley Brown. Born in Arkansas in 1922, Helen Gurley moved to Los Angeles with her mother and sister in 1936, after her father died in an elevator accident. She attended Woodbury Business College in Burbank, then worked in seventeen different offices before she joined the advertising agency Foote, Cone & Belding. When her boss, Don Belding, allowed her to write ad copy for the Sunkist Orange account, a career was born: by the mid-1950s, Helen Gurley was one of the top-paid female copywriters on the West Coast. At what was then considered the advanced age of thirty-seven, she married movie producer David Brown. She published her first book, *Sex and the Single Girl*, in 1962—and the rest is history.[2]

Secretarial guidebooks pointed to successful women like these as proof that a secretary with ambition could go far. "Many department store buyers, magazine editors, copywriters, personnel experts, public relations executives, television directors, real estate brokers, and other important women executives got their starts as secretaries. Opportunity knocks most enthusiastically for the girl with secretarial know-how," crowed *Strictly for Secretaries* (1965). But few secretaries ascended to the heights of fame and fortune attained by Helen Gurley Brown, or even my Aunt Norma, in part because moving up the proverbial ladder wasn't easy.[3]

Here's how one "young dynamo," Genevieve Staley, a domestic trade commissioner for the Los Angeles Chamber of Commerce, described the process in 1940. "Work for just one man," Staley told readers of the *Los Angeles Times*,

> Then you have more opportunity to make yourself indispensable. Lift the dull routine from his shoulders so he will have freedom for valuable work.
> Then study your field. Take night school or correspondence courses in allied subjects. Then, take an active part in the professional organizations

of your field. Read the trade publications. Learn the possibilities. Challenge yourself to discover new ways of making yourself useful. Work your imagination.[4]

The latter may have been the most useful bit of advice the would-be ladder climber could get. For in many offices, a secretary's dream of advancement, even after all the hard work she expended both at and outside the job site, remained a fantasy as management thanked her for work well done, then looked toward her male coworkers when promotion time rolled around.

Stepping Stone—or Millstone?

For the most part, the guidebooks conveniently didn't mention what came to be called, in the 1980s, the glass ceiling. Instead, they cheerfully suggested that secretarial work could be used as a stepping stone . . . to something, though opinions varied as to what. Early in the twentieth century, Eleanor Gilbert imagined an egalitarian workplace where women rose through the ranks just like men: "To the woman with high ideals about her own ability," a middle-management position such as the head of the stenographic department was "simply a stepping-stone to bigger things, exactly as it would be to a man," she wrote in *The Ambitious Woman in Business* (1916). Despite Gilbert's enthusiasm, head of the steno pool was as high as all but the most enlightened businesses would allow a woman to rise, and then only for a privileged few. "The current notion that a secretaryship is woman's most convenient stepping stone into other higher business positions seems to be by no means the general rule in practice. Once a secretary always a secretary would seem nearer to majority experience," noted the *New York Times* in 1931.[5]

Many advice writers who followed in Gilbert's wake had personal knowledge of this—they were or had been secretaries themselves—and tempered readers' expectations accordingly. Secretarial work was "an almost unexcelled way of getting a foothold" in whatever "field of activity" a woman was interested was the hopeful yet vague advice presented by Louise Hollister Scott in *How to Be a Successful Secretary* (1937). Clare H. Jennings, the president of the National Secretaries Association, barely even bothered with the ruse of advancement in "Should Your Child Be a Secretary?" one of a series of career-based ads for New York Life Insurance that appeared in magazines like *Life* and *Time* in the late 1950s and early 1960s. After mentioning she knew of "several" secretaries who became "editors, account executives, heads of purchasing departments, branch managers, and the like," she noted that a "prime requisite for success" was "approaching secretaryship as a chosen career—not as a . . . stepping stone to other positions."[6]

It's a Man's World—Get Used to It

When the ad featuring Jennings appeared in 1958, the words "stepping stone" and "secretary" had appeared in proximity to one another so frequently and in such an array of materials as to impart an immediately understood "truth" about secretarial work. A careful reader might discern clues to the contrary, most often in references to the fact that it was "a man's world." "Don't be too irritated if more efforts are expended by an organization in building up the men in the office than the girls," wrote Gladys Torson in *The Art of Being a Successful Business Girl* (1943). Like other advice writers of her generation, Torson prevaricated when it came to gender discrimination: "I don't believe that offices should discriminate between the sexes to quite the extent that some of them do," she wrote, as if there was an acceptable level of unjust treatment. There was "little to do but be philosophical" when men were advanced over equally competent—if not more so—women. "Comes the feminist revolution and things may be different, but with the business world constituted as it is today, you will have to work on the theory that this is a man's world."[7]

It was still a man's world when on the cusp of the feminist revolution, Lucy Graves Mayo recommended that women interested in using their secretarial skills to get a foot in the door of their chosen profession before advancing to "more and more important levels" look for "a large company with a broad 'mind' about women in high places." Otherwise, an ambitious

secretary could run into a stone wall when she asked for more responsibilities and was turned down because the company "didn't believe women
should be part of management."[8]

A woman's too apparent ambition could cause problems when she tried
to get a job at a less broadminded firm. A proofreader and copyeditor who
moved from New York to the West Coast in the mid-1960s ran into trouble
when she interviewed at several employment agencies in her new home.
Employers in Los Angeles, it seemed, were "very suspicious of hiring somebody [female] who either shows they are bright and interested in executive-
type problems, or who wants a career rather than just a secretarial job."[9]

The sad reality was that most employers didn't want to promote their
secretaries into positions of power and responsibility. In an "informal study"
of Cleveland-area companies in 1925, a female sociologist found that women
had supplanted men in secretarial roles in all workplaces but the electric
company and railroads. (There, the male secretaries viewed their work as "a
stepping stone to better jobs.") But what really shocked the sociologist was
management's cavalier attitude toward promoting women.

> It seems that for men secretarial work is just a step in their progress to
> bigger positions; to most women it is the end of the road. It has been a
> little amazing to hear men say they hire women because . . . [women] will
> stay and they offer no promotion because women will stay without the
> possibility of promotion.[10]

Employers wanted what historian Sharon Hartman Strom called "temporarily permanent" employees. Women who worked five or ten years in an
office "satisfied managers and handsomely repaid their investment in job
training, suited some women for positions requiring more responsibility and
longevity, and at the same time did not obligate employers to promote or pay
women wages comparable to those of men."[11]

In other words, because the vast majority of women left work after marriage, either because it was "what everybody did" or because their office
required it, management was consistently able to hire a crop of new employ-

ees at a lower rate than the older workers. At the same time, they could deny promotions to women because everybody knew that women would leave the office once they got married. According to the final Report of the President's Commission on the Status of Women (also known as "The Peterson Report"), published in October 1963,

> Because many personnel officers believe that women are less likely than men to want to make a career in industry, equally well-prepared young women are passed over in favor of men for posts that lead into management training programs and subsequent exercise of major executive responsibility.[12]

"You are told at the beginning that it's a stepping stone to something else," noted a secretary in 1974, "but the young men are courted, everybody is eager to help them learn and they get the promotions." The secretary simply reached a plateau and stayed there.[13]

The word "plateau" never appeared in the guidebooks, of course. There, the ambitious secretary might be advised to find a talented young executive, and stick to him like glue. A disgruntled 1970s-era secretary quoted in the *New York Times* called this "the coattail theory of advancement": as her boss climbed the ladder, so too would his secretary advance. "You're told to find a bright young man and rise with him," she explained. "I'm 25 years older than those bright young men, and I don't want to take a chance for 10 years while they rise. When did I sign a marriage contract? Why is my career advancement tied to my boss's?"[14]

The Career Woman: Unfeminine Freak?

If by dint of hard work a secretary was able to surpass the roadblocks strewn in her path and move up the ladder, she became—in guidebook parlance—a career woman. Make no mistake: a career woman was not the same thing as a career girl. Career girls—at least as they were portrayed in the popular press—were bouncy, kicky young things who spent their lunch hours shopping for new clothes that would appeal to both boss and boyfriend. It was generally assumed that as far as the career girl was concerned, secretarial work was a pleasant and remunerative way to fill the interlude between high school or college and marriage—or, if she did work after her nuptials, until the birth of her first child. Rare among the secretarial ranks was the woman who dreamed of "stepping up briskly forty years hence, amid co-worker applause, to receive the coveted company service award from the chairman of the board." Working with an eye to a promotion and the ultimate goal of a corner office marked an individual as a career woman, especially if she remained single or childless while she pursued her ambitions. In the eye of pop psychologists and other cultural commentators, this made her, like the office wife, an abnormal female. But where the office wife wrongly substituted her boss for a husband, the career woman far more ominously coveted the boss's job for her own.[15]

Like "office wife," "career woman" was not a positive label. "Do not have as your ideal . . . the woman who is carving out a career, as they call it," New York's Cardinal Hayes told a gathering of young clubwomen in 1934. "You will find them defying the laws of both God and man." When in 1952 *Good Housekeeping* urged readers to consider learning a trade lest family economic crises or empty-nest syndrome render a housewife broke or obsolete, it emphasized that doing so didn't "necessarily mean she should become a Career Woman," capitalizing the term as if it represented some kind of communicable—and fatal—disease. Even in a rare instance when the career woman was singled out for praise, the positive words came with a caveat. Chester Burger, in *Survival in the Executive Jungle* (1964), defined the "career gal" as the "older secretary"—over thirty-four years old. Whether she was married or had "abandoned hope of reaching the altar," the career gal expected to "continue working indefinitely" and brought to her job "a seriousness of mind and professionalism of attitude." But along with a highly tuned work ethic, she also brought with her what a later generation would call baggage:

> Her job is more than a job. It is her raison d'etre, the center around which her life revolves. It is more than an opportunity to earn her daily bread,

for it provides an outlet for her drives, her dreams, her ambitions, her emotional needs. In the words of the women's magazines, she seeks fulfillment in her job for many of her emotional needs.[16]

The career gal, Burger concluded, was "a very special type" who required "equally special handling by her boss" lest her identification with her job morph into boss-challenging officiousness. Examples of this very special type sometimes could be found in secretarial manuals, where she was easily recognized by her mannish style of dress and her glasses. *The Mademoiselle Handbook* (1946) inveighed against the "squint-eyed rugged female in mantailored suits and angular eyeglasses. . . . Our bet is that the pretty girl, being bright enough to stay pretty, has lots more intelligence all around the block than Miss Mantailored Anachronism." Twenty years later, she made an appearance in *Strictly for Secretaries* as "Miss Bun-in-the-Back who strides around in oxfords and severely tailored dark suits."[17]

Hendrik de Leeuw, a travel writer who took a break from that genre to pen *Woman: The Dominant Sex, From Bloomers to Bikinis* (1957), "a disturbing, controversial and stimulating book that all women will *want* to read and all men will *have* to read" according to its preface, went a step further and anointed the career woman a "newer species of woman," one possessed of "firm step and bold eye, pleading smile and pretended helplessness." She could be picked out of a crowd by her heavy-rimmed spectacles and her "tendency to address one and all as 'Darling.'" Such tender endearments did not extend to the most intimate areas of her life apparently; de Leeuw believed that married career women made lousy lovers because they were "too busy, too sophisticated, too highstrung, [and] too frigid" to keep their husbands happy in the sack, at least "after the pre-marital business and honeymoon concupiscence" had "run their gamut." Unsound marriages, divorce, and juvenile delinquency were the result of such work-induced frigidity.[18]

De Leeuw was not alone in his assessment of the career woman's sex life. Arthur J. Mandy, M.D., was a psychiatrist and founder of the Obstetric and Gynecological Psychosomatic Clinic at Sinai Hospital in Baltimore (perhaps his patients only imagined they were pregnant). According to Mandy, "ambitious 'career women' who defeminize[d] themselves ruin[ed] marriages and lives—their own and their husbands." These were "bossy, competitive, 'masculine' females" who considered it "more important to scribble on a shorthand pad than to watch their own young children grow up!" When it came to marital relations, there was another "tragic result" when wives refused to be what Mandy considered "real homemakers":

> So-called freedom and frigidity often go hand in hand. In my practice of obstetrics, I almost always find that frigidity in women is of emotional rather than physical origin. The condition is evidence of a woman's rejection of her feminine role.[19]

Before you stay-at-home moms start counting your multiple orgasms in triumph, be assured that in Mandy's opinion there were also many "masculine" housewives who tried to "play golf like men, bowl like men and, yes, drink like men. They even try to dress like men in their male shirts, slacks, walking shorts and clipped haircuts."[20]

What's surprising, other than that Mandy apparently lived in the butchest suburb east of the Mississippi, was that so few mid-twentieth-century medical professionals suggested that twelve-hour days at the office might wreak havoc with a male executive's fragile libido. Nor did they consider that the combination of childcare, household chores, and a full day at the office might have led to, not frigidity, but sheer exhaustion on the part of a woman executive.

If anything, the male libido perked up in an effort to prove itself when threatened. "Career Women Blamed for Men's Moral Lapses" was an eye-catching headline in the *Los Angeles Times* in 1948. According to Dr. Henry C. Schumacher, a U.S. Public Health Service consultant, the "intrusion of women into nearly every field that was once considered purely a masculine endeavor" was "giving the human male an inferiority complex." Apparently, the thought of strong, dominant women ruling over them was giving men more than that: Schumacher believed they turned to promiscuity and the intriguingly termed "moral carelessness" to combat their low self-esteem. Alas, the article failed to explain just how the good doctor concluded that this was women's fault.[21]

The idea was that while the secretary brought her femininity into the workplace and attended to her boss with almost wife-like servitude and loyalty, the crafty career woman usurped man's rightful position in the corner office—and thus became masculine herself. If a woman had "a sufficient number of what we commonly conceive as masculine characteristics such as aggressiveness, dominance and extreme objectivity," she could "make the grade" as an executive. "Thank god, though, a majority of women do not possess these characteristics," opined Dr. Samuel N. Stevens in 1939. "You rarely find a 'feminine' woman in a position of executive responsibility." (He also argued that because working women were loathe to organize for equal pay and persisted in primarily looking to men for leadership, it remained unlikely that they could "organize a pressure group big enough to elect a woman as President." If a woman did make it to the White House, he reassured his interviewer that it would be "at such a remote time that none of us will have to worry about it.")[22]

Even Rosalind Russell, justly famous for her portraits of spunky working women in multiple films throughout *her* screen career (including an ace reporter in *His Gal Friday* (1940) and a college dean in *A Woman of Distinction* (1950)), unloosed a torrent of bile on career women in a *Los Angeles Times* Sunday magazine supplement published in 1957. Career women were confused, Russell suggested. *"Most of them are driving and driven women, lonely and vulnerable, leading dissatisfied and empty lives,"* she began, in italics. The problem was not that women worked (heck, she'd "been putting on greasepaint . . . for some 20 years" herself), rather that some women devalued domestic pursuits in their belief that "anyone could get married," but "it took a special flair to become, say, an interior decorator rather than a housewife." To compound their initial error, these women then went on to "put their careers above everything else—" that is, husband and children. "Girls" came to the "mistaken conviction" that work always trumped family in many ways:

. . . lack of popularity with boys during their awkward teens, an unsuccessful marriage or even a feeling that children will tie them down, that they can put off having a family if they have the prestige of a good job.

More than anything else, women long for love; a feeling of being wanted. Denied this, many try frantically to prove their desirability by identifying with success. [23]

Russell of course meant men's success at the office, not the "true" female success of marriage and motherhood. Indeed, her analysis touched on all the bogeymen of the feminine mystique: teenaged unpopularity that sidled into divorced, childless, unlovable adulthood. It practically went without saying that the women who eventually found their way into the executive suite were spinsters:

When a career woman reaches her late thirties, the trap starts to close. She begins to realize that her business life, no matter how successful, does not bring fulfillment. . . .

But the trouble is that, though still slim and carefully manicured, she is no longer womanly. She has hidden the qualities of softness, sympathy and compassion for so long that it is hard for men to believe that she could fit into that little cottage.

Even if she succeeded in becoming "tender and thoughtful," the men around her would consider it "just an act," so jaded were they by "the girl at the top." What finally happened to these successful-in-business, unsuccessful-in-love career women Russell didn't say outright, but she immediately went on to describe the only time she "played a working-girl role straight and honest," a portrayal in which an "old-maid schoolteacher" ended up on her knees "begging [a] man to marry her."[24]

How much Russell herself contributed to the article ("Why I'm Sorry for Career Women") that bore her byline "as told to" another author is unknown (when it appeared, she was busy on Broadway as the iconoclastic Auntie Mame), but the essay was a brisk about-face from her previous dealings with working women. She was frequently lauded by both local and national chapters of the National Federation of Business and Professional Women's Clubs (NFBPWC) for "her contribution towards a better understanding and interpretation of women in the business and professional world," to quote an award bestowed on her in 1950. Russell appeared to be equally enthusiastic about the organization's members. When a local chapter of the NFBPWC gave her a plaque commemorating her "outstanding helpfulness to women" in 1943, she expressed her respect and admiration for the achievements of businesswomen.[25]

One might expect a former-secretary-turned-guidebook-writer like Patricia Flynn to admire the female executive, both in her own right and for the chutzpah it took to make it to the top. But like Rosalind Russell, the author of *So You Want to Be an Executive Secretary* (1963) blasted the career woman's lack of femininity:

> I have seen a lot of girls on their way up to the top who seem to drop a little bit of the femininity on each step. When they reach the top, they no longer quite resemble women. They are described by those around them as "that awful female executive"—or even harsher terms. It's perfectly fine to think like a man, but it's disastrous to act like one.

Flynn concluded that there was "nothing quite so attractive as a truly feminine woman"—cold comfort to the secretary who understood that "masculine" traits such as competitiveness and ambition were exactly what she needed to get ahead in "a man's world."[26] It took Jean Vermes, who quoted both Helen Gurley Brown and Simone de Beauvoir in *The Secretary's Guide to Dealing with People* (1964), to finally, in the same book, call out the notion that working made women less feminine for the canard that it was:

> Studies show that a woman must limit her business career ambitions if she is to be considered feminine. Somehow, if she develops her brain to its capacity, people think that this makes her less womanly. . . . This is utter

nonsense, of course. There is no reason why her feminine roles of wife-
hood and motherhood should be an end in themselves, and prevent her
from having a business career as well. No man makes a career of father-
hood alone. He would laugh at the suggestion. So why should a woman
make a career of her biological functions?

Vermes was right on the money, but cultural fears about women in
power continued to be alleviated by slander about their femininity. An article about the women who entered the newly coeducational Harvard Business School in 1964 included a quote from a first-year student who said
she enrolled "with the hope of obtaining the same goals and rewards as
men." As if to balance such fire-breathing feminism, the paper immediately noted, "That doesn't mean the 22 women students aren't interested
in dates, marriages and children. They are, and they believe their studies
will be worthwhile no matter how their lives are spent." Translation: After
spending all that money on an M.B.A., they'll drop out of the workforce
after the wedding.[27]

Competition: A Menace to Marriage

When it came right down to it, however, the career woman's major fault
was competing with men—at home as well as at the office. Competitiveness was a "menace" to marriage; it was bad enough when the wife worked
"a job in the bargain basement" but infinitely worse when she worked in "a
plush-lined office on the sixty-fifth floor." Either way, she needed to carefully
check her killer instincts at the door when she returned to the "glow of the
living-room lamp" because "no man" could "be happy in competition with
his wife," wrote psychiatrist Olga Knopf in *Ladies' Home Journal*. Men, she
continued, were incapable of "adjust[ing] themselves" to a wife who lost "her
essential femininity" and became "aggressive and dominating in her relations
at home," much as the boss detested an officious secretary.[28]

In particular, the career woman had to worry if she brought home a paycheck higher than her spouse's. The guidebooks disagreed on the issue: was it better for two breadwinners to funnel their checks into a single account, or should the wife's earnings be kept separate? *Independent Woman* stood for the former proposition:

> Pool your joint incomes and budget them so there can be no feeling who bought what for the home (this is particularly important if you earn more than your husband). Encourage your husband to get into the work which would interest him most; adapt your needs to those of your family. Seek your husband's advice.[29]

Other advice writers suggested that at least part of the wife's salary be used to pay for domestic needs. "We see no reason why she should not contribute her full share . . . toward food expenditures and as much toward each of the other principal types of expenditure as seems fair," suggested a guide from the early 1940s on balancing the household budget. The cost of her replacement was expected to come directly out of her purse. "If it is necessary or desirable to employ a cook or part time housekeeper the pay for this help should come from the wife's earnings." She was allowed to keep the remainder of her income for clothing and "personal" items. In this way, both career woman and spouse could pretend that her income was little more than pin money.[30]

Jean Vermes devoted an entire section of *The Secretary's Guide to Dealing with People* to what to do "WHEN THE WIFE EARNS MORE." But the problem started before that:

> Your salary has been regularly increased . . . and now you earn as much as he does, although you haven't told him about your last raise. You are afraid it will hurt his ego to discover that he is not the major support of the family. Should you continue to keep your income a secret or confess?[31]

Vermes counseled against lying to one's husband, if for no other reason than he'd find out about her new, larger paycheck when the two of them went over their returns together at tax time. The working wife could, however, ameliorate the situation by putting aside every week the amount of her last raise "for some special purpose, like a fur coat or some new furniture. This way your husband will still be making the major contribution to the weekly support of the household."[32]

Perhaps the thought of the household chaos that might result from a wife's higher salary was more than Vermes could handle, for despite the section's title, she never did explain what to do if the wife earned MORE than her husband. The "grim fact" remained that "few marriages, indeed, have remained happy after the wife has gone up the ladder of income, leaving her husband on one of the lower rungs."[33]

"But Where Would I Be without You, Miss Jones?": Getting Stuck in the Steno Pool

Even if she worked in a company or industry with a liberal attitude toward female advancement, secretarial work was not in and of itself "an open sesame to other careers," as *The Mademoiselle Handbook* (1946) expressed it. In fact, the woman who wanted to move up from her secretarial position faced many roadblocks. There was, for example, the purely practical matter of how to stop people—herself as much as those who benefited most from her clerical labor—from seeing her as "just a secretary." If the ambitious secretary followed Genevieve Staley's advice to make herself an indispensable assistant, she might well find her path blocked by a boss who deemed her too valuable to lose ("whereas a young man in her place would normally graduate to a junior partnership and go on up from there," noted the *New York Times* in 1930). Unless he was "more unselfish than most bosses," an executive would likely want to keep a good secretary "right there at *his* side, making smooth *his* path," not helping her to move up the career ladder. This was such a common pitfall that in the early 1970s, the director of Vassar's Vocational Bureau went so far as to advise girls not to learn shorthand because the "bright girl" who took dictation was "such a treasure" she might find herself permanently ensconced by her boss's side, steno pad in hand.[34]

Another decided obstacle in her path to career advancement was the way the secretary was supposed to "hide her light." Just as she wasn't supposed to mind when her boss, having shown up an hour late for an appointment she'd reminded him of multiple times in the past several days, excused his tardiness by telling his fuming client that his secretary had forgotten to calendar their meeting, so too was she supposed to take it on the chin when he presented one of her suggestions as his own idea. "If you originate a good idea, you give the credit to your boss because you know when he advances you advance with him. You give credit to others when it is due . . . sometimes when it is not, just to keep them happy. You never 'steal the show' because you don't have to . . . without your shouting it, word gets around that you are GOOD." Or so said *How to Be a Super-Secretary* (1949), though who knows exactly how the word got out when both boss and secretary allegedly kept mum about the origin of "his" fabulous new idea.[35]

All bets were off, however, if somebody else in the office staked a claim to the secretary's idea. Stranger things had happened. *Secretaries on the Spot* (1967) used the example of a clerk who "pirated" the idea of a secretary who assisted him part-time. "When she made a suggestion, he would say it was of no value, but later would present it to his superior as his own. The boss often commended him for his alertness; frequently, the ideas were adopted." *Secretaries on the Spot* suggested that the next time the secretary had an idea, she write it up as a memo and present it directly to the boss. This plan of action was seconded by *The Secretary's Guide to Dealing with People*: "Any ideas you have should be relayed to your own executive. If he takes credit for them, at least he will show his appreciation to you, and the chances are he will give credit where credit is due," the last clause being a stunning example of cockeyed optimism if ever there was one.[36]

"Madame Boss": Understanding Older Sister or Ballbuster?

If she did finally climb out of the steno pool, through the secretarial ranks, and into the executive suite, the woman boss often found herself between a rock and a hard place. A frequently given explanation of why women didn't advance into executive ranks was that they were "too emotional," as if the hormones coursing through their bodies made them unstable. Should an emergency arise during a woman executive's menstrual period, she might collapse into a pool of her own tears rather than taking decisive, testosterone-fueled action. But if she acted like a leader, she was slapped with the charge of "unfeminine." The dean of the University College at Northwestern University was blunt: there was "no future for the average woman in business," he told the *Los Angeles Times* in 1939. "Even the brilliant career women who are exceptions prove this rule because in every such case there is some freak explanation." When pressed for an example of the latter, the dean "cited the woman head of a large company who got the job . . . because she was the secretary to the former owner who had no relatives and left her the business." Women simply didn't get ahead on their own merits, he believed, in part because—you guessed it—their "normal and healthy" desire for home and family meant they quit after marriage.[37]

A 1947 *Fortune* magazine biographical sketch of Olive Ann Beech (the secretary-treasurer of Beech Aircraft) not only pointed to innuendo that she got her job through connections, not merit, but also painted her as an unfeminine ball-buster who wore the pants in her marriage. Beech was "a self-possessed and coldly practical businesswoman. . . . Some say she is merely a shrewd gal who married her boss. . . . Others take the view that the peculiar talents of O.A. Beech are largely responsible for the present success and affluence of Walter Beech. The truth probably lies somewhere in between." She did not "call office workers by their first names. . . . No sentimentalist, she quick-freezes any idea of Walter's of retaining an incompetent worker for the sake of old times."[38]

"Cold," "self-possessed," "unsentimental"—the words used to describe Olive Ann Beech did not suggest she shared the feminine warmth with which the *Secrets of Charm* (1954) suggested "famous women executives" were imbued. These business professionals were the "most womanly and gracious persons" who were "never career-minded to the exclusion of femininity":

> They accomplish their ends in women's clothing—not men's. Their manner is never brusque, but couples charm with ability. While they scorn to play the coquette at the conference table, they would not dream of playing the heavy role. Their goals are won through the gentle arts of persuasion, reasoning and sensitivity to the feelings of others.[39]

The Mademoiselle Handbook portrayed her as a kindly mother figure in a business suit:

> She will treat you as a human being, not a machine. . . . She realizes that every girl has to go Christmas shopping, and that on occasion you need a long lunch hour to see the dentist or buy a new suit. . . . If she is a woman worth her salt, she senses when you're in difficulties—when someone is sick at home, or when some other problem is furrowing your brow—and she's willing to make allowances and to go easy on you for a spell.[40]

"Madame Boss" also rated high with "most girls" who worked for her "because she isn't a wolf!" In addition to a magic sixth sense that allowed her to unerringly read her secretary's emotional life (frequently referred to as "feminine intuition"), the woman boss possessed such sensitivity because it was generally assumed she had spent time in the secretarial trenches herself. Sounding much like *The Mademoiselle Handbook*, which predated it by two decades, *Charm: The Career Girl's Guide to Business and Personal Success* (1964) explained that the female executive had "probably worked her way up through the ranks":

As a result, she is likely to be more considerate in many ways than her male counterpart, who entered via the training squad. She remembers what it was like to be an underling—to discover at the end of a long report that the carbon was in backwards, to have the boss's cigar ashes scorch a long and perfectly typed rush letter. In all probability, she will be more understanding whenever the going gets rough.[41]

Yet when the *Chicago Tribune* asked some National Federation of Business and Professional Women's Club members their thoughts about working with female executives in 1962, they said sisterly perception between the woman boss and her same-sex secretary was as much a burden as a balm. "A woman intuitively understands another too well. I think that's the main trouble," said one.[42]

The woman executive was "too filled with tension and emotions another woman understands all too well" to be a good boss to female underlings. What were these vague tensions and emotions that all women intuitively understood about one another? "A woman is used to competition with another woman in the field of husband hunting, and she carries this competition into the business arena," opined yet another club member.[43]

Jean Vermes thought that the impression that women executives were hard to work with, though "not commonly true," had "some basis in fact." The problem was that even though educators and guidance counselors were "trying to imbue" young women with the realization that they could "take on practically any job or responsibility," most women had been brought up to think of themselves in a "secondary role" to men. Thus, when a woman did "find herself in an executive position, all her basic feelings of inferiority, built up over the years," had to be overcome:

> Dominated as she is by a male world, she tries to compete by either acting humble, or adopting a high and mighty attitude. She is apt to be fussy and over-precise. Her efforts to equal men in achievement produce tension. She is unable to lose herself in her work as a man can because she

The Business Dinner

(T) here came a time in every career woman's life when she found it expedient to conduct business with male associates over a meal at a restaurant. Doing so required finesse, or even subterfuge, on her part because, despite the guidebooks' insistence that office etiquette differed from that practiced socially, no businesswoman could risk embarrassing a male guest by paying for his dinner in public. A "modern woman" prepared to "meet the situation gracefully" by arranging beforehand with the restaurant manager to forward the bill to her office, explained *The Ambitious Woman in Business* (1916). Almost fifty years later, *The Secretary's Guide to Dealing with People* (1964) offered a new gloss on virtually the same advice. In a section called "Paying the Bill Discreetly," author Jean Vermes suggested the career woman acquire a restaurant credit card as "for some reason, a man who will blanch if his woman [lunch] partner brings out her purse to pay a bill with money, will be quite undisturbed if that same woman just takes a pencil and signs her name."*

* Eleanor Gilbert, *The Ambitious Woman in Business* (New York: Funk and Wagnalls, 1916), 146–47; Jean C. Vermes, *The Secretary's Guide to Dealing with People* (West Nyack, N.Y.: Parker Publishing, 1964 (fourth printing, 1969)), 97.

is always self-conscious. A woman executive often vacillates between too great or too little an air of authority. In order to overcome her natural attitude of feminine compliance, she may adopt a stern and arbitrary manner.[44]

It's also not as if a girl growing up prior to the 1980s or so had much in the way of role models when it came to the business world. "What do you know about earning a living?" asked the *Ladies' Home Journal* in 1950. The double-page spread, aimed at young readers recently graduated from high school or college, featured men on the left and women on the right. A photo panel labeled "How would you like to be boss?" pictured men such as "John H. Ballard . . . at 16, $4-a-week errand boy for Bulova Watch company . . . Rose to president of firm." The corresponding layout on the opposite page was titled "How would you like to marry the boss?" and included "Mrs. Gordon Gibbs . . . graduated Katharine Gibbs School, hired by head New York school. Married, now vice-president." Gibbs was an executive in her own right, but the *Journal* clearly chose to emphasize the jobsite as marriage market, rather than focus on Gibbs's business success.[45]

Learning How to Have a Secretary, Not Be One

Another problem faced by the secretary-turned-executive was that long after she had moved out from behind the typewriter, men in the office frequently expected her to do secretarial tasks. "Don't let them stick you with taking notes in meetings . . . ," counseled former secretary Helen Gurley Brown. "Otherwise you'll be transcribing notes far into the afternoon while the other people are getting on with what the meeting was called about."[46]

The secretarial profession had been identified for so long with women that, in the office, men were "inclined to see in every successful woman a kind of supersecretary," there to answer his phone and take dictation, even if she had risen to a rank equal to his. The executive's refusal to see his secretary as anything other than his office helpmeet is why, in a book titled *Success!* (1977), legendary publisher Michael Korda (among his other authors at Simon & Schuster was Jacqueline Susann) gave women "obliged to start" as secretaries some rules to use on their rise to the executive ranks. Korda's previous guide to office politics, *Power!* (1975), had been excoriated as "amoral" and "Machiavellian." Korda later swore it had been meant as satire, but when *Power!* shot up the *New York Times* bestseller lists, he followed up with what he claimed was a real guidebook: *Success!* A reviewer for the *New York Times* called it "inconsistent and sloppy"—he could not have read much prescriptive literature or he would have realized Korda's tone and pacing were par for the course—but also noted its "savvy" information for women trying to get ahead.

Korda picked up where Brown left off. Women who hoped to move up the ladder needed to replace "mothering and errand-running" with brisk efficiency "directed outward as much as possible." It was important to keep her own boss happy, of course, but what the ambitious woman needed to do was make sure the higher-ups noticed her as well. Mostly this meant investing in the visible trappings of power, such as dressing as if one was already an executive, or leaving a few minutes late—not because you were at your desk doing extra chores, but in order to time your departure to that of the big boys. Riding down in the elevator with the execs, with an industry journal or a bundle of letters tucked under her arm, made her look like a go-getter. No one would be the wiser that the letters were dummies, "properly addressed and stamped . . . kept in your desk drawer and used over every night, as long as you are always careful to never actually mail" them.[47]

Conversely, it was important that the woman on the rise never sew, knit, or crochet at her desk. Neither should she "write greeting cards or attempt to balance" her checkbook—that's what secretaries were for, after all. Activities such as these struck "the wrong note," as did photographs of pets or small children. On the other hand, a "neat wall chart of some kind, however meaningless," showed managerial initiative (she could get away with this subterfuge because nobody was "likely to inquire very closely" about what the chart represented). Executives on the way up needed to show the masculine qualities of toughness and loyalty to the workplace; even if it was a fake, the wall chart said, "I'm interested in the office," as loudly as pictures of kids said, "I'd rather be at home."[48]

Once she had been given a position of authority, however small, Korda counseled the newly minted female executive to remove all vestiges of her secretarial past from her behavior as well as her desktop. She was under no circumstances to answer the telephone herself even if that meant missing calls, or allow her male colleagues to use her as a convenient "go-fer" (by ordering food for a meeting they are attending, for example). She was to similarly get rid of all the office supplies on top of her desk, lest her coworkers make the mental connection between her and the menial secretarial tasks she used to perform.[49]

A male secretary ("just as efficient, careful and subservient as any woman" when it came to answering the phones and taking dictation) provided the pièce de résistance; located outside the female boss's office door, his presence was a preemptive strike at the power of visiting men:

> There are few things that strike more direct terror into the hearts of male executives than the sound of a masculine voice saying, "I'm sorry, but Mrs. Judson is on the other phone, may she call you back?" Each then sees himself in the subordinate role, as a kind of nightmare vision of the future, taking dictation instead of giving it.[50]

Presumably this left the visiting executive so shell-shocked that he immediately acquiesced to "Mrs. Judson's" every dictate before scuttling back to his office and hiring a new-fangled secretary boy of his own.

Korda's tongue was probably firmly planted in his cheek when he penned those words in the late 1970s, but the male secretary was in fact undergoing a renaissance of sorts, thanks to a secretary shortage caused when young women who otherwise might have become secretaries instead applied to law or other professional programs. There were, for example, eleven women among several hundred men in Harvard Business School's first coed class in 1964 (the "girls" were required to wear dresses, of course). Meanwhile, back at the office, female secretaries, inspired by the women's liberation movement, were demanding better pay, bigger opportunities, and—horror of horrors!—refusing to make and serve coffee to the boss and his guests.

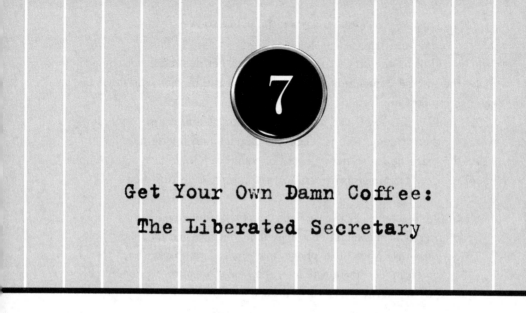

Get Your Own Damn Coffee:
The Liberated Secretary

What if an entire generation of women refused to learn how to type?

Gloria Steinem, Commencement Address,
Smith College, 1971

On September 7, 1968, visitors to Atlantic City's famous boardwalk were startled by the sight of over one hundred angry women protesting the Miss America pageant taking place inside Convention Hall. Picket signs denounced "the degrading mindless-boob-girlie symbol" and proclaimed, "I Am a Woman—Not a Toy, a Pet or Mascot!" Protestors shouted, "Liberation now!" and sang, "There She Is, Miss America" to a confused sheep (who at least one news report asserted was a ram). They also threw "assorted items of female oppression" into a "Freedom Trash Can," among them padded bras, girdles, false eyelashes, women's magazines, and two enduring symbols of the secretarial profession: steno pads and typing books. They might as well have hung Katharine Gibbs in effigy—she was certainly rolling over in her grave.[1]

In addition to giving rise to the persistent myth that the women's liberationists were bra burners (a plan to burn the contents of the trash can was
nixed by the city in advance), the Miss America protest was a first shot across
the bow in a skirmish between the women's movement and secretaries. On
one side were feminists—office workers among them—who deemed secretarial work "mind-rotting" and "spirit-breaking," as did the National Organization of Women's Image of Women Committee in 1972. On the other side
were traditional secretaries, represented by the National Secretaries Association (NSA), who, while admittedly "a little irked" (in the words of a *New
York Times* headline) by sexism in the office, prided themselves on their work
habits, didn't mind running an occasional errand for the boss—and were
offended by the new characterization of their jobs.[2]

Protesting the Perfect Secretary

To the women protesting on the boardwalk, steno books and typing manuals
represented the dashed hopes of all those aspiring young females who were
told women became medical or legal secretaries, not doctors or lawyers, or
who graduated with degrees in chemistry or engineering and discovered the
only jobs open to them were secretarial. An exasperated Vassar graduate
spoke for untold women in a letter she wrote to her English professor after
an unsuccessful job search in New York City: "Men don't have to type and
take dictation to earn a chance to begin learning!"[3] Given that many of the
early women's liberationists had a background in New Left campus politics,
the tossing of the typing manuals may also have been a comment on an
occurrence at Columbia University. There, on the eve of the student upris-
ing in April 1968, a male member of the Strike Coordinating Committee
marched into the midst of a group of women working to complete an analytical position statement on the action and demanded "a chick to do some
typing" for him.[4]

Despite the junking of steno pads in the Freedom Trash Can, the Miss
America protest was ultimately focused on the tyranny of beauty and its
rituals. Two years later, capping a day of demonstrations designated as the

Women's Strike for Equality, an action centered directly on secretarial work began when sixty women broke away from a huge march down Manhattan's Fifth Avenue celebrating the fiftieth anniversary of the American woman's right to vote. The women crammed themselves into the reception area at the Park Avenue campus of the Katharine Gibbs School and demanded to meet with its president, Alan L. Baker. The women told the obliging Baker that by training women for secretarial positions, Gibbs was "'fortifying' and 'exploiting' a system that kept women in subservient roles in business." In response, Baker promised to "take a good look" at the question.[5]

It's easy to make such a pledge when your office is occupied by a bunch of angry women. But two years later the Gibbs School announced a new evening class in management training for secretaries. "Management for Today's Woman" included instruction in "financial planning, business writing, personnel function and office systems." Of course, the school may have been prodded along by knowledge of Revised Order 4, which went into effect in 1971 and required companies working with the federal government to "initiate affirmative action programs" for the hiring and advancement of women, as part of Title VII's larger mandate to end employment discrimination. There was also the American Management Association's assessment that the general conception of the position of executive secretary as a "dead-end job" was an "important psychological factor" in deterring female employees who aspired upward. The class also made sense from a business standpoint: if there were going to be more management-level jobs for women, Gibbs could profit from their training. (Not that Gibbs had turned into a bastion of feminism by a long shot—in the mid-1970s, its curriculum was still based "on the needs of the men," in the words of the school's executive vice president.)[6]

The Olivetti Girl

At the same time the Gibbs School took a baby step toward a new, more professional image of the secretary, the Olivetti corporation was busy reinforcing the image of the secretarial sex bomb. Open up a glossy magazine— *Life* or *New York*, perhaps—from the spring of 1972, and you may see an

*The not-too-bright secretary who was more interested
in her manicure than her workload was one of the
stereotypes the women's movement worked to eradicate,
here in a 1970 ad from* BusinessWeek. *Just three weeks
later, an article titled "Women's Liberation Counts
a Victory" explained the Labor Department's new
antidiscrimination guidelines to readers of the same
magazine.*

ad featuring "The Olivetti Girl." The campaign, created by controversial ad
man George Lois, featured a new line of electric typewriters from the Italian
manufacturer—and a bevy of sexy girls to promote them. In one, a pretty
brunette is seated behind the typewriter. She smiles up at the camera while
a flock of business suit–clad executives lean close to her pretty face. "Why

be just an ordinary typist when you can be an Olivetti Girl?" asked the copy. An Olivetti Girl was "sharper, looser, never uptight," and "had more fun" than other secretaries (the phrase "or those killjoy feminists" was implied).[7]

Another ad was headlined "True Confessions of an Olivetti Girl (or, How a change in typewriters changed my life)" and showed a young blonde, with her hand over her mouth in the classic "oopsy!" position. "I was the jumpiest, touchiest, grouchiest secretary in the office. I used to dress sloppy, just like my typing. . . . But when I got an Olivetti Electric Typewriter—heaven! Don't laugh. It's got a brain inside. A brain that makes the four most common typing mistakes absolutely impossible. So I no longer go 'oooops.' . . . And now that I type sharper, I *look* sharper. People are starting to like me. In fact, there's not a man in the office who isn't crazy about me!"[8]

A television commercial from the same campaign featured another blonde Olivetti Girl, her hands flying over the keyboard, and the tagline, "The typewriter that's so smart she doesn't have to be."

Appalled by the "very unflattering manner" in which the Olivetti Girl campaign portrayed secretaries as dumb-bunny sex bombs, not to mention its infantilizing use of the word "girl," members of the New York chapter of the National Organization for Women picketed the Park Avenue offices of advertising agency Lois Holland Callaway on March 15, 1972. Among them was model Shere Hite, who would go on to a celebrated career as a sex researcher. She was the "Olivetti Girl" in the TV ad—and was so disgusted when she heard the voice-over on the final product that she joined the protest. "The offensive ads, N.O.W. said, show all secretaries as 'dizzy-headed sexpots.' And who'd hire one of them?" snarked a *New York Times* reporter who deigned to mention the protest on the paper's business page.[9]

George Lois was out of the country when the activists showed up at his office, but he responded in the form of yet another television ad for Olivetti. In this one, a sexy female boss pulls a sheet of typing paper out of her male secretary's typewriter. "I'm very pleased with your work, Joseph," she says. "By the way, what are you doing for dinner tonight?" The secretary—played by football star and sex symbol Joe Namath—turns toward the camera and grins lustily. When a delegation of feminists, invited to preview the new ad, walked out of a screening, Lois allegedly called after them, "What's the problem? The boss *always* tries to make the secretary."[10]

A *Little* Irked?

Given its mission to uphold the image of the professional secretary, the NSA could not have been happy about the Olivetti Girl campaign. Yet it and the other secretarial trade organizations were less than supportive of the efforts the women's liberation movement made on behalf of secretaries. When asked by a journalist whether the National Federation of Business and Professional Women's Clubs would be participating in the Women's Strike for Equality, its female director responded with more than a little antipathy toward the liberationists: "We're going to be dignified and ladylike. . . . We're not exhibitionists and we don't carry signs."[11]

"We just do not appreciate it," the president of the NSA, Mrs. Margaret Dillon, told the *New York Times* a few months after sign-carrying NOW members picketed George Lois's office. "We just do not feel we're subservient or put down. . . . And we're perfectly capable of being our own spokesmen since we know firsthand what secretaries think are their problems, and their ambitions. The truth is, we're not unhappy," she concluded, presumably speaking for herself and members of the NSA (who in 1972 numbered close to 30,000 out of the nine million women working as secretaries). Dillon dismissed the allegation that secretarial work led nowhere: "Even an executive's job can be a dead end, if you wanted to call things that."[12]

Dillon spoke to the press to publicize the release of a survey of 206 secretaries commissioned by the NSA in response to feminist critiques of secretarial work. But the sample was stacked with 125 members of the NSA, who, given their devotion to the tradition-minded organization, might not have been the most reliable sources regarding what the nonmember secretaries thought. As paraphrased by the *New York Times*, the survey found that the "average secretary" preferred "Mrs. to Ms.," respected her boss, and believed she could "advance into management." But cracks in the facade were beginning to show: Dillon had to admit that some women didn't like to "be called a secretary." Nor, according to the survey, did they like to be called "girls."[13]

In fact, Dillon and the NSA missed the boat. It was true that many older secretaries looked askance at the women's movement. According to the pro-liberation female head of the American Association of University Women, the older woman who had "been in shackles all her life" was threatened by liberation because it was "a rejection of everything she stands for" and because she had "been conditioned" to accept her role. But many secretaries—old and young both—hated the subservient aspects of the job and the infantilizing aspects of being called a girl. These women may not have identified as feminists, but they were ready to challenge their bosses as well as cultural assumptions about secretaries. The women's liberation movement gave them a blueprint for action even as it first missed the mark with its leaders' tin-eared declarations about secretarial work.[14]

By using the secretary as a symbol of the underemployed woman, the feminists helped to force open the professions to female workers—and that was a very good thing indeed. But when Gloria Steinem wondered what would happen if an entire generation of women didn't take typing, she neglected to mention—as did most of the women's movement in the early 1970s—that not everyone aspired to be an executive or other professional. ("They wanted everyone to be a brain surgeon," recalled a veteran secretary in the early 1980s.) For many women, even those with a college education, typing was a satisfactory way to support themselves and their families—or mostly satisfactory, anyway. The pay was low, after all, and a woman who complained about the office fanny-patter was likely to lose her job. But what really got a secretary's goat, now that the feminists brought up the subject of unfairness, was being treated like a waitress. In fact, what the Miss America protestors should have thrown into the Freedom Trash Can was a coffee pot, because when it came to gender politics in the office, the battle was fought over coffee—and who should make it.[15]

Grounds for Protest

Making coffee was a simple task infused with domestic mythology. A wife's inability to make a good pot of coffee was the punch line of many an ancient joke. At least apocryphally, good coffee equaled happy marriage. "Learn to make good coffee" was one of the suggestions on "How to Stay Married" a woman celebrating her thirtieth anniversary sent to the editor of the *New York Times* in 1935. "Poor coffee has caused many divorces," she concluded. Indeed, you don't have to dig too deeply in newspaper files to find headlines like "Charges Bad Coffee to Wife" (in 1900, an Oklahoma man filed for divorce after five years of marriage because his wife's coffee-making skill hadn't improved and he couldn't "stand it any longer"). Married or not, women were the designated coffee makers: it was revealed in 1927 that one Isidor Garfunkel left his daughter only $50 of his $10,000 estate because she "once refused to make coffee for him." Not surprisingly, when feminists in Miami rallied in support of the Women's Strike for Equality, they staged a "mock coffee-cup-breaking garden party."[16]

The secretary manuals were largely silent on the subject of coffee making—perhaps because it already fell into the much-discussed categories of errand running (in the days before in-office coffee service) and housekeeping (in the percolator era), or perhaps because there was no way to sugarcoat the fact that it turned the professional secretary into little more than a gofer or kitchen maid. What was the new secretary's "first assignment the day she reports for work, clad in her most becoming yet businesslike outfit?" asked a bemused *Los Angeles Times* columnist in 1956. "Why, to make the coffee, of course!"[17]

Though I certainly hope a few brave souls questioned long before the mid-1970s the assumption that making and serving coffee was part of the secretary's job description, that was when regular reports from the front lines of the coffee wars began to show up from across the country. A Los Angeles–based secretary, Leonor Pendleton, was fired in 1973 for "incompetence, insubordination, and failure to comply with job instructions," according to her employer's attorney, or "because she refused to follow a sexist practice

Pants in the Office

Prior to the early 1970s, women wore skirts or dresses to the office—period. Pants were purely for casual wear, rarely appropriate outside the house, and never worn on city streets. Couturier Andrés Courrèges offered pantsuits "for town" (as the *New York Times* quaintly described it) in the early 1960s, but only the bravest fashionistas wore them on the street—and definitely not to work. Television producer William S. Todman spoke for many executives when he explained why he would object to his secretaries wearing pants: "I find the looks of a neatly crossed leg in stockings more attractive."*

Two things helped make pants acceptable office wear: emphasis by the women's liberation movement on individuality and choice, and a near-universal loathing of the mid-calf-length, or midi, skirt that hit stores in 1969. Tired of being manipulated by the fashion industry ("One week we're going to the moon, then they try to lower our skirts. It doesn't jibe," a mini-skirted housewife told the *Times*), many women turned to pants. They were comfortable and, when worn at the office, practical. No longer did a secretary have to think twice before she stooped to pick up a dropped pencil or climbed a ladder to reach a file stored on a high shelf.†

Not all employers shared its workers' enthusiasm for the new style. When a memo appeared on a CBS news department bulletin board in January 1970 advising that it was not "Company Policy . . . for female employees to wear slacks during the course of their normal working hours," secretaries responded with a hastily organized "pants-in." "Girls Fight for Your Rights, Wear Pants Tomorrow," read a flyer. (The male personnel director said he would let the protest "go by" without consequence to those who participated.) Much to the chagrin of Revlon's female employees, the cosmetics giant instituted a written dress code in

---

* Angela Taylor, "Pants Suits for the City Stir Debate," *New York Times*, August 20, 1964, 32.
† Marilyn Bender, "Lower the Hem? Never Say the Girls," *New York Times*, August 8, 1969, 41.

1971—deemed "awful" and "archaic" by women workers—that barred both pantsuits and the ultra-short shorts known as hot pants from its corporate headquarters in Manhattan. Secretaries in the White House press office were banned from wearing pantsuits until 1973, when the energy crisis led to lowered thermostats and chillier working conditions.‡

Today, pants are an accepted workday fashion choice—except when a woman is going to a job interview, of course.

‡ Marilyn Bender, "Pants-Ban Tempest at C.B.S.," *New York Times*, January 21, 1970, 42; Nadine Brozan, "At Revlon, a Controversy over Who Wears the Pants," *New York Times*, June 7, 1972, 56; "White House Lifts Ban on Women in Pants," *New York Times*, November 26, 1973, 36.

based on the erroneous stereotype that only females, even in their employment situation, should perform household chores," in her counsel's words. Pendleton had refused to make coffee and wash the cups, a task performed by all the secretaries in her office, all of whom were female. Also that year, Alice H. Johnson, a civilian secretary working at the Brunswick (Maine) Naval Air Station, filed suit when she was fired for "her refusal to make coffee for the guys"; the Navy claimed she was let go for economic reasons, then hired a successor before "her chair had hardly a chance to cool," in the words of the Civil Service Commission examiner assigned to her case. She was later reinstated. In Manhattan, a secretary (who asked to remain nameless when she told her story to a meeting of Women Office Workers in 1975) was fired twenty minutes after she refused to get "four regulars" from a nearby coffee-shop for a man who stopped her in the hallway—he turned out to be a vice president of the company.[18]

A couple of weeks after Iris Rivera, a non-coffee drinker who worked for the state public defender's office in Chicago, was given a two-week termination notice in 1977 for refusing to comply with an office directive that secretaries (all female) make coffee for the attorneys (all male), forty women showed up at her workplace during the noon hour. Organized by advocacy

Miss, Mrs., ... Ms.?

Ⓣ he majority of the secretaries who responded to the National Secretaries Association survey in 1972 said they preferred "Mrs." to
"Ms." By that time, "Ms." had become a grammatical hot potato that
marked a woman with feminist leanings, who used the title because she
believed her marital status was nobody's business but her own.[*]

This wasn't always the case. Editor and columnist Ben Zimmer has
traced the use of "Ms." back to 1901, when an unnamed writer in the
pages of a local Springfield, Massachusetts, newspaper suggested that
the "embarrassing position" of calling "a maiden Mrs." or "insult[ing] a
matron with the inferior title Miss" could be avoided by using a new
term: Ms., to be pronounced "Mizz." According to Zimmer, the article
made "a minor splash," and was reprinted over the next few weeks in
newspapers "from Iowa to Minnesota to Utah."[†]

While feminists have been linked with the word as far back as 1949
(philologist Mario Pei made the connection that year in his book *The
Story of Language*), "some guides to business correspondence" from the
mid-twentieth century suggested Ms. be used in much the same way the
newspaper writer suggested in 1901: in Zimmer's words, as a matter of
"simple etiquette and expediency."[‡]

Most secretarial guidebooks, however, suggested the word "Miss"
be used if a woman's marital status was unknown. An exception was
the *Complete Secretary's Handbook* (1960), though the advice it offered
was tentative at best. "For some time," noted authors Lillian Doris and
Besse May Miller, "there has been a movement to popularize the use
of *Ms.* when a woman's marital status is not known, but the practice

---

[*] Judy Klemesrud, "In Defense of the Secretary: 'Truth Is We're Not Unhappy,'" *New York Times*, December 13, 1972, 43.
[†] Ben Zimmer, "Ms. The Origin of the Title Explained," *New York Times Magazine*, October 25, 2009, 16.
[‡] Ibid.

has not been widely accepted. We do not recommend this usage to secretaries."§

§ Lillian Doris and Besse May Miller, *Complete Secretary's Handbook*, rev. ed. (Englewood Cliffs, N.J.: Prentice Hall, 1960), 143.

group Women Employed and armed with a coffee pot—plus a bag of soggy grounds for Rivera's boss—they proposed to teach the attorneys how to make coffee. The tongue-in-cheek lesson ended with step 5: "Turn switch to on. This is the most difficult step but even an attorney can master it." Rivera, who filed a sex discrimination suit, was rehired a few weeks later—her boss left the office—and the rule was revised so that only those who drank coffee took turns making it.[19]

Women Employed had also been involved in a protest outside Litton Industries, after it discovered the company had sent its secretarial trainees to a special program to learn the finer points of coffee service. "A secretary learns to vary the strength of the coffee according to her boss' mood," recommended the chef who conducted the seminar. "At breakfast, she can give him toast and jam or sweet rolls or french bread but later in the day, there isn't much she can do to glorify coffee breaks." Members of the Secretaries Committee, a subsidiary of Women Employed dedicated to office work, confronted executives at the company's headquarters—and as a result, the coffee-making program was killed. "We've had a few out-and-out, bread-and-butter wins that have encouraged us to stop feeling like second-class citizens," said one of the protestors. "My entire self-image has changed."[20]

Coffee making had become a flashpoint, perhaps because brewing java for the men in the office was so clearly a servile and domestic act that had nothing to do with the secretary's actual job description. Women who never gave a second thought to gofering, or who previously merely grumbled under their breath in protest, had their feminist consciousness raised over the break-room coffee pot, and all the other "girls"-only office housekeeping tasks it symbolized. In offices across the nation, the question that divided the young and radicalized from the not-so-young and reactionary quickly became not "Whose side are you on?" but "Would you make and serve coffee to your boss?" Asked in 1974 whether secretarial work was "women's work," the public relations director of the Los Angeles chapter of Executives' Secretaries, Inc. (an invitation-only organization whose representatives worked together "to further the interests of their member firms") responded affirmatively and pointed to coffee making to support her reply. "Do you think a man would do that? He might find it demeaning." A woman wouldn't find it so, she went on, because it was her job at home. "If a man's married, maybe he has a wife to do it. He might not know how," hence his secretary better do it for him at the office.[21]

The coffee issue was pegged as "trivial" by antifeminists. A "suburban housewife" weighed in on "the ongoing tempest over the coffeepot" in a 1977 *Chicago Tribune* op-ed. Among her duties at her "first paying job" in a newspaper's editorial office the summer she turned eighteen was filling the male publisher's water carafe when he was in town, and purchasing milk for the "very much pregnant" society editor. "My womanhood wasn't compromised by these allegedly menial chores. I didn't find them degrading, . . . as the current crop of militant feminists charge. These gals are creating havoc over trivia," she concluded. Making coffee for the boss wouldn't subtract from her self-worth because she had "always been comfortable and secure" with her "role as a woman."[22]

"I recently hired a male secretary because a string of 'liberated young women' drove me up the wall 'asserting their rights,' [and] magnifying trivia," read a letter to the editor of the *New York Times Magazine* in response to a 1981 article about male secretaries. The writer, a woman, believed that getting the coffee was "not a feminist issue, but one of equitable division of labor," which the existence of male secretaries "put into proper perspective." Simply put, the office was "not a democracy!"[23] *Somebody* (male or female) needed to get the coffee—and that somebody was not the boss (male or female). Of course some might say that if the "equitable division of labor" wasn't a feminist issue then nothing was—and when it came right down to it, what was keeping the boss from getting his or her own coffee? She or he couldn't be THAT busy all the time.

Today, at least in the offices I've worked, coffee making is a more egalitarian chore, done by the person who gets to the office first, or whoever takes the last cup. But the hypothetical question of whether you would or wouldn't make, serve, or fetch coffee for your boss still invokes a spirited discussion—even at my current office, which doesn't have a coffee service. Just about everybody agrees that "it depends on the situation." If asking you to run out and get a cup is a display of his or her power, then no way. But if your boss returns the favor, then yes, no problem.

The Return of the Male Secretary

It was readily apparent by the mid to late 1970s that women were leaving the secretarial ranks in droves. "Why stay on secretarial work and make $10,000 a year when an unskilled laborer is making $16,000 a year?" asked a former legal secretary looking for a blue-collar job in 1977. There were new professional opportunities for women as well. "Many women who would have gone to Gibbs after college now go to law school," admitted a marketing executive for the secretarial school two years later. By then, the word "secretary" had acquired what an employment officer for Pacific Telephone called "a bad connotation." At least it did among women—but, in a demographic blip that led to reams of newsprint describing the phenomenon, some of the people who stepped in to fill the newly available jobs were men.[24]

"Thousands of men are entering the world of office work, a field vacated by many followers of the women's rights movement," reported the *New York Times* in 1975. These men took office jobs in hopes that "the secretarial route" might "be the surest step up the corporate ladder" in what was by all accounts a depressed economy. A man who could type wouldn't "need a secretary assigned to him at the beginning of his career," thus saving a company money, a Gibbs School vice president told the *Times*. Secretarial positions were also attractive to men because, by virtue of their gender alone, they were paid better than women secretaries. They could also expect to advance from the position. Men interviewed for these articles made clear they were planning on doing "something larger" with their lives. "When they advertise for a male secretary, it's usually not the run-of-the-mill job," said a man who worked as an executive secretary to the president and chairman of the board of a local newspaper (like my Aunt Norma, he was also the secretary of the corporation).[25]

Despite all the media coverage, however, men still made up a tiny portion of all secretaries. In 1972, for example, just 12 of the NSA's 28,000 members were men. In 1980, only one man attended the National Secretaries' Convention—and he felt compelled to remind a reporter for the *Times* that men had been secretaries for "at least 2,400 years," and named as examples Meriwether Lewis (personal secretary to Thomas Jefferson before he went exploring with Clark) and the unnamed male secretary who brought Mark Antony to Cleopatra "so they could die together." The male secretary was a "rare bird," according to a 1984 article in the *Los Angeles Times*, who made up a mere 1 percent of the secretarial workforce, "too few to represent a trend."[26]

The new crop of male secretaries faced the same suspicions about their sexuality as did their forebears: they were often viewed by both male and female coworkers as what the *New York Times* in 1986 termed "vocational eccentrics who cannot make it in a 'real man's' job." Real men were in management; only women, and less-than-real men, were secretaries. Men were still supposed to be barking orders, not following them like all those submissively ideal female secretaries. As the female president of the National Association of Temporary Services (NASD) explained to the *New York Times*, "Male executives have always perceived men who are secretaries as less than macho and somewhat quirky."[27]

In a macho world, a man didn't ask another man to do womanly stuff. "You're a man and you're working for a man and you're talking man to man. . . . A woman gets loaded up with shopping and stuff. My boss wouldn't dare do that to me," said a male secretary in 1972. "They're not treated the same," explained the NASD president in 1983. "A man will not ask a male secretary to get coffee. I've seen a guy go and get it himself rather than ask." On the other hand, some male secretaries complained that they were frequently asked to do heavy lifting and furniture moving, tasks that would rarely, if ever, be asked of women. A male legal secretary, who had been the only man in his class at Katharine Gibbs and was currently the only full-time male secretary at his firm, confessed to the *New York Times* in 1986 that "when people ask what I do I hedge; I tend to say I'm a legal assistant. I just don't want to expose myself to all the stereotypes."[28]

There was plenty of stereotyping to go around. The manager of Kelly Services (a temporary staffing agency forced to change its name from "Kelly Girls" in the early 1970s) told the *New York Times* that "all kinds of companies" wanted to hire male secretaries because they were "such diligent workers." A college sophomore who worked as a temp secretary opined that employers liked male secretaries because men were "used to getting the job done. . . . The women spent 20 minutes on coffee breaks chatting with their friends while we did the typing." Another male secretary said that executives gave men in his position "more responsibility" because, among other things, they knew that "a man is usually the breadwinner for his family and anxious to get promoted so they notice him more and take a greater interest in his career." The belief that a man was the head of a household is probably why, in 1972, a male secretary earned on average $34 a week more than a female in the position (the *Times* noted that the salary gap was closing due to equal-rights legislation).[29]

In 1982, Ellsworth Filhe Jr., "a 48-year-old bachelor" who worked for five woman bosses at Legal Assistance Foundation, was named Chicago's first male secretary of the year. He told the *Los Angeles Times* that he didn't mind making coffee, but was "spared the chore" at his present job because they had a coffee machine.[30]

B Y THE EARLY 1980s, the big secretarial organizations had adopted at least some of the rhetoric of the women's movement, as had the culture at large. A seminar on "How to Be Assertive without Being Aggressive" at the 1980 NSA convention was filled to capacity. After an exercise in which audience members orally completed the sentence "I have a perfect right to . . ." ("be adequately compensated" and "receive more compensation" were two popular replies), the therapist-researcher-career counselor who led the session concluded,

> Our biggest problem is to show them [bosses and coworkers who "might not like it when you become assertive"] we are not the traditional woman. She never rocks the boat, believes if you can't say something nice you shouldn't say anything, she serves, she meets the needs of everyone, she is cheerful. Don't beat them at tennis, don't let them see you are too smart, if something's wrong it's your fault.[31]

Of course it was a big problem! If secretaries were "stuck with this traditional role," as the speaker said, it was in large part because the experts—the NSA among them—had for the past eighty-some years been pushing exactly this model of womanhood as the secretarial ideal. A good secretary never rocked the boat, only said nice things, was cheerful, met her boss's needs, didn't let him see she was too smart, and took the blame if he did something wrong. In the unlikely event she found herself on a tennis court with him, without doubt the guidebooks would have counseled that she let him win. Now it was *her* job to fight the stereotype by becoming assertive ("without being aggressive," certainly an exercise in mixed messaging if ever there was one). No wonder some of the older secretaries had trouble switching gears. But the women's movement was only one of the forces in the 1970s and '80s that combined to kill dead the traditional office wife, not to mention the advice books that guided her. The other was technology—in the guise of the desktop computer and word-processing programs.

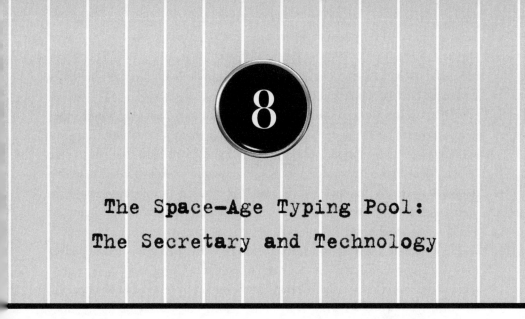

The Space-Age Typing Pool: The Secretary and Technology

Could be this conquest of space and time is prophetic with the abolishment of all human frailties and we arrive at a point when the "Ideal Secretary of 2000" actually turns out to be a robot. But I have yet to see a robot who looked good in a sweater and a skirt.

Anson Campbell, *Kitty Unfoiled* (1952)

From time immemorial (or at least since the Remington No. 1 typewriter went on the market in 1874), office procedure went like this: the boss dictated, his secretary took it down and then translated the squiggles into type. In 1913, Mr. John B. Flowers, "a young electrical engineer of Brooklyn," did his best to eliminate the middleman (or, most likely, middlewoman) with an early example of voice-activated technology. Flowers's device tried to re-create the human ear and hand. As explained by *Scientific American*, "In his apparatus a telephone diaphragm takes the place of the human ear drum; instead of the fibers, he employs a set of steel reeds, respectively tuned to the different overtone frequencies of the alphabet; for nerves he uses electric currents, and for the human hand [on the typewriter keyboard] a bank of solenoids."[1]

There were "serious limitations" with Flowers's voice-operated typewriter, *Scientific American* noted, chief among them its inability to distinguish between homophones like "to," "too," and "two," and that words like "laugh" would have to be pronounced phonetically in order for the machine to spell it correctly. Luckily, Flowers did "not present his invention as a complete solution of the problem of the voice-operated typewriter, but merely as a step toward that end."[2]

Almost half a century later, in the fall of 1961, just a few months after President John F. Kennedy announced his support for the *Apollo* space program and commitment to land a man on the moon by the end of the decade, an "I.B.M. man" tossed cold water on at least one aspect of the technologically assisted future. "There's a lot of talk about voice-activated typewriters," he told the *New York Times*. "They sound great, but they won't work. How will they ever distinguish between 'ate' and 'eight,' or pretty up the boss' English?"

Flash forward to today. While the copy churned out by voice-activated technology still requires a careful proofreader, it is much more accurate now than even fifteen years ago, when a go-getter associate attorney at the law firm I worked at suggested that management buy the software and replace all of us inefficient humans in the word-processing department. That never came to pass, thank goodness, but voice-activated technology perfectly illustrates the point where technology stops being a help to the secretary and instead becomes a menace to her job, something an astute observer recognized back in 1955. "The scientists say 'we could make a machine that would type when we talked into it,'" wrote syndicated financial columnist Sam Dawson. "This idea might please neither the stenographer nor the makers of dictating machines."[3]

Office Technology—Helpful
or Hurtful?

Like most complicated relationships, the one between the secretary and technology started out strong. The invention of the typewriter got the secretary her job in the first place, and it's still the piece of office machinery with which she's most associated, even if the bulk of her daily work is now done on a computer keyboard. As the twentieth century progressed, however, things got rocky. Sometimes automation made the secretary's job easier for her—with no strings attached. Before the introduction of the first plain-paper copier in 1959 (the Xerox model 914), secretaries made duplicates or triplicates of correspondence, memos, and other documents with carbon paper. This was a laborious process that involved proper alignment of stationery and carbon sheets—and woe to the secretary who made a typo. Prior to the advent of correction fluid or tape, making an invisible correction of even a single botched character was tricky, to say the least.

Gladys Torson explained how to correct a minor mistake armed only with a typewriter eraser and manual typewriter in *The Art of Being a Successful Business Girl* (1943). "No, you don't strike over the wrong letter," she reminded readers who no doubt ached to do just that.

> You start with the bottom carbon and erase carefully; then you insert a small piece of paper to prevent smudging (wide enough so it juts out beyond the margin on the side closest to the error and can be easily removed) and go on to the next carbon, inserting another piece of paper, and so on to the original, which you erase with particular care. . . . Remove the blank papers that you had inserted and type over the erasure. If your machine is in good order, you should have no trouble in making the correction so that the letters are in proper alignment.[4]

It was even harder to get the letters aligned if you didn't notice your mistake until you removed the stack of paper and carbons from the typewriter.

Technology—here in the form of her faithful friend
and working partner, the typewriter—made sure the
secretary had a life outside the office, 1957.

No wonder *How to Be a Good Secretary* (1969) declared, "The most popular office machine today is the copying machine." (Originals still had to be perfect, of course—it wasn't until the advent of word processing in the 1980s that correcting errors really became a breeze.)[5]

Other types of automation had less benefit for the secretary, and more for management. In the early 1950s, a dictating telephone solved what an ad called the "secretary shortage" by allowing one woman to do the work of "three, six, even twenty people, if you like." Even before the age of voice-activated technology, some machines promised to replace the secretary

Office technology as a threat to the secretary. Here, an ad for a telephone answering machine plays with the cliché of office romance to suggest that technology was superior to the ultimately expendable human being, 1962.

altogether. An ad from the early 1960s showed the boss hugging his new automated phone answering machine while a secretary looked on, perplexed, from the other room. After all, why bother with a wage-earning, vacation-taking, lunch-going human female when a machine could do her job without asking for a single benefit or sick day? "Our optical reader can do anything your keypunch operators do" was the tagline of a 1966 ad for the "Electronic Retina Computing Reader." Instead of a picture of the machine it was selling,

Bette C. Graham: The Mother of Liquid Paper

Ⓦ hen a 1946 divorce from her high school sweetheart left twenty-two-year-old Bette Graham a single mom with a young son to raise (Michael Nesmith, later world famous as a member of the 1960s "prefab four" pop group The Monkees), she turned to her secretarial skills for support. By 1951, she had risen to the level of executive secretary at the Texas Bank & Trust in Dallas, while still finding time on the side to do the freelance art projects she loved. Fed up with the mess left behind when she tried to make corrections on documents typed with her new IBM electric typewriter, she brought a bottle of white tempera paint to the office along with one of her watercolor brushes. Then she simply painted over the botched typed character, waited for it to dry, and typed in the correct one. While at least one of her bosses requested that Graham not use "any of that white stuff on my letters," the girls in the typing pool clamored for their own bottles of what Graham was soon hand-labeling "Mistake Out."[*] Encouraged by a local office-supply dealer, she came up with the formula for what she eventually trademarked as "Liquid Paper."

For secretaries and typists working on manual and electric typewriters, Liquid Paper was—and remains!—a godsend, allowing quick and easy corrections on both originals and carbon copies. Sales were brisk, especially after Bette went on a marketing trip around the Southwest in the early 1960s.[†] Near the end of the decade, the bottling plant moved out of her backyard and into an 11,000-square-foot factory, where over 10,000 bottles of Liquid Paper were produced every day.

Bette Graham sold the Liquid Paper Company to Gillette in 1979

[*] Edith Ann Vare and Greg Ptacek, *Mothers of Invention* (New York: William Morrow, 1988), 40, 41.
[†] "Betty C. Graham," at http://www.gihon.com/ (accessed April 4, 2008).

for $47.5 million and a royalty on every bottle sold through the year 2000. After her unexpected death the following year, half of her fortune went to her son (who filled thousands of bottles of Mistake Out when the operation was still headquartered at the house) and the other half to her philanthropic arts organization, the Gihon Foundation.

the ad featured a cute, young blonde wearing shorts and seated on the back of a motor scooter who teasingly tipped her hat at the reader. "Well, almost," continued the text. "It can't come back from a two-week vacation with a third degree sunburn. Or get sick. Or go to the little girls' room. But it *can* read." If the implication that keypunch operators were illiterate wasn't insulting enough, the ad came right out and suggested that one scanner "could replace your entire keypunch department, which costs your company about $8,000 per keypunch operator per year. Count your keypunch operators and ask your Financial VP what this would save your company. Then drop us a line." That was the problem with human beings: they needed bathroom breaks and demanded salaries. Machines were cheaper and more efficient.

Another ad that appeared in the very same issue of *Fortune* as the one advocating the firing of the keypunch department reminded executives of a reason why they might not want to pink slip all the humans just yet—at least not the female ones. "This one handles paper, and is fun to watch, talk to, kid with and tease" was the text beneath a series of photos of a mod, young secretary with file in hand. Beneath that was a photo of a rotary filing system with the caption "This one just handles paper." The filing system wasn't "exactly a fun thing," the copy continued, but it sped order processing by, among other things, cutting "chit-chat." The latter seemed unlikely as the four workers were seated within chatting distance to one another around the machine, but reducing the time employees wasted on nonwork tasks like socializing was a generally accepted goal since the days of scientific management.[6]

The Telephone That Registers Calls in One's Absence

The "Telephone That Registers Calls in One's Absence" sounds like something from the satirical newspaper *Onion*, but it was an actual invention described in the pages of *Scientific American* in 1919. The brainchild of a nameless "California inventor" (so much for his fifteen minutes of fame), the device was a recording telegraph meant to be installed in "the base of the telephone instrument." It sounds ingenious, but there were two major drawbacks. First, it required the operator (remember her?) to pull "the telephone receiver out," then put the telegraph into the circuit if no one was there to answer the call. Next— and this was perhaps the fatal flaw—the operator had to translate the caller's message into Morse code, which was "recorded on the [paper] tape in the base of the telephone." So when the secretary returned to her desk, all she had to do was decode any messages "with the aid of the code card supplied with the apparatus." Of course, human agency meant that simple miscommunication or a lack of Morse code literacy turned "Bob says to call back" into "Babs says the caulk's bad" in the wink of an eye, which is probably why successful early answering machines were the ones that recorded messages verbatim onto a magnetic wire.*

* "Telephone That Registers Calls in One's Absence," *Scientific American*, September 13, 1919, 261, 272.

The Secretary and Technophobia

The irony, of course, is that—at least once upon a time—secretaries who were willing to learn how to use a Dictaphone, mimeograph (a hand-cranked copier that used a purple ink whose distinct fragrance induces in some of us a sense memory as overwhelming as Proust's madeleines), addressograph, comptometer, or any one of a number of now forgotten but once cutting-edge office machines stood to make more money. From the way the guidebooks presented the information—often in terms of a cautionary tale—it seems that many secretaries may have been reluctant to do so. *The Efficient Secretary* (1917) used the example of an experienced secretary who was making $15 a week when her boss bought a "business phonograph" (i.e., transcribing recorder). She "refused to try" to learn the newfangled machine—and was promptly replaced with a stenographer with only two years' experience, at a salary of $18 a week (roughly $50 more per week adjusted to today's dollars). Mindful of the difference in pay scale between those who were comfortable with technology and those who weren't—and conscious as well of the fondness with which man-

"It can't come back from a two-week vacation with a third degree sunburn. Or get sick. Or go to the little girls' room. But it can read," 1966.

Cute, fun, . . . and expendable, 1966.

agement viewed deferential workers—Gladys Torson warned readers, "Don't be like the office boy, who, when offered a handy envelop-sealing machine to use in getting out the mail, said, 'Thanks, but I'd rather lick 'em.'"[7]

As for her typewriter, the guidebooks clearly expected the secretary to, at a minimum, dust and cover Old Faithful before she left the office every evening. Along with her ability to replace the ribbon (which was no easy task until the invention of the ribbon cartridge in the 1970s), this was probably the extent of the secretary's knowledge of typewriter mechanics—a situation deplored by Eleanor Gilbert in *The Ambitious Woman in Business* (1916):

Men are constantly amazed at the ignorance and awkwardness of office women with tools—the very tools they use. The average typist, even after many years of experience, is unable to make the simplest repairs to her machine. The office boy knows more about the mechanism of her typewriter than she does.

The "underlying reason" for this sorry state of affairs was, in Gilbert's opinion, "the difference in the education of boys and girls, and the peculiar superstition instilled in the latter that it is unladylike for a woman to know how to handle a hammer, a plane or a saw. Nevertheless, she can always learn," she concluded.[8]

"A typewriter cannot be expected to perform miracles by itself. A clean, well-aligned typewriter will turn out a clean, evenly typed letter." The Executive Secretary, 1959.

Bernice Fitz-Gibbon was a successful advertising executive whose humorous essays about office life occasionally appeared in the *New York Times*. "Since like most women bosses, I have little mechanical ability," she wrote in 1959, tongue mostly in cheek, explaining why a typewriter that took dictation would never catch on. "I am sure it is easier to deal with a secretary's machinations than with a machine's machinations. The machine would have a bewildering assortment of levers and pulleys and sprockets and spindles. It would be sure to leak, or its gears would grind." It might blow a fuse, and figuring which one to replace "would be like fixing the Christmas tree lights," a next-to-impossible task, she implied. Eleanor Gilbert would no doubt have been disgusted by her attitude.[9]

Knowledge of how to use a hammer—or the secret of fixing the Christmas lights—was not going to help a secretary if her typewriter's keys were jammed, but the charge that women are at best reluctant around technology and at worst afraid of it still resonates. Even a reasonably technologically savvy individual can doubt herself if, when something goes wrong with her computer at work, she has to call a "help" desk staffed seemingly exclusively by skeptical men. The advice, given by a secretary newly converted to word processing in 1983, to learn some computer jargon so "you can at least appear semi-intelligent when requesting service rather than just saying, 'Something is wrong with that thingamajig'" remains as wise today as it was when first proffered—though even that can't always save a woman from the tech support staff's attitude.[10]

Dictaphone or Steno Pad?

Women are most often tarred as technophobes, but male reluctance to use the dictation recording device known as a Dictaphone perplexed both efficient experts and Dictaphone manufacturers for much of the twentieth century. As a word processor, I used one every day; essentially, the device was a tape recorder that could be operated by a foot pedal to either speed up or slow down the playback, which greatly assists the operator with transcription. The boss doing the dictating used a version equipped with a hand-held microphone with stop, start, backspace, and fast forward controls. This made it possible for him to erase mistakes as he went along. (At least in theory—instead of backing up and starting over, some dictators preferred to dramatically intone "strike that" whenever they made a mistake. Of course, this left the humble word processor to figure out exactly what was supposed to be left out: the last word or the last paragraph?) There was a desktop model that used standard cassette tapes (previous incarnations used either a wax cylinder, thin vinyl disc, magnetic wire, or plastic cylinder called a "belt"). A handheld model used mini-tapes and allowed a busy executive to dictate when he was away from the office. Of course, digital technology means that many of today's transcriptionists never see a tape—let alone the person whose dictation they're typing.

Invented by Alexander Graham Bell in 1886 (using sound recording technology pioneered by Thomas Edison), the Dictaphone should have been a big hit with both bosses and secretaries: he could record dictation whenever he found it convenient, and she didn't have to drop everything she was doing to rush into his office with steno pad in hand (efficiency experts loved Dictaphones for just these reasons). Some large corporations had been using Dictaphone-based steno pools since the 1920s—and yet the technology didn't catch on the way it should have. "Dictating and transcribing machines" were "a thoroughly demonstrated success and on the market for years," remarked efficiency expert William Henry Leffingwell in 1932, but were still not "so extensively used as they should be."[11]

The situation hadn't changed much two decades later. In 1952, *Today's Secretary* polled 365 bosses on which secretarial duties they considered most important. "Typed transcripts from a voice-recording machine" was ranked thirty-seventh of the forty-four tasks listed in the survey. Ensconced in first place was the old standby "Took dictation and transcribed" (presumably from shorthand notes). More secretaries took dictation straight to the typewriter (which is incredibly difficult to do well even with computer technology) than used one of an array of dictation/transcription machines on the market. Perhaps not surprisingly, the same issue of the magazine included an article titled "Do You Know How to Transcribe Machine Dictation?"[12]

*When technology helped workers: the Dictaphone
provided gainful employment to this woman, as well as
other blind people, circa 1910s.*

Part of the Dictaphone's problem was due to the technological limitations of its earliest models. The turn-of-the-twentieth-century wax cylinder
machines often yielded recordings that were unintelligible—and not just
because the boss was smoking a cigar during dictation. Electric microphones
and amplifiers were added to the machines only in the late 1930s; prior to
that the dictator had to shout down an acoustic speaking tube, which he had
to hold at a proper distance from his mouth while speaking at the correct
speed and volume lest the recording be rendered impossible for the secretary
to comprehend. The problem was so large that a negative reputation dogged
the Dictaphone even years after improvements were made.[13]

Other objections to the Dictaphone had nothing to do with technology—and everything to do with its users. According to historian David Morton, some executives reported they "felt awkward or silly talking to a machine." Others discovered that they hated the sound of their voice coming back at them from the wax cylinder. Most important, many bosses didn't want to replace their secretary with a machine. "Too many men in the executive echelons are dependent upon the *personality* of the secretaries or stenographers to whom they dictate for a cold machine to ever replace the human presence," noted a corporate history of McGraw-Hill (publishers of the Gregg secretarial textbooks). They were too well "accustomed to secretarial thinking, memory, interpretive ability, understanding of the boss's peculiarities," and despite what the secretarial guidebooks said was proper, her "correction of the boss's mistakes" as he made them. Furthermore, if he was one of those executives who hired a secretary based on her looks, why would he give up an activity that put him in close proximity to a pretty face on a daily basis? Even where a "girl" was not hired for her looks, a secretary remained the most visible mark of the boss's status—one that he was not willing to relinquish without a fight. (Conversely, when the portable machines came on the market in the late 1950s and early 1960s, they were viewed as status symbols—important executives traveled!—and sales were better than those of the desktop models, whose presence announced, "I'm too low on the totem pole to have a secretary.") Morton also suggests that secretaries themselves "rightly saw the installation of dictation equipment as an attempt to de-skill their jobs, and resisted its use as much as possible." Thus, manufacturers of dictation recording devices had to sell the product, literally as well as figuratively, to both boss and secretary.[14]

In just one issue of *Today's Secretary* magazine (September 1952), three different manufacturers of dictation machines took out advertisements for their products. The secretary herself was not going to purchase one of these machines, of course, but she could request her boss to do so. "Selling the Boss on a Dictating Machine" was even one of the case studies in *Secretaries on the Spot* (1967); the secretary in question talked her boss

"No more mussed-up hairdo's for me!" The dictating machine as fashion accessory, 1953.

into using the machine, which, after a two-week adjustment period, he discovered he loved).[15]

The ads tried to make the machines seem friendly to female users, which often meant emphasizing their "feminine" qualities rather than business capabilities—the assumption being that women were afraid of or incapable of understanding technology. "No hair-rumpling headbands," promised one, while another featured earphones "as light as one of those new wingback earrings. And it doesn't muss my hair, either!" continued the copy. Still

"A really modern secretary knows just what she needs . . . a dab of powder and lipstick to look *smart and her Gray Audograph to* be *smart," 1953.*

another affirmed that the machine would free up "The Smart young secretary" for better things, such as "being charming and efficient."[16] Advertised this way, the machine became fashion accessories for office wives, not potential threats to employment.

Compare this with advertising that appeared in magazines aimed at bosses, not secretaries. There, the emphasis was on the bottom line and the high cost of human help. "The process of shorthand can be a substantial drain on your profits. Why take the time of two people to do what one can do better? Let the Dictaphone Time-Master dictating machine take dictation for your secretary," read a 1961 ad in *Fortune* magazine. The Time-Master ad got it wrong—face-to-face dictation was at least one situation where a businessman was more than happy to give up some of his profits. A flesh-and-blood, word-supplying, grammar-correcting secretary was exactly what he wanted, a point not lost on the author of *So You Want to Be an Executive Secretary* (1963): "Even the most gadget-minded executive, I'm willing to bet, doesn't sit around dreaming of the day when he can replace his secretary with a mechanical woman clanking in and out of his office."[17]

But Would She Look Good in a Sweater? The Secretary of the Future

The Dictaphone was an anomaly. For the most part, in the eyes of both press and public, technology could do no wrong in the post–World War II era. The promise of the first vacuum tube–filled, room-sized computers (ENIAC in 1946 and the first UNIVAC in 1951) was more than fulfilled by the glamour and wonder of the space program. Assisted by computers and other futuristic gadgetry that would undoubtedly trickle down to the home front—jet packs, anyone?—life in the upcoming twenty-first century looked shiny and bright. A House of the Future, sponsored by chemical-maker Monsanto and built largely of synthetic materials, opened at Disneyland in 1957. A smash hit with visitors, its kitchen included an early model of that twenty-first-century break-room necessity, the microwave oven. *The Jetsons*, a prime-time cartoon that debuted in 1962, humorously showed what work and family life might be like one hundred years in the future. Paterfamilias George Jetson worked at Spacely Space Sprockets, where his desk job consisted of pushing a single computer button once a day. In one episode, a robot named Uniblab is brought in as his supervisor—a job George coveted. But despite his ultramodern trappings, Uniblab is a mechanical micromanager who tells Miss Gamma, Spacely Space Sprockets' sexy, southern-accented receptionist: "Polish your nails on your own time."

Steno pads and hot pants for the secretary of the future! 1968.

The combination of advanced technology and the same old midtwentieth-century gender stereotypes also colored more serious prognostications of the secretary's future. From the vantage point of 1961—the year John Glenn became the first human to orbit the earth—*Today's Secretary* imagined the office in the far future of 2000. Thanks to the "electronic computer," a secretary would be able to come in at noon, work for an hour or two, then leave—finished with the day's tasks. Best of all were the two-month vacations! (What they didn't factor in was that she would be paid for only those two hours and that her benefits would be cut to shreds—that is, if her job hadn't already been outsourced to a virtual assistant on another continent who could be paid still less.)[18]

According to a 1968 article, the "Secretary of the Future"—in this case the year 2018—was forced to work a grueling three- or four-hour day, albeit seated "in a large comfortable chair" in an office that resembled a living room. Instead of walking the hallways to another part of the building, she would "be transported via trackless plastic bubble." Except for the latter prediction—and the suggestion that puffy gold lamé–striped hotpants would be acceptable career wear—the article was remarkably prescient. Miss Williams is "employed by an independent company servicing many firms" (in current terms, she is a virtual assistant). She confers with her boss "via video phone from an office perhaps miles from his" (she telecommutes). She

> oversees the automatic typing equipment which prints out words as they are spoken. At the end of a letter, she pushes a button and the finished letter appears on the executive's video screen. . . . Now he tells Miss Williams how many copies he wants and where they should be sent via beamed messages picked up on home receivers. His own copy is stored in the memory bank of a central computer.

(Miss Williams and her boss share a voice-activated word-processing program and send draft and finished versions of documents to one another via email.) According to the article, there was only one problem with this idyllic vision of the future: "There'll be no sitting on the boss's lap. That will have to wait for the annual Christmas get-together."[19]

It was, in fact, the secretary's willingness to sit on laps or perform the duties of a traditional, gofering office wife that separated her from the machines—and allegedly protected her job from automation. "A machine is neither yellable at or blamable on," wrote Bernice Fitz-Gibbon. "Machines will never charm the boss' guests or cover up for him when he goofs. What they will do is free the secretary from petty jobs and make her a more important person," was the confident prediction from a UNIVAC representative who spoke to the *New York Times* on the occasion of the fiftieth anniversary of the Gibbs School. Around the same time, *Life* magazine noted that a newly invented voice-activated typewriter "wasn't likely to automate any secretaries out of their jobs very soon," as—and here the magazine mimicked the machine's phonetic output—the "klumsi masheen kan nivver make kawfi."[20]

Speaking to the *Los Angeles Times* in 1966, Dolores Lefevre (past president and publicity chairman of the local chapter of the National Secretaries Association) explained that secretaries should "cheerfully" empty ashtrays, sharpen pencils, water plants, and, yes, make coffee—because "that's your security against being replaced by a computer." A decade later, technology had made further inroads on the secretary's job description—but her ability to act as a combination wife and waitress still protected her from the unemployment line. A new word-processing system "couldn't bring you a cup of coffee, remember your daughter's birthday, or tell you if your tie is crooked," explained a *Los Angeles Times* reporter in 1975. More ominously, it could "produce 350 error-free words per minute for hours on end—something no human secretary or typist can manage." (Journalists simply could not get enough of the coffee angle. A mid-1990s article describing how secretaries used new forms of office technology ended a paragraph about personal computers with the notation that "none bring coffee.")[21]

Word Processing:
The Space-Age Typing Pool

We're so used to—and spoiled by—word-processing programs that allow us to delete or move words, sentences, and entire paragraphs that it's easy for some of us to forget what it was like to work on an electric typewriter, much less a manual model. Consider the panoply of details a simple letter required. First of all, the text had to be properly centered on the page. There was probably a company style the secretary had to follow, but unlike today when it's easy to pull up an empty template complete with margins and line spacing, she had to make sure she started in the proper horizontal and vertical space, or, as *Techniques of Teaching Typewriting* (1955) explained, "translate horizontal inches into pica or elite spaces, and vertical inches into single, double, or triple line spaces."

> If a writing line is to be 50 spaces long, subtract 50 from the whole line length (80, 85, 90, 95, 100) and divide the remainder by 2. This gives the left margin. Subtract that number representing to the left margin from the whole line length, and that will be the right margin. . . . Several methods may be used to estimate vertical placement. All are dependent on knowing that there are six single line spaces to an inch. This multiplied by the length of the paper in inches will give the number of single-spaced lines that may be written on that sized paper.[22]

The secretary had to guesstimate how many lines a letter would take up, accounting of course for double or triple spacing and type size, then count down from the top of the page to find the line on which to begin typing. She also had to successfully gauge where to break from page one to page two. If a letter or report included tables of information, she had to set her tab stops so that the rows and columns were perfectly aligned.

In addition to demonstrating the kind of mathematic ability such on-the-fly calculations required, a secretary needed strong English skills. It was up to her to decide whether or not words that fell along the right-hand margin needed to be hyphenated, and if they did, how to do so properly. It went without saying that she corrected the boss's grammar and that her spelling and punctuation were top notch. When you realize that if one word was dropped or a sentence was out of place, an entire multipage document might have to have been retyped, you begin to understand why accuracy was so very important. "A letter going outside your company should have no *visible* correction," advised *The Successful Secretary* (1964). "If the correction shows at all, type the letter over." Similarly, if she made a mistake on page ten of a twenty-page document, she typed pages ten through twenty again. Then, if, god forbid, she found another error, she did it again. And so on, until it was perfect.

Word processing eliminated much of this work. Software alone doesn't make for beautifully laid-out letters or tables, any more than spell-checking or, worse, grammar-checking programs make for well-written ones—but on the whole, few would argue that the computer is a huge improvement over the typewriter. (Of course, almost every office holds on to at least one type-writer; there's nothing like it for filling in some kinds of forms or typing up a quick envelope or label.) Generally accepted as the conceptual forebear of today's word-processing systems, IBM's Magnetic Tape Selectric Type-writer was introduced in 1964. The so-called MT/ST wasn't a computer, but it recorded the operator's keystrokes in coded form on a reusable half-inch-wide magnetic tape. She could then correct mistakes and delete or add words, sentences, or paragraphs before she printed out the final docu-ment. The document could be stored on the magnetic tape and revised at a later date. All this came at a price, both monetary (an MT/ST system cost a cool $10,000 in the mid-1960s) and intangible. In the words of a *New York Times* article introducing the MT/ST, though the new typewriter undoubt-edly would "eliminate much of the drudgery in a secretary's job. It may also eliminate a lot of secretaries."[23]

What the presence of word-processing machines like the MT/ST did most immediately was to split the secretarial workforce into what the *Times* quaintly referred to in 1974 as "Correspondence Secretaries," who did all the typing, and "Administrative Secretaries," who answered the phone, opened the mail, did the calendaring, and so on (in time, these positions solidified into "word processors" and "secretaries," respec-tively). Women who had been full-service secretaries highly resented being assigned to the "space-age typing pool" in the wake of office automation; it was, they believed, an "automated ghetto" that offered little, if any, chance for advancement. Meanwhile, freed from the drudgery of daily typing (at least the longer documents), an administrative secretary might find herself responsible for multiple bosses. Even if she previously had been happy to run errands for her boss, she simply didn't have time to under the new regime. In either case, word processing weakened the traditional relationship between boss and secretary. A word-processing consultant admitted that secretaries frequently looked forward to what the *Times* termed "the office divorce" because it meant they were "no longer the chattel of just one man."[24]

Almost ten years later, a survey found that one in five secretarial stations was installed with some form of word-processing system, and 87 percent of the respondents thought automation "had had a positive effect on their profession," mostly as regards efficiency. "Once you've used a machine," noted a secretary in 1982, "you're spoiled for life. You never want to go back to an electric typewriter." By that time too, the rigid division between secretaries and word processors described by the *Times* in 1974 had softened. Secretaries still typed; they just sent the longer stuff to the word-processing department. They sent little jobs too, if they got swamped, which was a more frequent occurrence as they were assigned a greater number of executives. A male secretary in 1984 noted that he typed, filed, and copied for twelve bosses; while that was an enormous number, it wasn't at all unusual for the secretaries at the law firm where I worked a decade after that to carry a load of three or four attorneys— a number that kept getting higher as management sought to squeeze as much as possible out of fewer and fewer workers.[25]

"All this automation isn't going to do away with secretaries, on the contrary, business expansion will mean millions more of them," the author of the "Secretary of the Future" article had confidently—and, as it turned out, completely incorrectly—stated back in 1968.[26] She and the other prognosticators had failed to predict at least two turns of events, in addition to a couple of economic downturns in the 1980s and '90s that had big businesses tightening their belts. There was the breakdown of the old one-to-one ratio between boss and secretary. Back in the 1960s, five bosses meant a minimum of five secretaries (some big fish might have had two or three "girls" working for him); by the 1980s and '90s, a single secretary might handle the workflow of all five. What made this possible (in addition to what I've already discussed, of course) was something that would have been absolutely unthinkable in previous decades: executives started typing.

"Don't Worry, Miss Jones, I'll Type It Myself"

The inability to type had always been a carefully maintained executive attribute, right up there in importance with not knowing how to run the copier—or make coffee. The personal computer changed the boss's relationship with typing, though not without some initial reluctance. Some executives responded to the keyboard "like Dracula confronted with a crucifix," wrote word-processing authority Peter McWilliams in 1984. "The keyboard is an extension of the lowly typewriter, they think. It's a secretarial, not an executive, machine. Well, times change." The ability to quickly and easily fix mistakes meant that rank amateurs no longer had to fear typing. McWilliams noted that even though he couldn't type "in the traditional sense of the word," he could "process words—three fingers at a time—with little trouble." The computer's macho affiliation with high technology was just icing on the cake for a gadget-obsessed executive.[27]

Cultural historian Ellen Lupton points out that "with the rise of the personal computer, the keyboard began to lose its association with 'women's work.'" Lupton described how in 1990s-era advertisements where men appeared in juxtaposition with computers, the men were shown in a context of "high-tech engineering and push-button control" (a managerial/masculine activity) rather than merely typing (secretarial/feminine). In fact, it was no longer called "typing"—it was "keyboarding," even though there was no difference between the two activities. Oh, sure, there were a couple of extra rows of function keys on a computer keyboard, but the act of touch typing remained exactly the same. Yet when it was removed from the "feminine" typewriter, keyboarding became an acceptable skill for men. Gloria Steinem noted the switch in her 2007 commencement speech at her alma mater:

In my generation, we were asked by the Smith [College] vocational office how many words we could type a minute, a question that was never asked of then all-male students at Harvard or Princeton. Female-only typing was rationalized by supposedly greater female verbal skills, attention to detail, smaller fingers, goodness knows what, but the public imagination just didn't include male typists, certainly not Ivy League-educated ones.

Now computers have come along, and "typing" is "keyboarding." Suddenly, voila! — men can type!

"Gives you faith in men's ability to change, doesn't it?" Steinem concluded.[28] This metamorphosis was generational in effect; at the office I worked at in the mid-2000s, almost all the older male executives continued to dictate their correspondence and other documents, while the younger ones did all their own typing. That was at least half a decade ago—an eon in technological terms. The newest crop of dictation software is almost eerily accurate, and I'll bet it won't be long before executives (female as well as male) forget how to type all over again.

Epilogue

The Virtual Secretary in a Paperless Office, or, We've Come a Long Way—Maybe?

Unfortunately, to some people the word [secretary] still means someone who only gets coffee for the boss.

Diane Engelhardt, President, Katharine Gibbs School, Melville, Long Island (2001)[1]

H ere's an experiment. The next time you're at the library, pull an old—say, from forty or more years ago—phone or business directory for your town off the shelf. Turn to the pages listing schools and take a look at the number of secretarial schools listed there. Chances are good it's higher than you ever suspected. Now check the directory's current edition. Along with many bowling alleys, drive-in theaters, and other former landmarks of the American scene, secretarial schools have gone to the great hereafter. Technology did them in.

Even the venerable Katie Gibbs is no longer the icon she once was. In February 2008, Career Education Corporation, "one of the country's largest for-profit educational companies," announced it would close seven of nine Katharine Gibbs School campuses, among them the historic branches in Boston (opened in 1917) and New York (opened 1918). Sold by the Gibbs family to Macmillan publishing in 1968, the company changed hands frequently in the 1990s. Change had been afoot for decades by then, spurred on by the women's movement, by technological advances in the way office work was accomplished, and by the necessity to keep up with the marketplace. More emphasis was placed on technology and less on the "finishing school" decorum that for so long differentiated the Gibbs girl from her peers. In the early 1980s, "Personal Development" became "Professional Development," and while the curriculum still incorporated something called "verbal poise," assertiveness training and "the legal rights of the individual" were also part of the course, as was office etiquette (according to the *New York Times*, the latter encompassed "who sits next to whom at board meetings"). But the course also touched on "diet, exercise, wardrobe, hairstyle and makeup" as well as posture ("Try tucking your legs under your chair while you're typing. . . . Pretend they're Scotch-taped together"), just the sort of finishing-school touches the school was allegedly trying to leave behind.

In 2000, the dress code was further relaxed (at least at the Melville, Long Island, campus): women were no longer required to wear stockings, and sandals joined pumps on the list of acceptable footwear; male students ditched neckties in favor of tee shirts. These concessions were hardly a slippery slope to muffin tops and flip-flops: at least when it came to job interviews, visible piercings and dyed hair were not allowed, women had to cover any leg tattoos with stockings, and a navy blue suit was "strongly suggested."[2]

Even as Gibbs moved away from the model of the navy-suited supersecretary, executive coach and author Jean Hollands offered a special "softening" class for executive women deemed by their employers as being too aggressive. The "Bully Broads" who attended Hollands's program in 2001 learned to curtail the tough, no-nonsense behavior that got them to the top of the ladder in the first place in favor of acting more like . . . ladies. Tears may have upset the boss when she was a secretary—but now that she was an executive, they made her so much less intimidating. "Talk right through the tears," she wrote in *Same Game, Different Rules* (2001). "You will look and sound more courageous if you can appear to be focused and steady, and the tears are just those little nonsense things running down your face. You will really make an impression when you finish." And I'll bet the board of directors remembered it at promotion time too.[3]

In another situation that could have come straight out of the 1970s, Tamara Klopfenstein, a part-time clerk and receptionist in a Pennsylvania office, had had enough. "I don't have a problem getting coffee and/or water for our guests when they come in," she wrote in an email to her two male bosses. "I don't expect to serve and wait on you by making and serving you coffee every day." She would be "happy to sit down and talk" to them about the matter, but she would not be making them a pot of coffee. Nine minutes after hitting the "send" button, she was fired. The year was 2007.

Klopfenstein sued, alleging sex discrimination. In ruling against her, the judge found that she couldn't show "that she was treated differently from any 'similarly situated' male employees" because "there was only one receptionist in the office and the job had always been held by a woman." Got that? Because Klopfenstein could not show that a male receptionist had been treated differently than she had—because the company only hired female receptionists, who were the only employees who made and served coffee to the male bosses—she couldn't show gender discrimination.[4]

Welcome to today's office, which is at once completely different and frighteningly the same as yesterday's. Shorthand for professional use in the office has all but gone the way of the dodo bird. A few two-year schools still teach it, but in the words of one professor, it's "a very slim enrollment"—why take all the time to learn those squiggles and dots when voice-recognition software lets executives dictate directly into their PDA (personal digital assistant) and print out the text later? But while technology makes it easier for the administrative assistant or secretary to get her work done, for example, it also makes it easier for her bosses to spend the day emailing pornography to one another—or to her.[5]

Therein lies the rub, so to speak. Changes in technology flash along at what seems like the speed of light, but despite the women's movement and mandatory sexual harassment training, in some offices gender relations are stuck in the smirking, pre-liberation 1970s. Compare, for example, the outcome of Tamara Kopfenstein's case with that of Diana Becker. Becker was a secretary at the Waterloo, Iowa, Community School District, who one day in 1977 refused to take her turn at the coffee pot. "All the years I made it," she later told the *New York Times*, "I thought, this is not right." Brewing coffee "had nothing to do with education" after all, though her ultimate reason for refusing to do it was stunningly simple. "I think it's stupid," she told the *Times*.[6]

Becker's boss immediately called her on the carpet. When she still refused to make coffee, he sent her a letter addressed to "Ms." Diana Becker (she believed this was a snide reference to what he perceived was her "libber" attitude) terminating her employment for her "direct refusal to carry out . . . assigned responsibilities," even though coffee making was not part of her job description.[7]

While her local job board believed the school district had not shown sufficient cause for Becker's dismissal, the Waterloo Association of Educational Secretaries declined to take her case to arbitration. So Becker sued on the grounds of sex discrimination—and won.

We can't know all the underlying facts that informed the judge's decision in either case. But Klopfenstein's dismissal—like the perceived need for a Bully Broads program—is a sharp reminder of how office culture remains mired in its predilection for servile women. Workers at Bell Telephone Laboratories in 1954 nicknamed an early answering machine "Amanda, the electronic receptionist" as "a tribute to the helpfulness of the woman office worker."[8] One doesn't have to look any farther than the development of the fully virtual assistant (as opposed to the off-site but as-yet-still-human virtual assistant) to see that the stereotype of the helpful, just-sexy-enough secretary is still with us. Among the first generation of telephone-based electronic personal assistants in the late 1990s were those called Wildfire and Portico, both of which used "a friendly but assertive female voice, giving the impression of an executive secretary" (another, Webley, impersonated an English butler). A Wildfire user told the *New York Times* in 1998 that one of his male clients was so charmed by what the *Times* characterized as its "friendly and rather seductive voice" that he "responded to Wildfire's statement 'I'll see if I can find him' with, 'Take your time, sweetheart.'"[9]

Wildfire and its competitors were simplistic automatons in comparison with today's sophisticated computerized virtual assistants. Perhaps the only thing the current models have in common with the earlier services is the use of a feminine persona—and the tendency of some men to treat them as if they were real women. "Jenn" is Alaska Airlines's virtual assistant, depicted on its Web site "as a young brunette with a nice smile." According to a business writer for the *New York Times*, if "Jenn" is presented with "a clumsy bar pickup line," she will politely suggest "getting back to business." (When I recently asked "Jenn" if there was a male virtual assistant working for Alaska Airlines, she referred me to the site's current job listings and gave me a direct link to a page titled "Executive Leadership." Oh, Jenn.) "Laura" is a prototype virtual personal assistant from Microsoft who appears on-screen as a talking head (no word yet as to whether the boss will be able to order up his choice of blonde, brunette, or redhead).[10]

As we continue to struggle through the worst economic times since the Great Depression, some offices simply make do without secretaries: as of May 2010, approximately 1.7 million clerical and administrative workers have lost their jobs. These positions very well may not come back; just as executives discovered they could type in the 1980s, they are now finding that they can handle their own calendars and travel arrangements.[11]

The future of the secretary is perhaps best typified by the flesh-and-blood virtual assistant. Working out of her own home office, she might provide a combination of administrative skills and tech support to any number of clients. A 2008 *New York Times* online profile of a successful virtual assistant suggested that the arrangement "turned the whole assistant/boss dynamic on its head. Rather than an assistant who reports to a boss, she has become a service provider who manages her clients." This was an optimistic way of saying that the virtual assistant could cobble together a decent living by working eight hours a week for one client, twelve hours for another, and so on—as long as she, like all freelancers, was willing to hustle like mad to get jobs and pay for her own health benefits and vacation time.

Most of the comments that followed came from virtual assistants fervently explaining why they loved the flexible nature of being one's own boss.

One pointed out that a virtual assistant was "not just your typical secretary who takes notes and types away," but a professional who provided "customer service"—it's hard not to remember the NSA representative who told secretaries back in the 1970s that "cheerfully" emptying ashtrays would save their jobs from automation. But another commenter pointed out a way in which the virtual office might well subvert some of the worst aspects of the bricks-and-mortar one, instead of just re-creating them online. In a physical office, the "traditional boss-subordinate" relationship was surrounded by "all kinds of symbols of social rank," including the corner office, expensive clothing, and work hours. A virtual assistant, however, "might well be making lots of money" while her client was still in "'pre-profit' stage. . . . For people (near the 'top' or the 'bottom' or the rank scale) who are comfortable with this sort of rank-based social system, the loss of 'the office' is regretful. For those of us who have always found the rank-based social system distasteful, the loss of 'the office' is liberating."[12]

Described this way, the virtual office is intriguing indeed—but I will probably finish out my career in a traditional fluorescent-lit, coffee-stained cubicle farm. After all, I choose to work at an office job to provide relief from the freelance scramble, not to mention collecting a regular paycheck and having access to health insurance.

Like many people these days, I worry that I'll never be able to retire. But if I do leave the workforce at some point in the next fifteen or twenty years (ideally before someone finds my skeleton hunched over the keyboard), I can consider moving to a special place for old secretarial workhorses. Della Herring was a secretary with a dream. She stood up at a meeting of the National Secretaries Association in 1947 and asked why there wasn't a retirement home for secretaries. Della put her money where her mouth was, and contributed the first dollar to just such a project. Located near Albuquerque, New Mexico, Vista Grande opened in 1972; it was, and remains, the world's only retirement community for secretaries.[13]

Notes

INTRODUCTION: OUT OF THE KITCHEN AND INTO THE OFFICE

1. *How to Be a Super-Secretary* (New York: Remington-Rand, Inc., 1949) unpaginated. For a while in the 1940s, the company manufactured guns as well as typewriters; it went on to produce the first UNIVAC computers in the 1950s.
2. U.S. Department of Labor, Bureau of Labor Statistics, Alphabetical List of SOC Occupations, at http://www.bls.gov/oes/current/oes_alph.htm. Figure includes SOC code numbers 43-6011, 43-6012, 43-6013, 43-6014.
3. Harford Powel, *Good Jobs for Good Girls* (New York: Vanguard Press, 1949), 4.
4. "The Stenographer in Fiction," *Writer*, March 1914, 40.
5. Arnold Kane, *Office Wife* (Fresno, Calif.: Saber Books, 1961), 33.
6. Marie L. Carney, *The Secretary and Her Job* (Charlottesville, Va.: Business Book, 1939), 5.
7. Agnes F. Perkins, ed., *Vocations for the Trained Woman* (Boston: Women's Educational and Industrial Union, 1910), 204; *Ladies' Home Journal* quoted in Alice Kessler-Harris, *Out to Work: A History of Wage-Earning Women in the United States* (New York: Oxford University Press, 1982), 149; Eunice Fuller Barnard, "A New School for Wives—The Office," *New York Times Magazine*, January 25, 1931, 18; Patricia Flynn, *So You Want to Be an Executive Secretary* (New York: Macfadden Books, 1963), 11.
8. Mary McGee Williams and Irene Kane, *On Becoming A Woman* (New York:

Dell, 1959), 69; Helen Whitcomb and Rosalind Lang, *Charm: The Career Girl's Guide to Business and Personal Success* (New York: Gregg Division, McGraw-Hill Book, 1964), 307.

9. "Two Heads or One," *Workingman's Advocate*, May 7, 1870, 4, quoted in Kessler-Harris, *Out to Work*, 84.

10. Elyce J. Rotella, "The Transformation of the American Office: Changes in Employment and Technology," *Journal of Economic History*, vol. 41, no. 1 (March 1981), 51–52; Margery W. Davies, *Woman's Place Is at the Typewriter: Office Work and Office Workers 1870–1930* (Philadelphia: Temple University Press, 1982), 17–19.

11. Cathryn L. Claussen, "Gendered Merit: Women and the Merit Concept in Federal Employment, 1864–1944," *The American Journal of Legal History*, vol. 40, no. 3 (July 1996), 229; "Uncle Sam As Woman's Boss," *New York Times*, April 18, 1926, 16.

12. "Women In The Treasury," *New York Times*, July 27, 1886, 6; "Uncle Sam as Woman's Boss," 16; Gloria Steinem, "'Anonymous' Was a Woman," *New York Times Book Review*, August 11, 1968, 8.

13. *Workingman's Advocate* quoted in Kessler-Harris, *Out to Work*, 143; McCulloch quoted in "Uncle Sam as Woman's Boss," 16.

14. Cindy S. Aron, "'To Barter Their Souls for Gold': Female Clerks in Federal Government Offices, 1862–1890," *Journal of American History*, vol. 67, no. 4 (March 1981), 848–849.

15. Sharon Hartman Strom, "'Light Manufacturing': The Feminization of American Office Work, 1900–1930," *Industrial and Labor Relations Review*, vol. 43, no. 1 (October 1989), 55. In 1866, the maximum salary established by federal law for a female clerk was $900; men earned between $1,200 and $1,800; Aron, "'To Barter Their Souls for Gold,'" 847.

16. Aron, "'To Barter Their Souls for Gold,'" 836, fn. 1; Kessler-Harris, *Out to Work*, 147; Davies, *Woman's Place Is at the Typewriter*, 207–8; Ellen Lupton, *Mechanical Brides: Women and Machines from Home to Office* (New York: Cooper Hewitt National Museum of Design and Princeton Architectural Press, 1993), 43.

17. Herkimer County Historical Society, *The Story of the Typewriter* (Herkimer, New York: Press of A. H. Kellogg Company, 1923), frontispiece, 1; Richard F. Snow, "Christopher Latham Sholes: the Seventy-Sixth Inventor of the Typewriter," *American Heritage Magazine*, vol. 33, no. 5 (August/

September 1982), at http://www.americanheritage.com/articles/magazine/ah/1982/5/1982_5_78.shtml accessed September 4, 2007).

18. Davies, *Woman's Place Is at the Typewriter*, 37.

19. Lupton, *Mechanical Brides*, 43; Herkimer County Historical Society, *Story of the Typewriter*, 14; Davies, *Woman's Place Is at the Typewriter*, 35, 54.

20. "In truth, much witticism has been spent upon the pretty typewriter, a witticism that has taken the place of that formerly bestowed upon the mother-in-law. Both are overdone." Mrs. Hester M. Poole, "Social Graces for Every-day Service in the Home," *Good Housekeeping*, March 1898, 94; James Shepp, *Shepp's New York City Illustrated: Scene and Story in the Metropolis of the Western World: how two million people live and die, work and play, eat and sleep, govern themselves and break the laws, win fortunes and lose them, and so build and maintain the New York of to-day* (Chicago: Globe Bible, ca. 1894), 178.

21. Harrison, John, *A Manual of the Type-Writer* (London: Isaac Pitman, 1888), 9, quoted in Keep, Christopher, "The Cultural Work of the Type-Writer Girl," *Victorian Studies*, Spring 1997, 405; *Scientific American* quoted in Herkimer County Historical Society, *Story of the Typewriter*, 109; C. E. Smith letter to the editor in response to "Are Men Better Typists Than Women?" *Scientific American*, vol. 109 (1913), 411, quoted in Davies, *Woman's Place Is at the Typewriter*, 90.

22. Aron, "'To Barter Their Souls for Gold,'" 847; Kessler-Harris, *Out to Work*, 148, 135.

23. Edward Jones Kilduff, *The Private Secretary: His Duties and Opportunities* (New York: Century, 1916), 37, 111, italics in the original.

24. Aron, "'To Barter Their Souls for Gold'", 848; "Poisoned by Ribbon Ink," *New York Times*, October 17, 1899, 1; Kessler-Harris, *Out to Work*, 148, 135.

25. Deborah Schoeneman with Spencer Morgan, "Intelligencer Briefing," New York Metro.com, April 26, 2004, at http://www.nymetro.com/nymetro/news/people/columns/intelligencer/in_10245.

CHAPTER 1: SO YOU WANT TO BE A SECRETARY

1. Lucy Graves Mayo, *You Can Be an Executive Secretary* (New York: Macmillan, 1965), 50; Elsie McCormick, "Every Woman Should Learn a Trade," *Good Housekeeping*, April 1952, 51, 154.

2. "Her Eternal Youth," *New York Times*, July 2, 1922, 74.

3. Kathleen M'Laughlin, "Sidelines Stressed for Girl Chemists," *New York Times*, April 16, 1939, 25.

4. M'Laughlin, *ibid.*; Rae Chatfield Ayer, "Are Men Better Secretaries? No!—Rae Chatfield Ayer," *Rotarian*, November 1940, 58.

5. Mayo, *Executive Secretary*, 5; Linda Stalter, "Where Shorthand Can Take You," *Junior Secretary*, November 1966, 3; Liberated secretary quoted in Pat Colander, "Secretaries Hoping to File Injustices for Good," *Chicago Tribune*, April 23, 1975, C3.

6. Dorothy Thompson, "The Employed Woman and Her Household," *Ladies' Home Journal*, September 1952, 11, emphasis is the author's; Ferdinand Lundberg and Marynia F. Farnham, September, *Modern Woman: The Lost Sex* (New York: Harper & Brothers, 1947), 366.

7. Harold Shryock, *Happiness for Husbands and Wives* (Washington, D.C.: Review and Herald, 1968), 105.

8. Ayer, "Are Men Better Secretaries?" 59; Brazilian secretarial school administrator quoted by Ruth McKay, "White Collar Girl," *Chicago Tribune*, April 20, 1943, 18; Lucy Graves Mayo, *Wendy Scott, Secretary* (New York: Dodd, Mead, 1961), 56, 57.

9. Sibyl Lee Gilmore, *The Successful Secretary* (Chicago: The Dartnell Corporation, 1951), 8–9; Enid F. Haupt, *The Seventeen Book of Young Living* (New York: David McKay, 1957), 186, 185; advertisement for Nancy Taylor Schools, *Mademoiselle*, June 1960, 105; advertisement for Grace Downs Air Career School, *Mademoiselle*, June 1960, 106; Frances Maule, "I Want to Be a Secretary," *Independent Woman*, March 1941, 95.

10. Janice Weiss, "Educating for Clerical Work: The Nineteenth-Century Private Commercial School," *Journal of Social History*, vol. 14, no. 3 (Spring 1981), 408–9.

11. Mary Caroline Crawford, *The College Girl of America and the Institutions Which Make Her What She Is* (Boston: L. C. Page, 1905), 276; Weiss, "Educating for Clerical Work," 410–11.

12. Weiss, "Educating for Clerical Work," 415; Lisa M. Fine, *The Souls of the Skyscraper: Female Clerical Workers in Chicago, 1870–1930* (Philadelphia: Temple University Press, 1990), 23, 24.

13. Both quoted in Weiss, 414.

14. Eleanor Gilbert, *The Ambitious Woman in Business* (New York: Funk and

Wagnalls, 1916), 247; Helen Christen Hoerle and Florence R. Saltzberg, *The Girl and the Job* (New York: Henry Holt, 1919), 18; Frances Maule, "I Want to Be a Secretary," *Independent Woman*, March 1941, 75, 95.

15.   Henry C. Link, "More Education or a Job?" *Rotarian*, May 1938, 15, 17.

16.   Lynn Lilliston, "Secretarial Skills Go Long Way in Employment Field," *Los Angeles Times*, June 5, 1966, D10; Jean A. Wells and Muriel B. Wool, *College Women Seven Years after Graduation: Resurvey of Women Graduates—Class of 1957*, Women's Bureau, Bulletin 292 (Washington, D.C.: U.S. Department of Labor, 1966), 14.

17.   Linda Stalter, "Where Shorthand Can Take You," *Junior Secretary*, November 1966, 3.

18.   Katharine Gibbs School ad, *Rotarian*, May 1941, 62; Link, "More Education or a Job?" 15.

19.   Sonia F. Gray, "Women in Rhode Island History—Making A Difference: Katharine Ryan Gibbs (1863–1934)," at http://www.projo.com/specials/ women/94root13.htm; Jane See White, "The Growing Secretary Shortage," *Los Angeles Times*, December 16, 1981, G16; "'Katie' Gibbs Grads Are Secretarial Elite," *BusinessWeek*, September 2, 1961, 43; Martha Weinman Lear, "The Amanuensis, Evolution and Revolution of the Secretary over Half a Century," *New York Times Magazine*, October 15, 1961, 28; History of Simmons College, at http://www.simmons.edu/overview/history /index.shtml; "College for Women Workers," *New York Times*, October 12, 1902, 27.

20.   Gray, "Women in Rhode Island History."

21.   "'Katie' Gibbs Grads Are Secretarial Elite," 43–44; White, "The Growing Secretary Shortage," G16, 17.

22.   Katharine Gibbs School, 1960–1961 catalog, 5; Carol Hymowitz, "If She Is Wearing Purple Eye Shadow, She Isn't from Gibbs," *Wall Street Journal*, April 5, 1984, 1; White, "Growing Secretary Shortage," 17; Marie Fontaine, "Mastering Computer Key to a Secretary's Success," *Providence Journal*, April 23, 1995, I-01.

23.   Katharine Gibbs School, 1960–1961 catalog, 5; "'Katie' Gibbs Grads Are Secretarial Elite," 43, 44, 46.

24.   Mayo, *You Can Be an Executive Secretary*, 50.

25.   Katharine Gibbs School catalog, 1960–1961, 18.

26.   "Speedwriting," in *World Book Encyclopedia*, (Chicago: Field Enterprises

Educational Corporation, 1965), 604; "Nathan Behrin, Court Reporter," *New York Times*, May 7, 1971, 44.

27. "Shorthand," in *Encyclopædia Britannica Online*, at http://www.search.eb.com/eb/article-53187 (accessed May 7, 2008); Leslie Cowan, *John Robert Gregg* (Oxford, UK: Pre-Raphaelite Press at Oxford, 1984), 12.

28. Cowan, *John Robert* Gregg, 12, 43.

29. Ibid., 72.

30. "The Easy Way," *Junior Secretary*, October 1967, 13.

31. "Take a Tip From Tony!" *Gregg Writer*, September 1946, 16.

32. "Girl Locked in Vault, Freed as Hole Is Bored For Her to Read Own Shorthand Combination," *New York Times*, June 17, 1928, 27.

33. Dorothy Townsend, "How Sweet It Is—a Masculine Aroma!" *Los Angeles Times*, March 23, 1963, B1.

34. Bernice C. Turner, *The Private Secretary's Manual: A Practical Handbook for Secretaries and Their Executives*, rev. ed. (New York: Prentice-Hall, 1943), 25.

35. Helen Dare, "Simply Made Up Her Mind Not to Be a Mediocrity," *San Francisco Chronicle*, December 9, 1915, 11; Ron Alexander, "Typists Compete in Keyboard Speed," *New York Times*, April 22, 1982, C3.

36. S.S. Packard quoted in Weiss, "Educating for Clerical Work," 414.

37. Maule, "I Want to Be a Secretary," 94.

38. Eunice Fuller Barnard, "Portrait of the New York Secretary," *New York Times*, February 1, 1931, 6; Courtenay Marvin, "Grooming for Business," *Independent Woman*, January 1940, 17; Fred S. Cook, ed., *Secretaries on the Spot*, 2d. ed. (Kansas City, Mo.: National Secretaries Association (International), 1967), 59.

39. "When a Woman Reaches Forty," *San Francisco Chronicle Magazine*, September 26, 1920, 3.

40. Classified ad, *Chicago Tribune*, March 14, 1943, B9; Ruth McKay, "White Collar Girl," *Chicago Tribune*, April 3, 1943, 18, and March 31, 1945, 22.

41. Classified ad, *Chicago Tribune*, May 16, 1943, C11.

42. Ruth McKay, "White Collar Girl," *Chicago Tribune*, March 31, 1945, 22.

43. Quoted in Maud Robinson Toombs, "When a Woman Reaches Forty," *San Francisco Chronicle*, September 26, 1920, SM3; Gladys Torson, *How to Be a Hero to Your Secretary: A Handbook for Bosses* (New York: Greenberg, 1941), 105, 106; Helen and John Whitcomb, *Strictly for Secretaries*, rev. ed. (New York: McGraw-Hill Book, 1965), 22.

44. Mayo, *You Can Be an Executive Secretary*, 22; Elizabeth Gregg MacGibbon, *Manners in Business* (New York: Macmillan, 1936), 18, 12.

45. Chester Burger, *Survival in the Executive Jungle* (New York: Macmillan, 1964), 224–25.

CHAPTER 2: YOU'RE IN THE OFFICE NOW, MISS SEC

1. Lloyd Wendt, "The 'Office Wife' Is Out!" *Chicago Tribune*, September 1, 1946, F3.

2. John Robert Powers and Mary Sue Miller, *Secrets of Charm* (Philadelphia: John C. Winston, 1954), vii; Marie Lauria, *How to Be a Good Secretary* (New York: Frederick Fell, 1969), 59, emotive italics in the original.

3. Lloyd Wendt, "Meet Miss Secretary," *Chicago Tribune*, November 16, 1941, E2; Frances Maule, "I Want to Be a Secretary," *Independent Woman*, March 1941, 94; Helen Whitcomb and Rosalind Lang, *Charm: The Career Girl's Guide to Business and Personal Success* (New York: Gregg Division, McGraw-Hill, 1964), 4.

4. Wendt, "Meet Miss Secretary," E2; Lauria, *How to Be a Good Secretary*, 72.

5. Whitcomb and Lang, *Charm*, 137.

6. Gilmore, *The Successful Secretary* (1951), 12; Parker Publishing Editorial Staff, *The Successful Secretary* (West Nyack, N.Y.: Parker Publishing, 1964), 61. There are two separate advice manuals titled *The Successful Secretary* referenced in this book. One is a pamphlet by Sybil Lee Gilmore, referred to in the text as *The Successful Secretary* (1951). The other is a hardcover book by the Parker Publishing Company Editorial Staff, referenced as *The Successful Secretary* (1964). (It could be worse. I own yet another pamphlet with the same title, but it didn't make the cut for inclusion here.)

7. Ibid.; Jean Vermes, *The Secretary's Guide to Dealing with People* (West Nyack, N.Y.: Parker Publishing, 1964), 57.

8. Ellen Lane Spencer, *The Efficient Secretary* (New York: Frederick A. Stokes, 1917) 26, 27; Helen Dare, "The Wifely Ban on the Pretty Girl in Her Husband's Employ," *San Francisco Chronicle*, January 23, 1912, 7.

9. Whitcomb and Lang, *Charm*, 137.

10. Joan Beck, "Women Bank Employees Invest in Charm Schools," *Chicago Tribune*, February 16, 1953, A1; Ruth McKay, "White Collar Girl," *Chicago Tribune*, December 20, 1961, B12.

11. Vermes, *Secretary's Guide to Dealing with People*, 36; Parker, Publishing Editorial Staff, *Successful Secretary*, 36.

12. Lucy Graves Mayo, *Executive Secretary*, 41; Eleanor Gilbert, *The Ambitious Woman in Business* (New York: Funk and Wagnalls, 1916), 138.

13. Marie L. Carney, *The Secretary and Her Job* (Charlottesville, Va.: Business Book, 1939), 279.

14. Classified ads, *New York Times*, January 30, 1923, 37.

15. "Wide Bias Found in Job Agencies," *New York Times*, July 21, 1963, 39.

16. "Connecticut Jobs Open to Negroes," *New York Times*, July 26, 1946, 23; "Says Washington Secretarial Schools Bar Negroes," *Jet*, January 31, 1963, 24; Donald Janson, "Kansas City Negroes Win Gain; 3 Schools to Integrate Classes," *New York Times*, June 23, 1963, 64.

17. Farnsworth Fowle, "Negroes to Train for Office Work," *New York Times*, October 4, 1963, 18; Charles Grutzner, "Skilled Negroes in Demand Here," *New York Times*, July 21, 1963, 1.

18. Helen Whitcomb and Jon Whitcomb, *Strictly for Secretaries*, rev. ed. (New York: McGraw-Hill Book, 1965), 118–19.

19. Vermes, *Secretary's Guide to Dealing with People*, 41.

20. Fred S. Cook, ed., *Secretaries on the Spot*, 2nd ed. (Kansas City, Mo.: National Secretaries Association (International), 1967), 55, 200.

21. Emily Post, *Etiquette* (New York: Funk & Wagnalls, 1943), 671–73.

22. Rae Chatfield Ayer, "Are Men Better Secretaries? No!—Rae Chatfield Ayer," *Rotarian*, November 1940, 58; T/Sgt Thomas F. Kerrigan, "'Classification 213,'" *Gregg Writer*, April 1946, 396; Donald Beisel, "You Never Can Tell," *Gregg Writer*, September 1946, 17; Jean Thomas, "Times Have Changed," *Gregg Writer*, February 1947, 282; Elias John Pepper as told to James Joseph, "Secretary in a Man's World," *Today's Secretary*, April 1953, 396.

23. Barbara H. Nalepa, "The World of the Typewriter," *Junior Secretary*, October 1967, 15.

24. Nellie Brighton, "'Heaven Protects the *Working* Girl': A Modern Concept of the Situation," *Gregg Writer*, April 1946, 406.

25. "Tessie Asks The Experts," *Today's Secretary*, January 1953, 229; Rae Chatfield Ayer, "Are Men Better Secretaries? No!— Rae Chatfield Ayer," *Rotarian*, November 1940, 32; Clare H. Jennings, "Should Your Child Be a Secretary?" New York Life Insurance Company ad, *Life*, March 17, 1958, 9.

26. Sharon Johnson, "More Men Are Diving into the Secretarial Pool," *New York Times*, November 5, 1975, 55.

27. John L. Scott, "'Take a Letter, Darling' Ingenious Light Comedy," *Los Angeles Times*, June 5, 1942, 17; Stanford M. Lyman, "From Matrimony to Malaise: Men and Women in the American Film, 1930–1980," *International Journal of Politics, Culture, and Society*, vol. 1, no. 2 (Winter 1987), 80; Christine Doudna, "Male Secretaries: New Men of Letters," *New York Times Magazine*, April 5, 1981, 121; Bernard F. Dick, *Forever Mame* (Jackson: University of Mississippi Press, 2006), 81.

28. Lucy Graves Mayo, *You Can Be an Executive Secretary* (New York: Macmillan, 1965) 239; Faith Baldwin, *The Office Wife* (New York: Grosset and Dunlap, 1930), 61–62; Gladys Torson, *The Art of Being a Successful Business Girl* (New York: New Home Library, 1943), 179; Gladys Torson, *How to Be a Hero to Your Secretary: A Handbook for Bosses* (New York: Greenburg, 1941), 89.

29. Abigail Van Buren, "She's Also the Boss's Secretary," *Los Angeles Times*, February 22, 1967, E5. Abby told her to tell the boss she was quitting unless her job resumed "its original character."

30. *Saturday Evening Post* photo in Lupton, *Mechanical Brides: Women and Machines from Home to Office* (New York: Princeton Architectural Press, 1993), 55.

31. Helen Dare, "The Wifely Ban on the Pretty Girl in Her Husband's Employ," *San Francisco Chronicle*, January 23, 1912, 7.

32. Bennett Cerf, ed., *Laughing Stock* (New York: Grossett and Dunlap, 1945), 153.

33. Margaret L. Helfrich, "The Generalized Role of the Executive's Wife," *Marriage and Family Living*, vol. 23, no. 4 (November 1961), 386.

34. Hubbard Hoover and Isabelle Macrae Hoover, "The Pursuit of Happiness," *Los Angeles Times*, December 26, 1948, C11.

35. Ibid.

36. "Secretaries Quash Idea They Like to Romance With Their Bosses," *Los Angeles Times*, October 2, 1949, 21; Dare, "Wifely Ban on the Pretty Girl in Her Husband's Employ," 7, secretary quoted in Ruth McKay, "White Collar Girl," *Chicago Tribune*, December 23, 1941, 21.

37. Bernice C. Turner, *The Private Secretary's Manual: A Practical Handbook for Secretaries and Their Executives*, rev. ed. (New York: Prentice Hall, 1943), 8.

38. Andrew Hamilton, "How About a Cup of Coffee?" *Los Angeles Times*, July 9, 1955, A5; Richard Rutter, "The Coffee Break, Asset or Liability, Seems Here to Stay," *New York Times*, February 10, 1956, 29.

39. Parker Publishing Company Editorial Staff, *Successful Secretary*, 38.

40. Mayo, *You Can Be an Executive Secretary*, 241.

41. Paula Fass, *The Damned and the Beautiful: American Youth in the 1920's* (New York: Oxford University Press, 1979), 294.

42. Parker Publishing Editorial Staff, *Successful Secretary*, 40–41.

CHAPTER 3: YOUR BOSS

1. Bolt quoted by Anson Campbell, *Kitty Unfoiled: An Informal Portrait of the American Secretary* (Pittsburgh: Reuter and Bragdon, 1952), 51.

2. Marie Lauria, *How to Be a Good Secretary* (New York: Frederick Fell, 1969), 40, 42.

3. Lucy Graves Mayo, *You Can Be an Executive Secretary*, (New York: Macmillan, 1965), 35, 37; Helen Gurley Brown, *Sex and the Office* (New York: Bernard Geis Associates, 1964), 135.

4. Chester Burger, *Survival in the Executive Jungle* (New York: Macmillan, 1964), 220.

5. Nadine Brozan, "A Demand to Be More Than Just 'Office Girls,'" *New York Times*, October 17, 1975, 45; "somebody's secretary," quoted in "On the Side with E.V. Durling," *Los Angeles Times*, October 6, 1938, A1.

6. Jean Vermes, *The Secretary's Guide to Dealing with People* (West Nyack, N.Y.: Parker Publishing, 1964), 89; Ruth McKay, "White Collar Girl," *Chicago Tribune*, December 6, 1941, 19.

7. Parker Publishing Editorial Staff, *The Successful Secretary* (West Nyack, N.Y.: Parker Publishing, 1964), 29.

8. Norma Lee Browning, "Secretary Who Wed Her Boss Finds Marriage Is a Job, Too," *Chicago Tribune*, March 27, 1952, A7.

9. Vermes, *The Secretary's Guide to Dealing with People*, 9.

10. Ruth McKay, "White Collar Girl," *Chicago Tribune*, December 1, 1941, 21.

11. Sarah Louise Arnold, "The College Woman as Secretary," in Agnes F. Perkins, ed., *Vocations for the Trained Woman* (New York: Longmans, Green, 1910), 204; Edward Jones Kilduff, *The Private Secretary: His Duties and Opportunities* (New York: Century, 1916), 294, 295, 298–99; Helen B. Glad-

wyn, "How I Became a Confidential Secretary," *Ladies' Home Journal*, September 1916, 32.

12. Gladys Torson, *The Art of Being a Successful Business Girl*, (New York: New Home Library, 1943), 142–43; Gladys Torson, *How to Be a Hero to Your Secretary: A Handbook for Bosses* (New York: Greenburg, 1941), 77–78.

13. Editors of *Esquire, Esquire Etiquette: A Guide to Business, Sports, and Social Conduct* (New York: J. B. Lippincott, 1953) 13, 14.

14. "Secretaries Pick Superlative One," *New York Times*, July 24, 1954, 15; Elizabeth Goodland, "The Boss Is Boss, Secretaries Advised," *Los Angeles Times*, July 20, 1961, A1; Helen Whitcomb and Rosalind Lang, *Charm: The Career Girl's Guide to Business and Personal Success* (New York: Gregg Division, McGraw-Hill, 1964), 301.

15. "Stores to Open Gift Boutiques for Christmas," *New York Times*, November 10, 1964, 52.

16. Ruth McKay, "White Collar Girl. Secretary to the President," *Chicago Tribune*, May 3, 1948, A7.

17. List quoted in Margery W. Davies, *Woman's Place Is at the Typewriter: Office Work and Office Workers, 1870–1930* (Philadelphia: Temple University Press, 1982) 155–56.

18. Bernice C. Turner, *The Private Secretary's Manual: A Practical Handbook for Secretaries and Their Executives*, rev. ed. (New York: Prentice Hall, 1943), 98.

19. Ruth McKay, "White Collar Girl," *Chicago Tribune*, March 2, 1942, 20.

20. Vermes, *Secretary's Guide to Dealing with People* 174; Browning "Secretary Who Wed Her Boss Finds Marriage Is a Job, Too," A7; Helen Gurley Brown, *Sex and the Single Girl* (originally pub. 1962; New York: Pocket Books, 1963), 93.

21. Parker Publishing Editorial Staff, *Successful Secretary*, 294.

22. Deirdre Carmody, "International Secretary of the Year Is One in 27,000," *New York Times*, July 17, 1970, 29.

23. Lucy Mayo, *You Can Be an Executive Secretary*, 39; Louise Hollister Scott, *How to Be a Successful Secretary* (New York: Harper & Brothers, 1937), 160.

24. *How to Be a Super-Secretary* (New York: Remington Rand, 1949), unpaginated; Lauria, *How to Be a Good Secretary*, 70; Vermes, *Secretary's Guide to Dealing with People*, 20; Ashley Montagu quoted in Betty Hannah Hoffman, "Femininity. What Is It? Who Has It? Do You?" *Ladies' Home Journal*, July 1962, 57.

25. Scott, *How to Be a Successful Secretary*, 89; Elizabeth Gregg MacGibbon, *Manners in Business* (New York: Macmillan, 1936), 66.

26. Scott, *How to Be a Successful Secretary*, 89, 90; Sybil Lee Gilmore, *The Successful Secretary* (Chicago: Dartnell, 1951), 53; *How to Be a Super-Secretary*, unpaginated, ellipses in the original; Torson, *Art of Being a Successful Business Girl*, 104; Sue Avery, "Bosses Receive Tips on the Treatment of Women," *Los Angeles Times*, September 8, 1968, SG B8; MacGibbon, *Manners in Business*, 55.

27. Lauria, *How to Be a Good Secretary*, 61.

28. Mary Kathleen Benét, The Secretarial Ghetto (New York: McGraw-Hill Book, 1973), 11; Parker Publishing Editorial Staff, *Successful Secretary*, 16; Whitcomb and Lang, *Charm*, 317.

29. *How to Be a Super-Secretary*, unpaginated; MacGibbon, *Manners in Business*, 66; Mary Elizabeth Wright, "Do You Act Like A Good Secretary?" *Today's Secretary*, April 1953, 404.

30. Vermes, *Secretary's Guide to Dealing with People*, 55.

31. Chester Burger, *Survival in the Executive Jungle* (New York: Macmillan, 1964), 231; MacGibbon, *Manners in Business*, 68.

32. MacGibbon, *Manners in Business*, 69; "New Year's Resolutions I Wish My Boss Would Make!" *Today's Secretary*, January 1953, 235, italics in original.

33. Editors of *Esquire*, *Esquire Etiquette*, 25; italics in original; Gilmore, *Successful Secretary*, 11.

34. *How to Be a Super-Secretary*, unpaginated; Burger, *Survival in the Executive Jungle*, 232.

35. Lucy Graves Mayo, *Wendy Scott: Secretary* (New York: Dodd, Mead, 1961), 29; "She was an officious busybody," at http://207.58.168.16/forum/viewtopic .php?f=29&t=1550; "an interfering old woman," at http://wordnetweb.princeton .edu/perl/webwn?s=officious; Scott, *How to Be a Successful Secretary*, 162; Parker Publishing Editorial Staff, *Successful Secretary*, 73–75.

36. Editors of *Esquire*, *Esquire Etiquette*, 25; Eleanor Gilbert, *The Ambitious Woman in Business* (New York: Funk and Wagnalls, 1916), 256.

37. Mayo, *You Can Be an Executive Secretary*, 10, 11; Vermes, *Secretary's Guide to Dealing with People*, 13.

38. Quoted in Benét, *Secretarial Ghetto*, 104.

39. Scott, *How to Be a Successful Secretary*, 64; Mayo, *You Can Be an Executive Secretary*, 90.

40. Harford Powel, *Good Jobs for Good Girls* (New York: Vanguard Press, 1949), 1; Turner, *Private Secretary's Manual*, 314, 315; Kiplinger, quoted in Caroline Bird, *Born Female*, rev. ed. (New York: David McKay, 1974), 84; Roy Rowan, "Can the C.E.O. Hang On to His Secret Weapon?" *Fortune*, March 12, 1979, 120.

41. Turner, *Private Secretary's Manual*, 10.

42. Ibid., 16.

43. "Cheer Up Your Chores," *Today's Secretary*, October 1952, 81.

44. Torson, *Art of Being a Successful Business Girl*, 121; Whitcomb and Lang, *Charm*, 301; "Secretaries Tell Job Types," *Los Angeles Times*, April 4, 1960, A1.

45. Monica L. Haynes, "Call Me Indispensable," *Pittsburgh Post-Gazette*, April 21, 1998, D1; Klemfuss quoted in Mamie J. Meredith, "'Mimeo Minnie,' 'Sadie, the Office Secretary,' and Other Women Office Workers in America," *American Speech,* December 1955, 300.

46. The observance has had its name changed twice so far: to "Professional Secretaries Day/Week" in the 1980s, then to "Administrative Professionals Day/Week" in 2000. *Time*, May 26, 1952, 96–97.

47. "Sidelights on the Financial and Business Developments of the Day," *New York Times*, May 28, 1952, 43; "Sidelights on the Financial and Business Developments of the Day," *New York Times*, April 15, 1953, 47.

48. "Does the Trained Nurse or the Stenographer Have the Better Chance of Matrimony?" *San Francisco Chronicle*, December 17, 1905, 7; Jerry Weil, *Office Wife* (New York: Signet Books, 1957), back cover copy.

CHAPTER 4: SINGLE SECS, MARRIED SECS, AND THE LOOMING SHADOW OF THE OFFICE WIFE

1. C. Wright Mills, *White Collar: The American Middle Classes* (New York: Oxford University Press, 1951), 203.

2. Elizabeth Cook and business teacher quoted in Sharon Hart Strom, *Beyond the Typewriter: Gender, Class, and the Origins of Modern American Office Work, 1900–1930* (Urbana: University of Illinois Press, 1992), 355; Taft quoted in Eleanor Gilbert, *The Ambitious Woman in Business* (New York: Funk and Wagnalls, 1916), 11–12.

3. Elizabeth Gregg MacGibbon, *Manners in Business* (New York: Macmillan,

1936), 60; Agnes F. Perkins, ed., *Vocations for the Trained Woman* (New York: Longmans, Green, 1910), 203; Ellen Lane Spencer, *The Efficient Secretary* (New York: Frederick A. Stokes, 1917), 167–68.

4. *Smith College News* quoted in Nancy F. Cott, *The Grounding of Modern Feminism* (New Haven: Yale University Press, 1987), 181; MacGibbon, *Manners in Business*, 60; Frances Avery Faunce, with Frederick G. Nichols, *Secretarial Efficiency* (New York: McGraw-Hill, 1939), 54, quoted in Margery W. Davies, *Woman's Place Is at the Typewriter*, 148.

5. May Christie, "America Only Country Where Girls Can Really Afford Not to Marry," *San Francisco Chronicle*, December 9, 1922, 13.

6. Lupton, Mechanical Brides, 45; Achmed Abdullah, "Ruth and Peter," *The Washington Post*, chapter 1, August 15, 1926, M13; and chapter 4, August 20, 1926, 9. Abdullah was the pseudonym of Russian-born author and screenwriter Alexander Nicholayevitch Romanoff.

7. Faith Baldwin, *The Office Wife* (New York: Grosset and Dunlap, 1930), 95.

8. Julia Collier Harris, "The Spirit of Revolt in Current Fiction," *Journal of Social Forces*, vol. 3, no. 3 (March 1925), 428.

9. Ellen Lupton, *Mechanical Brides: Women and Machines from Home to Office* (New York: Cooper Hewitt National Museum of Design and Princeton Architectural Press, 1993), 45; Baldwin, *Office Wife*, 11, 23.

10. Baldwin, *Office Wife*, 38.

11. Ibid., 42, 130, 204.

12. *Variety* quoted by Jeremy Arnold, "The Office Wife," *TCM Spotlight*, at http://www.tcm.com/tcmdb/title.jsp?stid=3497&category=Articles (accessed May 21, 2008).

13. Robert Van Gelder, "An Interview with Miss Faith Baldwin," *New York Times*, August 9, 1942, 2; Baldwin, *Office Wife*, xi, x; Thyra Sampter Winslow, "The Office Wife," *Washington Post Magazine*, August 9, 1931, 7, 11; Doris Blake, "Doris Warns Business Girls Office Devotee Ends an Emotional Bankrupt," *Chicago Tribune*, July 10, 1932, E6.

14. Ynez S. quoted in Alma Whitaker, "Let's Talk It Over!" *Los Angeles Times*, April 15, 1939, A5; "Secretaries Quash Idea They Like to Romance with Their Bosses," *Los Angeles Times*, October 2, 1949, 21.

15. Clifford R. Adams and Vance O. Packard, *How to Pick A Mate, The Guide to a Happy Marriage* (New York: E. P. Dutton, 1946), 16.

16. "Jilted 'Office Wife' Tells of Killing Lawyer," *Chicago Tribune*, October 18, 1938, 7; "Blonde Killer's Fate Near Jury; Friend Quizzed," *Chicago Tribune*, December 20, 1938, 5; "Office Wife May Learn Her Fate In Slaying Today," *Chicago Tribune*, December 21, 1938, 5; "Office Wife Gets 14 to 15 Yrs. For Killing Lawyer," *Chicago Tribune*, December 23, 1938, 16.

17. Lester David, "Could *You* Be Blackmailed?" *Los Angeles Times*, December 16, 1951, H7.

18. Norma Lee Browning, "Wanted: A Husband!" *Chicago Tribune*, February 17, 1952, C4.

19. Ibid.

20. Strom, *Beyond the Typewriter*, 8; "Wants a Bachelor Girl," *New York Times*, October 17, 1911, 20.

21. Louise Hollister Scott, *How to Be a Successful Secretary*, (New York: Harper and Brothers, 1937), 37.

22. Lloyd Wendt, "Meet Miss Secretary," *Chicago Tribune*, November 16, 1941, 8.

23. Kathleen McLaughlin, "Shall Wives Work?" *New York Times Magazine*, July 23, 1939, 5

24. Ibid.; Hilles quoted in"Call to Woman's Party," *New York Times*, October 16, 1933, 11.

25. Bess M. Wilson, "Must Career Women Be Single?" *Los Angeles Times*, March 23, 1941, I11.

26. Ruth McKay, "White Collar Girl," *Chicago Tribune*, November 15, 1941, 15.

27. Patricia Flynn, *So You Want to Be an Executive Secretary* (New York: Mac-fadden Books, 1963), 52, 53. Clairol's "Does she or doesn't she?" campaign debuted in 1956 and ran in print or on television through the 1970s.

28. MacGibbon, *Manners in Business*, 147, 149.

29. Jean Vermes, *The Secretary's Guide to Dealing with People* (West Nyack, N.Y.: Parker Publishing, 1964), 186–87.

30. Lucy Graves Mayo, *You Can Be an Executive Secretary* (New York: Macmillan, 1965), 234–35.

31. Service manager quoted in Strom, *Beyond the Typewriter*, 391; Sybil Lee Gilmore, *The Successful Secretary* (Chicago: Dartnell, 1951), 47; Frederick M. Rossiter, *Bride and Groom* (Los Angeles: Monogram Books, 1953), 168.

32. Clifford R. Adams, "Making Marriage Work," *Ladies' Home Journal*, January

1951, 26; and November 1955, 56; Ruth Shallcross, "Empty Cradles?" *Independent Woman*, October 1940, 342.

33. Ruth Shallcross, "Empty Cradles?" 342.

34. Vermes, *Secretary's Guide to Dealing with People*, 182.

CHAPTER 5: AROUND THE DESK WE GO

1. Helen Gurley Brown, "At Work, Sexual Electricity Sparks Creativity," *Wall Street Journal*, October 29, 1991, A22; Helen Gurley Brown, *Sex and the Office* (New York: Bernard Geis Associates, 1964), 285–86.

2. Brown, *Sex and the Office*, 286.

3. Carol Brock, "For the Hostess," *Good Housekeeping*, December 1949, 133.

4. Elizabeth Gregg MacGibbon, *Manners in Business* (New York: Macmillan, 1936), 116–17, 89; Louise Hollister Scott, *How to Be a Successful Secretary* (New York: Harper and Brothers, 1937), 102; Gladys Torson, *The Art of Being a Successful Business Girl*, (New York: New Home Library, 1943), 174; Emily Post, *Etiquette* (New York: Funk and Wagnalls, 1943), 661.

5. "Stenographers and Typewriters a Drug on the Labor Market," *New York Times Magazine*, April 17, 1904, 5.

6. Mary Mortimer Maxwell, "The School Teacher, The Stenographer, and Matrimony," *New York Times Magazine*, August 26, 1906, 2.

7. Ellen Lane Spencer, *The Efficient Secretary* (New York: Frederick A. Stokes, 1917), 99; Helen Whitcomb and Rosalind Lang, *Charm: The Career Girl's Guide to Business and Personal Success* (New York: Gregg Division, McGraw-Hill, 1964), 441; Alma Archer, *Your Power as a Woman* (New York: Hazel Bishop, Inc., 1957), 215, 211–12.

8. Archer, *Your Power as a Woman*, 211; Helen Whitcomb and Rosalind Lang, *Charm: The Career Girl's Guide to Business and Personal Success* (New York: Gregg Division, McGraw-Hill, 1964), 441.

9. Helen Gurley Brown, *Sex and the Office* (New York: Bernard Geis Associates, 1964), 22, 30.

10. Ibid, 59.

11. Ibid., 185, 193, 220–21.

12. Brown, "At Work," A22.

13. Spencer, *Efficient Secretary*, 99.

14. "Wanted a Typewriter," *New York Times*, October 10, 1888, 4.

15. "Youngest," *Time*, August 11, 1924, at http://www.time.com/time/magazine/article/0,9171,718892,00.html (accessed September 4, 2007). Fans of AMC's *Mad Men* television show will recognize a toned-down version of "scuttle" from the 2007 episode, "Nixon vs. Kennedy."

16. "Flirting Bosses to Be Listed," *Los Angeles Times*, June 15, 1922, I6; Julie Berebitsky, "The Joy of Work: Helen Gurley Brown, Gender, and Sexuality in the White-Collar Office," *Journal of the History of Sexuality*, vol. 15, no. 1, January 2006, 104; Lois Pemberton, *The Stork Didn't Bring You* (New York: Hermitage Press, 1948), 149, 113. In her article, Berebitsky goes on to show how Helen Gurley Brown, by "'outing' workplace sexuality" in the pages of *Sex and the Single Girl* and *Sex and the Office*, "hoped to give individual women a measure of the power that men derived from being sexual agents in the office." Berebitsky, "The Joy of Work," 93.

17. Mrs. Hester M. Poole, "Social Graces For Every-day Service In the Home," *Good Housekeeping*, March 1898, 94.

18. Eleanor Gilbert, *The Ambitious Woman in Business* (New York: Funk and Wagnalls, 1916), 141.

19. Scott, *How to Be a Successful Secretary*, 104; Torson, *Art of Being a Successful Business Girl*, 174, 173; Fred S. Cook, ed., *Secretaries on the Spot*, 2nd ed. (Kansas City, Mo.: National Secretaries Association (International), 1967), 148; MacGibbon, *Manners in Business*, 118.

20. Marie L. Carney, *The Secretary and Her Job* (Charlottesville, Va.: Business Book, 1939), 292.

21. Cook, *Secretaries on the Spot*, 108, 221.

22. Lloyd Wendt, "Meet Miss Secretary," *Chicago Tribune*, November 16, 1941, E2.

23. Mary Hamman and the Editors of *Mademoiselle*, *The Mademoiselle Handbook* (New York: McGraw-Hill Book, 1946), 55.

24. Amy Abbott, "Keep the Office Wolf Away," *Los Angeles Times*, July 13, 1958, D5.

25. "'White Lie' Condoned," *Los Angeles Times*, December 3, 1970, D3.

26. Gladys Torson, *How to Be a Hero to Your Secretary: A Handbook for Bosses* (New York: Greenburg, 1941), 84.

27. Scott, *How to Be a Successful Secretary*, 104; Hamman and the Editors of *Mademoiselle*, *Mademoiselle Handbook*, 52.

28. William Borders, "Holidays Getting Weekend Stretch," *New York Times*,

December 30, 1964, 23; Gordon Hake, "Office Party (Yule)," *New York Times Magazine*, December 21, 1952, 22; Hal Boyle, "Wives Take a Hand," *Los Angeles Times*, December 9, 1952, 12; "Man Bussed Office Girls; Home Busted," *Los Angeles Times*, October 4, 1958, B1; Warren Strugatch, "L.I. Work: Did the Grinch Steal the Office Party, Too?" *New York Times*, December 10, 2000, LI8.

29. A.E. Hotchner, "The Drunken Office Party," *Los Angeles Times*, December 13, 1953, J7; Hal Boyle, "Wives Take Hand," *Los Angeles Times*, December 9, 1952, 12, Brown, *Sex and the Office*, 138; "Boss Pays for Actions of Office Party-goer," *BusinessWeek*, May 1, 1954, 139; "Why Office Parties Go Wrong," *BusinessWeek*, November 30, 1957, 83; Dorothy Cameron Disney, "Can This Marriage Be Saved?" *Ladies' Home Journal*, December 1957, 55; "Office-Party Drinks Can Lead to Death, U.S. Adviser Warns," *New York Times*, December 17, 1966, 35; Philip Hager, "Company Found Responsible for Death After Office Party," *Los Angeles Times*, October 31, 1974, A1.

30. MacGibbon, *Manners in Business*, 133, 134.

31. Vermes, *Secretary's Guide to Dealing with People*, 89; Parker Publishing Editorial Staff, *The Successful Secretary*, (West Nyack, N.Y.: Parker Publishing, 1964), 46.

32. Strugatch, "L.I. Work: Did the Grinch Steal the Office Party, Too?" LI8; Kelley Holland, "The Office Party, as a Tightrope Walk," *New York Times*, November 25, 2007, 17.

CHAPTER 6: STEPPING STONE OR MILLSTONE?

1. "Women Who Lead the Way," *New York Times*, February 20, 1921, 5; "First Woman Officer Elected by a National Bank in Bronx," *New York Times*, May 17, 1931, 41.

2. Julie Berebitsky, "The Joy of Work: Helen Gurley Brown, Gender, and Sexuality in the White-Collar Office," *Journal of the History of Sexuality*, vol. 15, no. 1, (January 2006), 95.

3. Helen Whitcomb and John Whitcomb, *Strictly for Secretaries*, rev. ed. (New York: McGraw-Hill Book, 1965), 15.

4. "Career Women," *Los Angeles Times*, May 20, 1940, A7.

5. Eleanor Gilbert, *The Ambitious Woman in Business* (New York: Funk and

Wagnalls, 1916), 353; Eunice Fuller Barnard, "Portrait of the New York Secretary," *New York Times*, February 1, 1931, 6.

6. Louise Hollister Scott, *How to Be a Successful Secretary* (New York: Harper and Brothers, 1937), 4; Clare H. Jennings, "Should Your Child Be a Secretary?" New York Life Insurance Company ad, *Life*, March 17, 1958, 9.

7. Gladys Torson, *The Art of Being a Successful Business Girl* (New York: New Home Library, 1943), 119–20.

8. Lucy Graves Mayo, *You Can Be an Executive Secretary*, (New York: Macmillan, 1965), 6; Lynn Lilliston, "Secretarial Skills Go Long Way in Employment Field," *Los Angeles Times*, June 5, 1966, D10.

9. Lilliston, "Secretarial Skills Go Long Way," D10.

10. Mary Schauffler, "Impressions of Secretarial Work," 4, quoted in Sharon Hartman Strom, *Beyond the Typewriter: Gender, Class, and the Origins of Modern American Office Work, 1900–1930* (Urbana: University of Illinois Press, 1992), 191.

11. Strom, *Beyond the Typewriter*, 190.

12. Report quoted in Jean Vermes, *The Secretary's Guide to Dealing with People* (West Nyack, N.Y.: Parker Publishing, 1964), 194.

13. Bernadine Morris, "Secretaries: A Little Irked but Generally They're Happy," *New York Times*, July 8, 1974, 34.

14. Nadine Brozan, "A Demand to Be More Than Just 'Office Girls,'" *New York Times*, October 17, 1975, 45.

15. Patricia Flynn, *So You Want to Be an Executive Secretary* (New York: Macfadden Books, 1963), 23; Lucy Graves Mayo, *You Can Be an Executive Secretary*, (New York: Macmillan, 1965), 2.

16. "Cardinal Warns of 'Career' Women," *New York Times*, January 22, 1934, 9; Elsie McCormick, "Every Woman Should Learn a Trade," *Good Housekeeping*, April 1952, 51; Chester Burger, *Survival in the Executive Jungle* (New York: Macmillan, 1964), 230–31.

17. Ibid., 227; Mary Hamman and the Editors of *Mademoiselle*, *The Mademoiselle Handbook* (New York: McGraw-Hill Book, 1946), 26; Helen and John Whitcomb, *Strictly for Secretaries*, 53.

18. Hendrik de Leeuw, *Woman: The Dominant Sex, From Bloomers to Bikinis* (London, Arco Publishers, 1957), 32.

19. Arthur J. Mandy, as told to Jack Harrison Pollack, "American Wives Are Too Bossy!" *Los Angeles Times*, July 19, 1959, I7, I9.

20. Ibid., 17.

21. "Career Women Blamed for Men's Moral Lapses," *Los Angeles Times*, April 30, 1948, 13.

22. "Career Women Doused with Academic Cold Water," *New York Times*, June 16, 1939, 7.

23. Russell, as told to Jack Stewart, "Why I'm Sorry for Career Women," *Los Angeles Times*, January 27, 1957, N9.

24. Ibid., 9, 31; the role was that of Rosemary in *Picnic* (1955).

25. Lawrence E. Davies, "Peace Study Urged by Business Women," *New York Times*, July 6, 1950, 24; Bess M. Wilson, "Women's Activities," *Los Angeles Times*, October 17, 1943, D4.

26. Flynn, *So You Want to Be an Executive Secretary*, 13–14.

27. Vermes, *Secretary's Guide to Dealing with People*, 203; Elizabeth M. Fowler, "Harvard Business School Goes Coed With Ivy Aplomb," *New York Times*, February 21, 1964, 39.

28. Olga Knopf, "Marriage and a Job," *Ladies' Home Journal*, March 1941, 96.

29. Ruth Shallcross, "Empty Cradles?" *Independent Woman*, October 1940, 342.

30. "How to Make Your Budget Balance," quoted in Ruth McKay, "White Collar Girl," *Chicago Tribune*, November 25, 1941, 19.

31. Vermes, *Secretary's Guide to Dealing with People*, 191.

32. Ibid., 191–92.

33. Olga Knopf, "Marriage and a Job," *Ladies' Home Journal*, March 1941, 96.

34. Mary Hamman and the Editors of *Mademoiselle*, *The Mademoiselle Handbook* (New York: McGraw-Hill Book, 1946), 33, italics in original; Mildred Adams, "When the Career Woman Vies With Man," *New York Times Magazine*, October 26, 1930, 23.

35. *How to Be a Super-Secretary*, (New York: Remington Rand, 1949), unpaginated.

36. "Case 17: Clerk 'Steals' Secretary's Idea," in Fred S. Cook, ed., *Secretaries on the Spot*, 2nd ed. (Kansas City, Missouri: The National Secretaries Association [International], 1967), 56–57, 201; Vermes, *Secretary's Guide to Dealing with People*, 43.

37. "Career Women Doused with Academic Cold Water," *Los Angeles Times*, June 16, 1939, 7.

38. "Olive Ann Can Handle This," *Fortune*, May 1947, 144, 146.

39. John Robert Powers and Mary Sue Miller, *Secrets of Charm* (Philadelphia: John C. Winston, 1954), 363.

40. Hamman and the Editors of Mademoiselle, *Mademoiselle Handbook*, 53.

41. Helen Whitcomb and Rosalind Lang, *Charm: The Career Girl's Guide to Business and Personal Success* (New York: Gregg Division, McGraw-Hill Book, 1964), 316.

42. Mary Merryfield, "Where Am I Going besides the Office? *Chicago Tribune*, February 25, 1962, E1.

43. Ibid.

44. Vermes, *Secretary's Guide to Dealing with People*, 200.

45. "Profile of Youth: Earning a Living" *Ladies' Home Journal*, June 1950, 48, 49.

46. Helen Gurley Brown, *Sex and the Office* (New York: Bernard Geis Associates, 1964), 71.

47. Richard Reeves, "Power!" *New York Times Book Review*, September 21, 1975, 4; "Book Ends," *New York Times Book Review*, August 24, 1975, 33; Christopher Lehmann-Haupt, "Books of the Times," *New York Times*, October 21, 1977, C-29; Michael Korda, *Success!* (New York: Random House, 1977), 197.

48. Ibid., 187, 197.

49. Ibid., 192–93.

50. Ibid., 191.

CHAPTER 7: GET YOUR OWN DAMN COFFEE

1. Charlotte Curtis, "Miss America Pageant Is Picketed by 100 Women," *New York Times*, September 8, 1968, 81; Peter Babcox, "Meet the Women Of the Revolution, 1969," *New York Times Magazine*, February 9, 1969, 34; Alice Echols, *Daring to Be Bad: Radical Feminism in America 1967–1975* (Minneapolis: University of Minnesota Press, 1989), 93.

2. Bernadine Morris, "Secretaries: A Little Irked But Generally They're Happy," *New York Times*, July 8, 1974, 34.

3. Caroline Bird, *Born Female*, rev. ed. (New York: David Kay, 1974), 50.

4. Babcox, "Meet the Women of the Revolution," 91.

5. Linda Charlton, "Women March Down Fifth in Equality Drive," *New York Times*, August 27, 1970, 30.

6. Marilyn Bender, "A Good Woman Is Hard to Find," *New York Times*, August 6, 1972, 7.

7. Olivetti ad, *Life*, April 28, 1972, 25.

8. Olivetti ad, *New York*, March 20, 1972, 16.

9. Philip H. Dougherty, "Frank Agency Hails Longevity," *New York Times*, March 16, 1972, 80.

10. Olivetti ad at http://www.youtube.com/watch?v=a1dphpqOVDg; Lois quoted in Mark Kriegel, *Namath: A Biography* (New York: Penguin Books, 2004), 338–39.

11. Lacey Fosburgh, "Traditional Groups Prefer to Ignore Women's Lib," *New York Times*, August 26, 1970, 44.

12. Dillon quoted in Judy Klemesrud, "In Defense of the Secretary: 'Truth Is We're Not Unhappy,'" *New York Times*, December 13, 1972, 52; "nine million" in Judy Klemesrud, "Secretary Image A 'Tempest in a Typewriter'?" *New York Times*, March 7, 1972, 34.

13. "Secretary Self-Image on the Rise," *Los Angeles Times*, December 21, 1972, D13; Klemesrud, "In Defense of the Secretary," 52.

14. Fosburgh, "Traditional Groups Prefer to Ignore Women's Lib," 44.

15. Veteran secretary quoted in Walter Kiechel III, "Beyond the Liberated Secretary," *Fortune*, December 14, 1981, 173.

16. Anna Blumberg, "How to Stay Married," *New York Times*, September 10, 1935, 20; "Charges Bad Coffee to Wife," *New York Times*, May 17, 1900, 2; "Cow," *Time*, Monday, May 2, 1927, at http://www.time.com/time/magazine/article/0,9171,751699,00.html; Charlton, "Women March down Fifth in Equality Drive," 30.

17. Jack Geyer "She Does It All," *Los Angeles Times*, May 24, 1956, A5.

18. Harry Bernstein, "Coffee Chore," *Los Angeles Times*, November 9, 1974, D3; Mike Causey, "Secretary Wins in Coffee Pot Fight," *Washington Post*, March 21, 1974, F7; Nadine Brozan, "A Demand to Be More Than Just 'Office Girls,'" *New York Times*, October 17, 1975, 45.

19. "Won't Serve Coffee, She Files Suit," *Chicago Tribune*, February 3, 1977, 3; "Coffee Case—Grounds for Protest," *Chicago Tribune*, February 4, 1977, 3; Harriet Sigerman, ed., *The Columbia Documentary History of American Women Since 1941* (New York: Columbia University Press, 2003), 123; Edward Baumann, "Followup," *Chicago Tribune*, July 4, 1977, 12.

20. Both quoted in Pat Colander, "Secretaries Hoping to File Injustices for Good," *Chicago Tribune*, April 23, 1975, C3.

21. Kathleen Hendrix, "Executive Secretaries, Inc.: To Sir With Love," *Los Angeles Times*, October 20, 1974, G17.

22. Gloria Charnes, "Speak Out," *Chicago Tribune*, April 18, 1977, C4.

23. Letters to the Editor, *New York Times Magazine*, May 3, 1981, 39.

24. Barbara Bry, "Fewer Want to Be 'Just a Secretary,'" *Los Angeles Times*, October 6, 1979, 22; David Blum, "Take a Letter . . . Somebody? Please!" *New York Times*, November 13, 1977, F9.

25. Sharon Johnson, "More Men Are Diving into the Secretarial Pool," *New York Times*, November 5, 1975, 55; "More Secretaries," *Los Angeles Times*, March 29, 1972, B8.

26. Sharon Johnson, "More Men Are Diving Into the Secretarial Pool," *New York Times*, November 5, 1975, 55; "More Secretaries," B8; Laurie Johnson Albin Krebs, "Notes on People," *New York Times*, July 17, 1980, B8; Lynn Smith, "Ideas," *Los Angeles Times*, April 25, 1984, G1.

27. Andrew L. Yarrow, "Why Men Are Edging into the Secretarial Pool," *New York Times*, June 29, 1986, F6.

28. Olive Evans, "Secretary's Changing Office Role," *New York Times*, October 31, 1983, B12; "More Secretaries," B8.; Yarrow, "Why Men Are Edging into the Secretarial Pool," F6.

29. Johnson, "More Men Are Diving into the Secretarial Pool," 55. Converted to 2008 dollars, the wage gap was approximately $175 a week.

30. John Brownell, "Newsmakers. Watergate Break-In to Coffee Breakout," *Los Angeles Times*, January 28, 1982, OC2.

31. Edith Evans Asbury, "Secretaries, Taking a Break, Learn to Assert Rights, *New York Times*, July 16, 1980, B3.

CHAPTER 8: THE SPACE-AGE TYPING POOL

1. "The Voice-Operated Typewriter," *Scientific American*, February 8, 1913, 136, 147. A solenoid consists of a wire coil, often wrapped around a metallic core, that becomes magnetized when a current passes through it.

2. Ibid., 136, 147.

3. Martha Weinman Lear, The Amanuensis, Evolution and Revolution of the Secretary over Half a Century," *New York Times*, October 15, 1961, 121; Sam Dawson, "Where Will Sally Go?" *Evening Journal* (Lincoln, Neb.), February 7, 1955, 4, quoted in Mamie J. Meredith, "'Mimeo Minnie,' 'Sadie the Office Secretary,' and Other Women Office Workers in America," *American Speech*, December 1955, 299.

4. Gladys Torson, *The Art of Being a Successful Business Girl* (New York: New Home Library, 1943), 23–24.

5. Marie Lauria, *How to Be a Good Secretary* (New York: Frederick Fell, 1969), 253.

6. Recognition Equipment Incorporated ad, *Fortune*, July 15, 1966, 205; Acme Visible ad, *Fortune*, July 15, 1966, 178..

7. Ellen Lane Spencer, *The Efficient Secretary* (New York: Frederick A. Stokes, 1917), 19; Torson, *Art of Being a Successful Business Girl*, 62.

8. Eleanor Gilbert, *The Ambitious Woman in Business* (New York: Funk and Wagnalls, 1916), 234.

9. Bernice Fitz-Gibbon, "Machines for Dictators? Hardly," *New York Times Magazine*, December 6, 1959, 82.

10. Vivian Leigh Edwards, "Secretary's Fear of Word Processor Quickly Vanishes," *Los Angeles Times*, April 25, 1983, E2.

11. Leffingwell quoted in David Morton, *Off the Record: The Technology and Culture of Sound Recording in America* (New Brunswick, N.J.: Rutgers University Press, 2000), 74.

12. "S Is for Secretary," *Today's Secretary*, September 1952, 15; Seymour Rosen and Adrienne Frosch, "Do You Know How to Transcribe Machine Dictation?" *Today's Secretary*, September 1952, 18.

13. Morton, *Off the* Record, 86, 87.

14. Ibid., 87, 90, 91, 99–100, emphasis in the original.

15. Fred S. Cook, ed., *Secretaries on the Spot*, 2d. ed. (Kansas City, Mo.: National Secretaries Association (International), 1967), 98, 217–18.

16. Ads in *Today's Secretary,* September 1952, SoundScriber ad, 9; Dictaphone ad, 55; Gray Audograph ad, 8.

17. Dictaphone ad, *Fortune*, September 1961, 234; Patricia Flynn, *So You Want to Be an Executive Secretary* (New York: Macfadden Books, 1963), 45.

18. *Today's Secretary,* quoted in Lear, "The Amanuensis, Evolution and Revolution of the Secretary over Half a Century," 121.

19. Joan Heilman, "Secretary of the Future," *This Week Magazine*, November 24, 1968, 7.

20. Fitz-Gibbon, "Machines for Dictators?" 82; Lear, "The Amanuensis, Evolution and Revolution of the Secretary over Half a Century," 121; "Automation, Mr. Dooley," *Life*, March 3, 1961, 41.

21. Lefevre quoted in "Empty Boss' Ashtray," *Los Angeles Times*, September 7, 1966, SF10; Alexander Auerbach, "New Secretary Is Speedy but Lacks

Human Touch," *Los Angeles Times*, August 13, 1975, D11; "Secretaries in the Age of Satellites," *New York Times*, May 1, 1994, C43.

22. Jane E. Clem, *Techniques of Teaching Typewriting* (New York: Gregg Division, McGraw-Hill, 1955), 273, 274.

23. Parker Publishing Editorial Staff, *The Successful Secretary* (West Nyack, N.Y.: Parker Publishing, 1964), 119; IBM ad, *Fortune*, July 15, 1966, 166–67; "I.B.M. Introduces New Typewriter," *New York Times*, June 30, 1964, 46.

24. Georgia Dullea, "Is It a Boon for Secretaries—Or Just an Automated Ghetto?" *New York Times*, February 5, 1974, 32.

25. Anne-Marie Schiro, "Secretaries' Poll on Computers," *New York Times*, March 14, 1983, B7; Anne-Marie Schiro, "For Secretaries, Now It's Word Processors," *New York Times*, August 16, 1982, B12; Lynn Smith, "Men Are Taking a Plunge Into Secretarial Pool," *Los Angeles Times*, April 25, 1984, G1.

26. Heilman, "Secretary of the Future," 7.

27. Peter McWilliams, "Word Processing," *New York Times*, October 28, 1984, AS24.

28. Ellen Lupton, *Mechanical Brides: Women and Machines from Home to Office* (New York: Cooper Hewitt National Museum of Design and Princeton Architectural Press, 1993), 48, 49; "With Iraq War as a Backdrop, Speakers Reflect on the Future," *New York Times*, June 10, 2007, at http://www .nytimes.com/2007/06/10/us/10commencement.html?pagewanted=2&_ r=1&sq=gloria%20steinem%20commencement%20typing&st=nyt&scp=1 (accessed March 10, 2008).

EPILOGUE: THE VIRTUAL SECRETARY IN A PAPERLESS OFFICE

1. Englehardt quoted in Warren Strugatch, "L.I.@Work; The Indispensable Secretary, by Whatever Name," *New York Times*, April 22, 2001, LI6.

2. Bruce A. Mohl, "A New Type at Gibbs," *Boston Globe*, October 7, 1980, 1; Marcelle S. Fischler, "Long Island Journal; Unlikely School for Purple Hair and Tattoos," *New York Times*, October 22, 2000, LI4.

3. Hollands quoted in Neela Banerjee, "Some 'Bullies' Seek Ways to Soften Up," *New York Times*, August 10, 2001, C1.

4. Shannon P. Duffy, "Asking for Coffee Not Grounds for Sex Harassment

Suit," *Legal Intelligencer*, June 11, 2008, at http://www.law.com/jsp/article
.jsp?id=120422158304.

5. Gina Kim, "So Long, Shorthand: The Once Essential Secretarial Skill of
    Using Symbols to Take Notes Is an Art of the Past," *Seattle Times*, May 20,
    2003, E1.

6. Douglas Kneeland, "A Secretary Who Spurned the Coffee Detail," *New York
    Times*, October 28, 1977, A10.

7. *Ibid.*

8. Quoted in Mamie J. Meredith, "'Mimeo Minnie,' 'Sadie the Office Secretary,'
    and Other Women Office Workers in America," *American Speech*, December
    1955, 301.

9. Deborah Claymon, "Virtual Assistants, with Personality; Electronic Secretar-
    ies Can Be Charming, Funny and Frustrating," *New York Times*, December
    17, 1998, G1.

10. Joe Sharkey, "A Virtual Travel Agent With All the Answers," *New York Times*,
    March 4, 2008, C8; Ashlee Vance, "Microsoft Mapping Course to a Jetsons-
    Style Future," *New York Times*, March 2, 2009, B1.

11. Catherine Rampell, "In Job Market Shift, Some Workers Are Left Behind,"
    New York Times, May 12, 2010, A1.

12. Jocelyn, September 29, 2008, and Barbara Saunders, January 21, 2009,
    commenting on Marci Alboher, "When the Assistant Is an Entrepreneur,"
    August 17, 2008, NYTimes.com, at http://shiftingcareers.blogs.nytimes.com/
    2008/08/17/when-the-assistant-is-an-entrepreneur/?scp=1&sq=%22assistant
    +is+an+entrepreneur%22&st=Search&apage=2#comments.

13. Vista Grande FAQ at http://www.iaap-rtf.org/about/faq.html#VG. Preference
    is given to active members of the International Association of Administrative
    Professionals (formerly the National Secretaries Association), but nonmem-
    ber administrative professionals are welcome, too, as are civilians.

Selected Bibliography

Anonymous. "My Husband Had an 'Office Wife.'" *Coronet*, March 1949, 118.

Aron, Cindy S. "'To Barter Their Souls for Gold': Female Clerks in Federal Government Offices, 1862–1890." *Journal of American History*, vol. 67, no. 4 (March 1981), 835.

Baldwin, Faith. *The Office Wife*. New York: Grosset and Dunlap, 1930.

Benét, Mary Kathleen. *The Secretarial Ghetto*. New York: McGraw-Hill Book, 1972.

Berebitsky, Julie. "The Joy of Work: Helen Gurley Brown, Gender, and Sexuality in the White Collar Office." *Journal of the History of Sexuality*, vol. 15, no 1 (January 2006), 89.

Blum, David. "Take a Letter . . . Somebody? Please!" *New York Times*, November 13, 1977, F9.

Burger, Chester. *Survival in the Executive Jungle*. New York: Macmillan, 1964.

Campbell, Anson. *Kitty Unfoiled: An Informal Portrait of the American Secretary*. Pittsburgh: Reuter and Bragdon, 1952.

Carney, Marie L. *The Secretary and Her Job*. Charlottesville, Va.: Business Book House, 1939.

Cook, Fred S., ed. *Secretaries on the Spot*. 2nd ed. Kansas City, Mo.: National Secretaries Association (International), 1967.

Cowan, Leslie. *John Robert Gregg*. Oxford, UK: Pre-Raphaelite Press at Oxford, 1984.

Davies, Margery W. *Woman's Place Is at the Typewriter: Office Work and Office Workers, 1870–1930*. Philadelphia: Temple University Press, 1982.

Doris, Lillian, and Besse May Miller. *Complete Secretary's Handbook*. Rev. ed. Englewood Cliffs, N.J.: Prentice Hall, 1960.

Editors of *Esquire*. *Esquire Etiquette: A Guide to Business, Sports, and Social Conduct*. New York: J. B. Lippincott, 1953.

Ex-"Office Wife." "I'm Glad I Lost My Job." *Los Angeles Times*, June 18, 1933, H11.

Fitz-Gibbon, Bernice. "Machines for Dictators? Hardly." *New York Times Magazine*, December 6, 1959, 82.

Flynn, Patricia. *So You Want to Be an Executive Secretary*. New York: Macfadden Books, 1963.

Gilmore, Sybil Lee. *The Successful Secretary*. Chicago: Dartnell, 1951.

Hamman, Mary, and the Editors of *Mademoiselle*. *The Mademoiselle Handbook*. New York: McGraw-Hill Book, 1946.

Heilman, Joan. "Secretary of the Future." *This Week*, November 24, 1968, 7.

Herkimer County Historical Society. *The Story of the Typewriter*. Herkimer, N.Y.: Press of A.H. Kellogg Company, 1923.

How to Be a Super-Secretary. New York: Remington Rand, 1949 and 1951.

"'Katie' Gibbs Grads Are Secretarial Elite." *BusinessWeek*, September 2, 1961, 42.

Keep, Christopher. "The Cultural Work of the Type-Writer Girl." *Victorian Studies*, Spring 1997, 401.

Kessler-Harris, Alice. *Out to Work: A History of Wage-Earning Women in the United States*. New York: Oxford University Press, 1982.

Kilduff, Edward Jones. *The Private Secretary: His Duties and Opportunities*. New York: Century, 1916.

Kischel, Walter, III. "Beyond the Liberated Secretary." *Fortune*, December 14, 1981, 173.

Klemesrud, Judy. "Secretary Image a 'Tempest in a Typewriter'?" *New York Times*, March 7, 1972, 34.

———. "In Defense of the Secretary: 'Truth Is We're Not Unhappy.'" *New York Times*, December 13, 1972, 52.

Lauria, Marie. *How to Be a Good Secretary*. New York: Frederick Fell, 1969.

Lear, Martha Weinman. "The Amanuensis, Evolution and Revolution of the Secretary over Half a Century." *New York Times Magazine*, October 15, 1961, 28.

Lupton, Ellen. *Mechanical Brides: Women and Machines from Home to Office.* New York: Princeton Architectural Press, 1993.

MacGibbon, Elizabeth Gregg. *Manners in Business.* New York: Macmillan, 1936.

Maule, Frances. "I Want to Be a Secretary." *Independent Woman,* March 1941, 75.

Mayo, Lucy Graves. *You Can Be an Executive Secretary.* New York: Macmillan, 1965.

———. *Wendy Scott, Secretary.* New York: Dodd, Mead, 1961.

Morris, Bernadine. "Secretaries: A Little Irked but Generally They're Happy." *New York Times,* July 8, 1974, 34.

Parker Publishing Company Editorial Staff. *The Successful Secretary.* West Nyack, N.Y.: Parker Publishing, 1964.

Private Secretary #1. New York: Dell Publishing, December–February 1963.

Rowan, Roy. "Can the C.E.O. Hang On to His Secret Weapon?" *Fortune,* March 12, 1979, 120.

Scott, Louise Hollister. *How to Be a Successful Secretary.* New York: Harper and Brothers, 1937.

Segrave, Kerry. *The Sexual Harassment of Women in the Workplace, 1600 to 1993.* Jefferson, N.C.: McFarland, 1994.

Shepp, James. *Shepp's New York City Illustrated.* Chicago: Globe Bible, ca. 1894.

Spencer, Ellen Lane. *The Efficient Secretary.* New York: Frederick A. Stokes, 1917.

Strom, Sharon Hartman. "'Light Manufacturing': The Feminization of Office Work, 1900–1930." *Industrial and Labor Relations Review,* vol. 43, no. 1 (October 1989), 53.

———. *Beyond the Typewriter: Gender, Class, and the Origins of American Office Work, 1900–1930.* Urbana: University of Illinois Press, 1992.

Taylor, Angela. "Out from behind the Desk and into the Spotlight—Temporarily." *New York Times,* April 26, 1974, 32.

Torson, Gladys. *How to Be a Hero to Your Secretary.* New York: Greenberg, 1941.

———. *The Art of Being a Successful Business Girl.* New York: New Home Library, 1943.

Turner, Bernice C. *The Private Secretary's Manual.* Rev. ed. New York: Prentice Hall, 1943.

Vermes, Jean C. *The Secretary's Guide to Dealing with People.* West Nyack, N.Y.: Parker Publishing, 1964 (4th printing, 1969).

Weiss, Janice. "Educating for Clerical Work: The Nineteenth-Century Private

Commercial School." *Journal of Social History*, vol. 14, no. 3 (Spring 1981), 407.

Whitcomb, Helen, and Rosalind Lang. *Charm: The Career Girl's Guide to Business and Personal Success*. New York: Gregg Division, McGraw-Hill Book, 1964.

Whitcomb, Helen, and John Whitcomb. *Strictly for Secretaries*. Rev. ed. New York: McGraw-Hill Book, 1965.

Permissions/Illustrations Credits

Grateful acknowledgement is made to the following for providing permission to reprint copyrighted material.

Page v   Aunt Norma at her desk, circa 1970. Collection of the author.

Page 3   Advertisement for Remington Rand, 1954.

Page 6   Front cover, *Barbara Ames, Private Secretary*, by Jeanne Judson (New York: Ace Books, 1960).

Page 7   Front cover, *Very Private Secretary*, by Jack Hanley (Beacon Books / Universal Publishing and Distributing Corporation, 1960).

Page 17   Frontispiece, *The Story of the Typewriter*, by the Herkimer County Historical Society (Herkimer, N.Y.: Press of A. H. Kellogg Company, 1923). Courtesy of the Herkimer County Historical Society.

Page 18   Miss Remington, 1908. Library of Congress, Prints and Photographs Division, LC-USZ62-7376.

Page 19   Advertisement for World Typewriter, 1890.

Page 22   Postcard advertising giant Underwood typewriter. Collection of the author.

Page 27   Photograph of secretarial students at Hartford Secretarial School, circa 1940s. Collection of the author.

Page 29   Advertisement for School of Shorthand, 1911.

Page 31   Front cover, *Je Suis Secrétaire . . . Au Bureau Comme Chez Moi!*
           Couverture Henri Lievens ® Marabout Flash, © Editions Gérard et
           C°, Verviers, 1960/52 C.

Page 35   High school typing class, circa 1910–20. Library of Congress, Prints
           and Photographs Division, National Photo Company Collection,
           LC-DIG-npcc-30595.

Page 36   Advertisements for secretarial schools, *Glamour*, March 1959.

Page 41   Advertisement for Katharine Gibbs School, 1957.

Page 48   "Vinegar" valentine, 1940s. Collection of the author.

Page 51   Front cover, *The Living Method Shorthand Course*, by Lewis Robins
           and Reed Harris. Used by permission of Living Language, a division of
           Random House, Inc.

Page 53   Teen typist. Library of Congress, Prints and Photographs Division,
           National Child Labor Committee Collection, LC-DIG-nclc-05130.

Page 66   Office workers at work (one powdering her chin) at the Chrysler Cor-
           poration, 1942. Library of Congress, Prints and Photographs Division,
           FSA/OWI Collection, LC-USW3-016393-C.

Page 74   Miss Aurelia Toyer and Miss Torreceita E. Pinder, stenographers in the
           United States State Department, 1943. Library of Congress, Prints and
           Photographs Division, FSA/OWI Collection, LC-USW3-029277-C.

Page 84   "Pressing Business! You Deceitful Wretch!" Prints and Photographs
           Division, Library of Congress, LC-USZ6-262.

Page 85   "You Amorous Little Upstart! I'll Teach You Not to Hug Married Men!"
           Prints and Photographs Division, Library of Congress, LC-USZ6-262.

Page 89   Ink blotter, circa 1950s. Collection of the author.

Page 91   Novelty postcard, circa 1930s. Collection of the author.

Page 107   Stella Fischer, secretary to the director, Division of Information,
           Office of Emergency Management, early 1940s. Library of Congress,
           Prints and Photographs Division, FSA/OWI Collection, LC-USE6-
           D-001400. Text: Marie L. Carney, *The Secretary and Her Job*, 268.

Page 110   Advertisement for Celotex Sound Conditioning, 1942.

Page 118   Advertisement for Underwood Typewriters, 1952.

Page 122   "Vinegar" valentine, 1940s. Collection of the author.

Page 135   Front cover, *Private Secretary*, no. 1, December–February 1963, copy-
           right © 1963 by Dell, a division of Random House, Inc. Used by per-
           mission of Dell Publishing, a division of Random House, Inc.

Index

Page numbers in *italics* refer to illustrations.